# Gifts

# Gifts

## Two Hospice Professionals Reveal Messages from Those Passing On

**Anne Wallace Sharp and
Susan Handle Terbay**

New Horizon Press                                    Far Hills, NJ

Requests for permission should be addressed to:
New Horizon Press
P.O. Box 669
Far Hills, NJ 07931

Sharp, Anne Wallace and Terbay, Susan Handle.
        Gifts: Two Hospice Professionals
        Reveal Messages from Those Passing On

Library of Congress Catalog Card Number: Pending

ISBN: 0-88282-150-4

New Horizon Press

Manufactured in the U.S.A.

2000  1999  1998  1997 / 5 4 3 2 1

# Dedication

This book is dedicated to all those extraordinary—and ordinary—people who have given of themselves so completely and freely in their time spent at hospices—patients, family members, nurses, social workers, volunteers, counselors, office staff and chaplains. The stories in this book are theirs. Real names have not been used; and often, circumstances and details have been altered to protect the privacy of those who have lost loved ones.

Each story stands alone in tribute and commemoration of a special soul. They are stories of courage—faith—hope—love—inspiration. They speak of GIFTS—gifts given and received.

These are stories of death and dying—but they are also stories of life and eternity.

# Authors' Note

The word "hospice" describes a unique concept of care that was developed to help patients and their families deal with life-threatening illness. English in origin, the hospice philosophy has become the basis for world-wide health care programs that focus on the needs of the terminally ill. The goals of hospice service include: helping a terminally ill person live as fully as possible, supporting the family before, during and after a loved one's death, helping the patient remain at home and die there, as long as this is appropriate and possible, and advocating and enabling the patient to die with dignity.

These are true experiences. The personalities, events, actions, and conversations portrayed within the story have been reconstructed from extensive interviews and research, accounts, documents, letters and the memories of participants. In an effort to safeguard the privacy of certain individuals, the authors have changed their names, locales and in some cases, altered otherwise identifying characteristics. Events involving the characters happened as described; only minor details have been altered.

# Acknowledgements

WE WISH TO EXTEND OUR WARMEST AND SINCEREST
THANKS AND APPRECIATION TO ALL THOSE WHOSE
CONTRIBUTIONS MADE THIS BOOK POSSIBLE:

BEREAVEMENT COUNSELORS:
    Anne Kuntz
    Tom O'Neill
    Donna Smith
    Kristie Williams

CHAPLAINS
    Pete Hood
    Lynn Gitzinger

SOCIAL WORKERS
    Dee Baughman
    Marilyn Thomas

## VOLUNTEERS
Ann Brubaker
Persha Price
Elmer Sensel

## REGISTERED NURSES
Maggie Bauer
Sandy Bonamassa
Lynn Cox
Clarissa Crooks
Roberta Erwin
Oda Holliday
Sonia Kreider
Jan Jessen
Debbie McMillan
Gretchen Root
Kathy Skarzynski
Kim Vesey
Elaine Wheaton
Susan Wohlfarth

# Contents

# Introduction

A man experiences visions of his long dead sister preparing him for his wife's imminent death ...

A little girl, tormented by her aunt's untimely death only finds comfort when her aunt appears before her smiling ...

A woman, saddened by her family's disbelief in heaven, prays that they be given a sign of the after-life. The family and a hospice nurse are startled by the sound of a chariot racing through the hospice and stopping suddenly at the dying patient's door ...

These have been our experiences. We, at Hospice, no longer believe in coincidences. We have witnessed too many miracles. We know that God is working hand-in-hand, side-by-side with all of us. And when someone dies with love and compassion, we, as well as the family survivors, often stand back filled with joy, awe and gratitude that we were present for this final transition in the journey from life to death.

However, many people die as they lived—quietly, dignified and with a sense of purpose. Some people fight death as they fight life and others struggle with death as they struggle with life. For some, the struggle continues until the last breath is taken.

Some die tragically, some suffer needlessly. And we, as hospice professionals, grieve for what "might have been" and wonder what we could have done differently—for we know how it can be—and we each have an image of how 'it should be". We have been honored guests at the birth of many souls as people navigate the passage from life to death and beyond.

The stories and other material contained in this book speak of miracles. We have gathered together not only our own witnessing of revelations—extraordinary and ordinary—but reports by nurses, social workers, bereavement counselors, chaplains, volunteers and other hospice staff. These reports offer a new perception of death, grounded in reality, but transcending it and celebrate the lives of people who have touched us in many significant ways. As these individuals journeyed through life to death, they walked with courage, hope, peace, love and faith, as well as a sense of humor. They have given us the greatest of gifts —glimpses of eternity and memories that we will cherish and we continue to celebrate:

The experience of a young man dying in winter, afraid he won't find his way to the light when the sun somehow shines on his face, three times in his last moments; the mother who has been almost comatose, rousing herself to tell her young children before leaving, "It's so beautiful."

Using these epiphanies, we reveal new insights into the miraculous transition from life to death and the many lessons and awakenings; some of which can be explained, others which cannot. *Gifts* is also a moving look at the profound relationships formed between terminal patients as guides and the hospice professionals who are themselves enlightened by what happens as life unfolds into death. We offer a powerful new vision of death as a profound process of personal and spiritual discovery in the journey of each individual soul toward enlightenment.

Most of the people who have worked at a hospice for any

length of time will tell you that what they do is more than a job —it is a vocation—a ministry. In other words, a hospice is where they are meant to be. Hospice Chaplain V. "Pete" Hood says, "In working here I have found that special joy of doing what I like and getting paid for it." Most of us feel that way. Many of us left higher paying jobs to work at a hospice. Many of us stay despite other more lucrative offers and the temptation of less demanding and stress-filled hours. We stay because the hospice offers us life in the midst of death, joy in the midst of sorrow, hope in the midst of despair, and faith in the midst of doubt.

Listen to some of the reasons we stay:

Elmer Sensel (volunteer): "My experiences as a volunteer for the hospice have proven to be the most rewarding activities of my life. As a golfer, I have had three holes-in-one. As a sales manager, I once successfully negotiated a contract worth ten million dollars. But none of these experiences compares to the smiles of appreciation and pleasure I have received from patients during my visits with them."

Kathy Skarzynski (RN): "After spending five weeks working at Hospice as a student nurse, I knew that I had found the type of nursing I wanted to do... I have never been able to picture myself doing anything different."

Persha Price (Volunteer): "Working with these patients makes me realize more than ever the importance of accepting death as part of life. The strongest feeling I sense is one of peace."

Anne Kuntz (Bereavement): "Little did I know that these extraordinary young people would change my outlook on life."

Elaine Wheaton (RN): "I was a privileged witness ... My patients taught me about loyalty, faithfulness, and unconditional acceptance and love—gifts that I carry with me on my own journey."

Susan Terbay: "It is the eyes of patients—those penetrating, mysterious windows of the soul—that keeps me working at the hospice. How can I learn about life if I've never known death?"

Anne Sharp (RN): "I have been an honored guest at the birth of many souls as people have made their final passage from life to death. I have rejoiced in miracles, despaired at senseless tragedies, marvelled at the indestructibility of the human spirit, and mourned the loss of many special people, who in the brief time we shared together became my friends. And I have learned and grown, as both a nurse and a human being, because of my interaction with these individuals."

Gretchen Root (RN): "I was out walking and praying — 'Where do you want me, Lord?' Several ideas came to mind and were dismissed immediately, but then I thought, 'hospice,' and knew I had my answer. I had prayed for a job that would give me a challenge and an opportunity to use my gifts. I have never had a doubt that I am where I belong."

# Reflections by the Authors

What brought me, Sue, to a hospice and how can I continue to work here? I hear these questions repeatedly and, for me, there are no easy answers.

My mother died when I was young and, since that time, I have had a fear of death and dying. This fear was intensified by the death of a dear friend nine years ago. I hated death, despised the word cancer, couldn't understand why bad things happened to such good people, and would never in my wildest imagination have pictured myself working for an agency whose very philosophy was based on death.

So how did I end up at a hospice? And more importantly, why can I honestly say that a hospice is where I belong—where I'm supposed to be.

Nine years ago, I needed a job. Looking through the want ads, I noticed an opening at a hospice for a receptionist. I was skeptical, but a friend of mine who was a hospice chaplain urged me to apply. He told me that I'd be good at the job. Right! Working on a day-to-day basis with death was more devastating than I had imagined.

Despite these misgivings, I decided to send in an application. To this day, I'm not sure why I did it. To my amazement, I was hired.

It's been a fantastic nine years. I have learned so much! I found the staff to be sensitive, compassionate and very patient with the "new kid on the block." I have learned from the patients, as my involvement with them has increased.

What keeps me going? Why do I continue to work at a hospice? I can sum it up in one word—eyes.

A very wise person once said, "The eyes are the windows of the soul." Nowhere is this more true than at a hospice.

A person's eyes often speak volumes. A face, ravaged and destroyed by disease, loses resemblance to the person that dwells within the body. But the eyes bear witness to the indestructibility of the human spirit. The eyes reflect the inner soul. At a time when all hope has seemingly vanished, the eyes reveal the real truth of redemption. The eyes communicate in ways that words cannot.

I remember, not long after I started working at the hospice, asking one of the nurses, "How can you take care of patients when they are so deformed and ravaged by disease?"

The nurse smiled at me, "Sue, sometime when you're with one of our patients, look at his or her eyes. You'll see who that person really is."

I never really understood what she was talking about until years later. One day, as I was walking down the hallway, I looked into one of the patient's rooms. Lying there was a man in his early sixty's. He beckoned me to enter.

I hesitated. I had never been in a patient's room before—had, in fact, avoided contact with all patients. Apprehensively, I approached his bed and asked if I could be of some assistance. "Is there someone out there waiting for me?" he asked. I heard his question—but what I noticed were his eyes. They penetrated my very being, challenging me to understand what he was trying to say. As I stood there, I couldn't help but think of all those extravagant Hollywood productions about the life of Christ. The actor chosen to play the lead always has deep penetrating eyes. This man could have gotten the role, hands down.

"I don't see anyone," I told him. 'But I'll look again and if I see somebody, I'll send them in."

His eyes never broke contact with mine. To this day, I can still see and feel the intensity and pleading in those eyes.

Since that time, I have gazed into hundreds of eyes. I am both fascinated and renewed by what I have seen. In spite of profound pain, loss of physical attractiveness, helplessness, and an inability to stop the course of the disease, the eyes reveal peace, beauty and hope.

It is the eyes—those penetrating, mysterious windows of the soul—that keep me working at the hospice. I have come to realize that it is not outward appearances that define who we are. Rather, it is the soul and those eyes tell it all!

The death of my mother at a young age and the loss of a very dear friend hurt deeply and has affected me profoundly my entire life. Because of these and other "losses" in my life, I have suffered pain and, as a result, I have grown. Each encounter I have with people contributes to who I am. How can I know love if I have never loved? How can I know happiness, pain, sadness, loss, passion, if I have never encountered it? How can I learn about life if I've never known death?

I feel I have found my vocation here at the hospice as I listen to and walk with others as they experience their life and death.

The question for me, Anne, isn't so much why I came to a hospice but why I stay. Working with the terminally ill is a stressful and exhausting job and "burnout" is frequent. But those of us who persist and stay, day after day, year after year, have come to look at what we do, not so much as a job, but as a vocation— a calling. I am where I need to be, doing what I'm supposed to be doing.

I have worked at this hospice twice, with a three year hiatus spent doing emergency room nursing. Why did I leave the first time? Burnout, plain and simple. I had been doing on-call nursing, handling emergency situations on weekends, evenings, and nights. Initially I loved it—enjoyed the challenge of crisis intervention and responding to a variety of problems. When I became "numb" and cut off from my feelings — when I hated the thought of going out in the middle of the night to comfort a family whose loved one had died—I knew I needed a break and a change.

So I turned to another stress-filled position—a different kind of crisis intervention—that of an evening shift leader in a chaotic inner city emergency room. Once again, I rose to the challenge. I loved the fast pace, the unpredictability, the nonstop life and death situations. I thrived on the adrenaline surge of treating a gunshot wound, a trauma—having to utilize all my professional skill and ingenuity. After three years of constant chaos, I began to feel trapped. Hospital politics became very abusive and the welfare of the patient and the staff became secondary to making a profit. I was desperate for a change and called my former supervisor at Hospice on the off chance that something might be available.

She asked me to send in a copy of my resume and told me that if something opened up in the near future, she would call. The next day, one of the team leaders called and offered me a job —no interview, no application. I could start whenever I was ready, doing home care.

When I walked into the hospice a few days later, I knew that I had made the right decision. People, who I had worked with previously, greeted me with hugs and "welcome back." I was home. I was back where I belonged.

For the past four years, I have been a home care nurse. I find it very rewarding and extremely fulfilling. On the downside, I also find it tiring, stressful and filled with emotional ups and downs. It's not easy to watch someone die, but I find great satisfaction in knowing that, in some small way, I have helped and made a difference.

I have met a lot of wonderful people and formed new friendships. I grieve when my friends die, but I have also come to celebrate the time spent together, the special moments, their courage and faith. I have also learned to appreciate the struggle, the fears, the doubts—even the pain. Walking with someone on their journey from life to death is a sacred gift. I feel gifted by their trust, their openness, their honesty. The dying process strips away our walls and other defense mechanisms. And when I allow my own walls to come down, when I can trust my own feelings, then I can meet someone heart to heart, soul to soul. And a bond is formed that I cherish, celebrate and mourn.

Hospice is where I am supposed to be. I can't explain it fully, but I know in my heart that this is what I have been called to do. There are times when I hate it—times when I feel I can't give any more—moments when I feel burned out, drained, exhausted and times when the sadness and grief reach up and overwhelm me. But on my own journey, I have also learned to take better care of myself. I take a step back, rest, renew myself and then return for more, because I have found that when I reach that point where I think I can't give anymore, I always find something else to give.

And I receive so much. Whatever gifts I am able to give, the patients repay those gifts tenfold. They aren't always aware of their gifts—whether it be a gift of courage, faith or unconditional love, but they give nonetheless. I see God's presence all around me—in the tears of those who grieve, in the love so freely given and received, in the hugs of family members, in the eyes of those who question and search, and in the small glimpses of heaven I have been privileged to share.

In the midst of death, I continually find life and, for me, that is the most profound gift of all. My job, my vocation, my calling is life giving.

# 1

# Glimpses of Eternity

*Many hospice professionals, as well as the two authors
contribute stories of patients who, as they were dying,
gave glimpses of the world to come.*

## SALAH

Salah Hosseini was a beautiful Muslim woman whose faith
was inspiring. Her strength, courage, love and determination left
a legacy for her family, and for those of us fortunate enough to
have known her.

Salah was a woman of fifty who had been diagnosed with
pancreatic cancer. She had moved to live with her son Ammar
and his wife Patty. She was a proud and dignified woman and the
obvious matriarch of this tight-knit family. Her younger son
Aziz lived in New York.

Salah, the oldest daughter of a Muslim merchant, was originally from Tanzania. She married at an early age and quickly had
two sons. She immigrated to the United States alone, found
employment and one by one brought the rest of her family to this
country. The family lived in Texas for years where her husband
ran a hotel business until he went bankrupt, fell into poor health,
had a stroke and became an invalid. Salah continued to learn

new skills, became a computer programmer and supported her family. Moving to New York, she worked, raised her two sons, and took care of her invalid husband. Diagnosed with pancreatic cancer in 1991, she underwent extensive surgery and slowly recuperated. Chemotherapy and radiation were prescribed and despite her adverse reactions to these treatments, she continued caring for her ailing husband. His death in March of 1993 devastated her. She moved in briefly with her son Aziz in New York, but as her condition deteriorated, she moved to be with her son Ammar.

Her physician referred Salah to the Hospice program not long after her arrival in the area. Her life expectancy was very limited, as the disease was rapidly consuming her body and depleting her strength. I remember vividly the first time I saw Salah. She was sitting up in bed in a small bedroom off the living room. Her eyes were magnificent—dark brownish black and penetrating. So much depth there—so much spirit—so much pain—and yet so much life. Her olive colored skin was without blemish and her hair was the darkest black I have ever seen. Flowing down to her waist, her hair glistened and was kept perfectly in place by a small hairclip in the shape of a star. She was tall and very gaunt. She smiled at me and her smile was genuine, warm and inviting.

She pointed to a small chair at her bedside and I introduced myself as Anne Sharp, her nurse and I sat down. Her daughter-in-law excused herself, "I'll let you and Mrs. Hosseini talk alone." In the three months that I cared for Salah, I never heard her daughter-in-law refer to her in any manner except as "Mrs. Hosseini," obviously a tribute to the matriarch that she was.

"Please call me Salah," she said. "And tell me what I might expect."

I explained about home care nursing, and the visits I would be making. She wanted more information. "No, what can I expect from this disease?"

# GIFTS

We talked of her pain, diminished appetite, the weight loss, nausea and weakness. We discussed pain medication. We spoke of her desire to not die within her son's home—she did not want to burden him, or his family (wife and young son). She asked if I knew how long she had to live. I told her how difficult this question was to answer, but that I would be honest with her as things went along and let her know my thoughts, opinions and best guesses.

She was very open about her feelings, talking about her husband's death and how she did not really want to live without him. She spoke of yearning for the peace found in heaven and of being without pain and struggle. She denied being afraid of death. "I actually yearn for death, sometimes. And yet I value this life also. I have been fortunate. A loving husband, two wonderful sons, two devoted daughter-in-laws, a grandson and many friends. But I feel very alone right now."

"Why is that? Why do you feel alone?"

"I am uncomfortable talking to my sons about my feelings. I don't want to upset them. Aziz is such a baby— my pain becomes his. He is not handling my sickness well. He cannot bring himself to talk about it. His tears come so quickly and they upset me so. So, I must laugh and make merry when he is here."

"And what of your other son, Ammar?" I asked.

"Ammar is my rock. He is my oldest. He is most like me. He knows what to do and I feel comfortable here in his house. But I hesitate to upset him. He has such an important job and is so busy. I do not wish to burden him with my problems."

I encouraged Salah to consider sharing her thoughts and feelings with her family, and offered to make a referral to one of our bereavement counselors. But she refused. "I will talk to you. I like you and you will tell me what to expect. No one else. I am a very private person and I have no need to share my thoughts with strangers."

13

Salah and I had many wonderful talks during the next few months. She spoke often of her faith and belief in Allah. She asked me one day what I believed and I told her that I believed the body dies, but the soul lives on. She said, "My religion teaches something similar. Your God—my Allah—I think they are very much the same. Loving, kind, patient. I do not fear death for I know I go to a better place. I don't know if it is an actual place. I think what I believe is that I am like a drop of rain. When I die I will return to earth and eventually find my way to a great river and be reunited with all the other drops of water."

"Kind of like a collective spirit?" I asked.

"Yes, exactly. My soul will live on. And I think when I die I will finally know the answers to all my questions."

Her mind was amazing. She always had something to ask, something to question, some issue she needed clarification about. She wanted explanations about the changes that were happening to her body; how it was that she could take so much pain medication and still function. We talked of all these things and more.

Meanwhile her physical condition continued to deteriorate. Her weight dropped precipitously as her appetite diminished even further. Her pain continued to escalate and she began to sleep more and more each day. Her thoughts became confused and I knew that this confusion weighed heavily on her mind. She continued to function as independently as she could. She detested having to ask for help. Her daughter-in-law was extremely devoted and ready to assist with anything, but Salah insisted on doing what she could, without assistance. This independence resulted in a fall, and Salah was forced to begin to rely on her family to provide some of her care.

She became very restless and her pain increased. I asked her one day what was going on. "I do not think I can relax here. I am so concerned about being a burden to my son, and to Patty. They have so much going on in their lives. I hate their having to take care of me." Despite protestations from her family that she was not a burden, Salah would not accept their assurances. She continued to be restless and fought against "letting go" of the need to manage her own care. She had been taking care of her family for so long, that she couldn't allow herself to be on the receiving end. She admitted, "I've always been in control. It's always been me who accomplished things. I don't know how to let others care for me."

This issue of control was clearly a big one. Salah was close to death and yet was still fighting "tooth and nail." She said, "I want to let go, but I can't do it here." So after discussion with her family, we opted for an admission to the Inpatient Unit. Maybe in a neutral place, where she wouldn't spend her entire day worrying about her family, Salah could relax enough to die.

Even in the Hospice Unit, Salah had difficulty "letting go." She tried to control her medication schedule and became irate with nurses and other staff members. Eventually her physical condition deteriorated even further and she sank into a semi-comatose state.

One morning I got a call from her son Ammar. "Mom is so restless. She keeps talking out of her head, telling me that she wants to go home," he said. "Can you go down to see her? I'll meet you there."

I met Ammar, his wife Patty and their son in the Hospice Unit later that morning. We walked into Salah's room together. She opened her eyes and in a clear and distinct voice said, "It's about time you got here. I need to talk to you all." We sat down around her bed. Ammar held one hand, while I held the other. Salah began to talk.

"I had a horrible dream last night." Her speech was now slow and slightly labored, but the words were clear.

"What did you dream, Mom?" Ammar asked.

"I dreamed I died, but that wasn't the bad part. The bad part was that I woke up again and here I was—still hurting, still alive."

"Tell us about your dream," I encouraged.

"It was very dark. Black and dark and there was no light and I was in pain and hurting and struggling. It was so black that I was frightened, but I knew I had to go on. And then it was light. And I knew Allah was there."

"Did you see eternity?" Ammar asked. I was impressed with how intuitive and understanding he was.

"Yes. Yes. It was eternity." Salah seemed so relieved.

"And was it beautiful?" Ammar asked.

"Unbelievably beautiful. A place of light and peace and serenity. And I saw your father there."

"Was he still suffering?" Ammar asked.

"No. He was whole, and walking and he beckoned to me. And Allah was there. And suddenly I knew the answers to all my questions. I knew all the answers. The reasons. And I felt whole. I was whole again. I was complete." She paused to catch her breath and her dark eyes glistened with tears. "And then I woke up."

"Why do you think you had to come back from there?" Ammar asked.

She looked at her son and smiled. "So I could tell you about it. You will have to tell Aziz. Then he will know also."

Ammar began to cry and held his mother's hand even tighter. He began to talk to her in her native tongue. The communication between mother and son was very intimate. Not understanding a word of it, I understood it all.

Salah lingered a few more days before quietly and peacefully dying with both her sons at her bedside. Her funeral in New York was reportedly attended by over a thousand friends, family members and work associates.

Salah was a magnificent woman. I will never forget that morning in the Hospice Unit and her description of eternity. I felt blessed to be there and honored that Salah wanted me there. In the end, religion, culture and other differences really didn't matter. Love, faith, courage, dignity and family did. She left a legacy to her family that they will hold close to their hearts forever.
Submitted by Anne Wallace Sharp

# GIFTS

## DADDY

It was a chilly day in November when I received a call that my dad's physician wanted to talk to me. A week earlier Daddy had been admitted to the hospital for extreme fatigue and dehydration. He had undergone every imaginable test in an effort to determine the cause of his problems. The call from the doctor came while I was at work. As a social worker, I happened to work at the same hospital where my Dad was a patient, so I offered to meet the doctor at the fifth floor nurses' station. Although I had walked the fifth floor hallway a thousand times, I never remembered it being as long as it was that day.

I sat motionless as Dr. Morgan told me that my Dad had pancreatic cancer. His best guess was that my Dad had only a couple of weeks to live. A numbness swept over my body and mind. Although I had suspected Daddy had cancer, to hear its finality severed my heart.

I loved Daddy. He was the best friend I had. He loved me unconditionally. He had nurtured me through two divorces and had sheltered me and my son from an alcoholic ex-spouse. My dad and I had survived the death of my mom—together. He had always been my rock and now I realized I would have to become my own foundation. I hated it!!

The physician and I went to Dad's room together. The doctor sat on the bed and gently cradled my dad in his arms. Softly, he explained the reality of the diagnosis. We all wept together.

I knew I did not want to miss a moment of Daddy's final journey, but I also knew I would have to share Dad with the rest of my siblings. I subconsciously decided that I would be with him in whatever way he wanted me to be.

Each of my sisters and my brother took on a different role during Dad's final days. One helped Dad settle his finances; another took care of physical matters around the house; while a third provided prayer. For me, I needed to just sit, hold Daddy's hand and be where he was. During the next two weeks, I learned the lessons of a lifetime.

Daddy remained at the hospital until a bed was secured for him at the local hospice. I traveled that fifth floor hallway daily, eager, yet sad to see Dad. He shared family history during these visits, and, as always, was eager to share his memories. One day as we spoke, he looked up at the ceiling and told me to look at the modules being built. I looked but could not see. He explained that the center of the universe was being recreated and that the modules were part of the scheme. He later told me that when the modules were completed, his time on earth would be finished and he'd be ready to leave.

Once Daddy was at the hospice, he continued to see the module work being done. He explained it in such scientific detail that I really could not comprehend what he was describing. But I could—and did—listen. Then we would sing, pray and eventually just sit and look at one another. He leaned toward me one afternoon and softly stroked my cheek. He told me I looked just like a cherub sitting there. Tears welled up inside of me. I laughed and told him I was quite sure no one else had ever described me as a cherub. But he did! And I knew I would never experience such unconditional love again on my own journey.

Even during the last few days of his life, Daddy continued to converse with me. Thankfully, he did not experience the pain we had feared and anticipated. I rejoice that his pain was minimal. As he slept, I watched the gentle rising and falling of his chest, knowing that this might be his last day and last breath. I felt so heavy.

But Daddy ... that was another story. He was delighted! He told me that although he did not want to leave his kids, he was ever so excited about going to heaven and being with my Mom again. It was a strange feeling to hear him speak like this. But I followed my heart and told him I was excited for him also.

# GIFTS

One morning he was lying in bed swinging his head back and forth and drumming in the air. He said he heard the sweetest music coming to greet him and he wished that I could hear it. He asked me to listen, but this was a private symphony.

Later the same day, he gazed at the door and turned his head towards the top of the bed. He almost giggled and looked at me with a smirk on his face. His blue eyes were gleaming beneath his bushy gray eyebrows. "I don't suppose you saw the lady with the purple dress come in and just sit at the head of the bed, did you?"

I shared with him that I had not had the privilege. "But, I believe you." I also guessed that it was Mom he was seeing. Daddy then shared that for the past two weeks he'd felt someone sitting on his left side, gently stroking his leg and offering sweet reassurance.

During one of my final visits, all four kids were at the bedside. Daddy went around the room and detailed how each child had helped make his transition from this world a little easier. For one, it was thanks for the financial help; for another, thanks for helping with the chores at home. The third I can no longer remember. But what he told me made a difference in my future. Daddy told me that I had guided his spirit so it would be ready to depart this world.

That night Daddy told me the module would be completed the next day. He died the next afternoon.

The following year I came to work at Hospice—where, with Daddy's spirit guiding me, I help others make their final life journey.

Submitted by Dee Baughman

# SHARP AND TERBAY

## LISA

Lisa was nineteen years old. Diagnosed at age sixteen with bone cancer, she was nearing the end of her life. She was an incredible young woman who had learned to cope with a devastating disease. A year before I met Lisa, she had lost a leg to the cancer, but had adapted to that loss as she had adapted to everything—with courage and a positive outlook.

When she was referred to the hospice, she had just finished a round of chemotherapy which had resulted in the loss of her hair, but not her spirit. At nineteen, she was an extremely wise young woman.

She had a strong support system, including teachers and friends and a priest who visited at least twice weekly. Her Catholic faith provided much comfort to her. She was comfortable talking to me about her faith and her beliefs. However, when the subject of angels came up, Lisa became very tearful.

"I don't see angels as being helpers," she told me one day. "They scare me." So we didn't talk about angels.

But I was very concerned and shared my concerns with Dee, the social worker who was working with Lisa. "Who is going to help her over to the other side? She has no relatives or friends that I know of in Heaven. What can we do to make this transition easier for Lisa?" Dee and I talked and conferred on how best to prepare Lisa for her journey.

Lisa finally opened the door herself. On one visit, she broached the subject. "Debbie, I gotta tell you ... and you gotta help me. I was lying here and watching teevee the other night. Suddenly I could just feel it ... could feel someone sitting just above my head on the corner of the bed. I knew someone was there but I was afraid to look. Finally, I just had to look. I looked over my right shoulder and there was this gray haired old lady sitting on the corner of my bed. I only saw her briefly and then she was gone, but I knew she'd been sitting there a long time."

"Did she say anything to you?"

"No ... Debbie, I'm not ready to die," Lisa cried.

"You don't have to die, Lisa, just because the spirits or angels come to see you. Sometimes they just come to check on you. They're there to help you .. to make sure you're doing okay. They'll leave and just come back to check on you, but that doesn't mean you have to go with them just yet. They're there in case you need them."

This seemed to reassure Lisa ... and we went on to talk of other things.

A week later, I had a somewhat frantic telephone call from Lisa's father. "You're never going to believe this, Debbie. My sister (who lives in Minnesota) had this dream last night. She called me this morning ... because she was so excited and concerned. Deb, I had to call you because I don't know what to do about it."

I encouraged him to continue. "My sister dreamed that my mother—Grandma Rose—had come to her in a dream. Grandma Rose told my sister not to worry about Lisa, that she'd take care of Lisa." He paused. "What I need to know, Debbie, is whether we should tell Lisa about this dream. You know how she is about angels and spirits and stuff ... and we don't want to upset her."

Lisa's dad decided to go ahead and tell Lisa about the dream. And when I next saw Lisa, she, too, told me about the dream. "I don't remember much about Grandma ... I was really young when she died. I don't remember what she looks like and don't remember my folks talking about her."

The family got busy and searched the house for pictures. They finally located one and brought it in for Lisa to see. "Oh!!!! That's my gray haired lady ... So that's who came to check on me."

Lisa seemed very comforted that someone cared enough to come to her from Heaven ... and that they would take care of her whenever "it" happened.

# SHARP AND TERBAY

Over the course of the next two weeks, Lisa's condition changed for the worse. The family readied themselves for her death. I visited one last time with Lisa on the afternoon before her death. I told her I loved her, and Lisa took my hand and said, "I love you, too, Debbie."

I reassured her, "You're okay. Grandma Rose is waiting for you. She's going to be with you ... she'll be there when you need her."

The whole family was present. They had called friends and relatives and offered everyone a last chance to say goodbye to Lisa. One by one, each person said their goodbyes. All that day there was a steady stream of loved ones with Lisa.

Finally as it became close to 10:30 p.m., Lisa's seven year old nephew asked for one last chance to be with Lisa. He sat down—alone in the room—holding her hand. No words were exchanged. He was still sitting there when Lisa took her last breath.

Submitted by Debbie McMillan


## THE VISITOR

Jeannie was a fourteen year old girl whose mother had terminal cancer. She was an extraordinarily composed young person who seemed to be coping remarkably well. She was saddened by her mother's illness, grief-stricken at the thought of her mother dying, yet strangely at peace.

Prior to her mother's death, Jeannie related the story of a man who had visited her on several occasions. Initially, she spoke of her confusion about this man — for no one else ever noticed him. She wondered who he was, why she could see him and what he wanted.

# GIFTS

She drew a picture of him and described him in great detail. He was an elderly man dressed in a black suit with cuffed pants. He always wore red socks and brown shoes, and had a pronounced scar down one side of his face. He appeared to her at various times, in different places, but he never spoke.

When Jeannie talked of this man, she expressed no fear. "I know he's not human, but I wonder why he keeps appearing and won't speak."

The man, himself, finally provided the answer. One day Jeannie was on the bus and this man walked through the bus and sat down beside her. He spoke, telling her that her mother was dying. He reassured her that her mother was going to a special place, where nothing could ever harm her again. He told Jeannie that Jesus was going to take good care of her mother. After speaking these words, he got up and left the bus. Jeannie never saw the man again.

A few days later Jeannie's mother died. Jeannie grieved, but felt somehow reassured by this stranger's words and his presence in her life.

Submitted by Tom O'Neill

## A GLIMPSE OF LIFE

In my role as bereavement counselor, I've met many different people from various backgrounds, circumstances and situations. Everyone I've encountered had unique personalities and coping skills. Each one impacted my life in some way. There is one particular patient, however, that I will never forget ... for she touched my life in a special way and taught me many things. Her memory lives on within me.

# SHARP AND TERBAY

I make Sunday visits to the Hospice Care Center. I have found it is a good time to meet with patients and their families. Sundays are usually quiet days—without much of the hecticness and bustle of the work week. The quiet allows for a more peaceful and meaningful time to talk with patients.

I remember the Sunday I met Geneva. She was a petite woman wearing a bright yellow blouse and pant set. What I probably noticed most though were her beautifully manicured pink nails and the fact that she was pacing the room, tethered to a long oxygen tubing.

I introduced myself, telling her that I was available for emotional support. She was reluctant to talk, openly admitting that she didn't trust too many people and wasn't sure about trusting me. I told her that was okay. "We can talk about anything you like ... or nothing at all."

That first day Geneva shared very little but did tell me that she had been fighting her breast cancer for over twenty years. Shortness of breath was her biggest complaint. "I don't like being hooked up to this thing." She further explained that she was scheduled for more radiation treatments during her stay at Hospice. I asked many things about her life and feelings at this time, but didn't prod her for answers. "I'm still going to beat this thing," she proclaimed. And then asked me, "Why do you have so many questions?"

Over the course of the next few weeks, Geneva gradually relaxed and began to trust me. She confided in me about her life: her grief over her husband's sudden death twenty years earlier, her fears about death and dying, her son's bout with cancer—and her struggle and questions with her faith. She was frustrated that the radiation treatments were making her so weak. And she voiced appreciation for the volunteers who were coming in and helping her with her nails. "Although I'd rather do it myself." Her ability to care for herself (and her looks) seemed like a real source of strength—and frustration.

# GIFTS

Geneva was able to go home briefly, but a few weeks later she was back to be treated for increased pain and weakness. I could see the struggle on her face as she attempted to deal with her fatigue, weight loss and advancing disease. Sadly, I knew she wouldn't be with us long.

I spoke with Geneva's daughter, Karen, about her mother's condition. Karen shared with me that she knew her mother was dying. Her biggest concern, however, centered around her own daughter, Shelly, who was coming home to visit from college. Karen was worried about Shelly's reaction when she saw her grandmother.

This was a valid concern, for Geneva had become extremely anxious and confused and was doing moaning and incoherently babbling. Because of the confusion, she was secured in bed by a vest restraint ... and she didn't like this ... not one little bit.

When Shelly arrived, I tried to prepare the young woman for what she might see. Shelly was amazingly calm. "I just want to see Grandma."

She walked into Geneva's room and went over to the bed. She took her grandmother's hand and said softly, "Grandma, it's Shelly. I'm here. And I love you."

Almost immediately, Geneva's breathing slowed. Her face became more peaceful as she looked directly at her granddaughter.

"Shelly," she said, "see those bags down there, honey. I'm going on a trip. I'm going to see my mom, my dog and some friends. Your grandpa is outside the room and he's waiting for me. I'll be okay ... and I want you to know how much I love you ... how much I love everybody."

Three generations of family were in the room, sharing this incredible moment. I felt blessed to be part of such a natural transition. I was especially impressed because I knew that Geneva was not a religious woman. She had been, in fact, a woman who felt alienated from her church. Yet in her closing moments, she was able to instill comfort to her family ... and a message of faith that I know I'll never forget.

In our journey together, Geneva taught me about courage, the will to fight, the need to surrender—she taught me about death.

Her final moments were filled with peace ... surrounded by those she loved ... and those who loved her.

Prayer of Faith
(author unknown)

We trust that beyond absence ... there is a presence.
That beyond the pain ... there can be healing.
That beyond the brokenness ... there can be wholeness.
That beyond the anger ... there may be peace.
That beyond the hurting ... there may be forgiveness.
That beyond the silence ... there may be the Word.
That beyond the Word ... there may be understanding.
That through understanding ... there is love.

Submitted by Kristie Williams

## JEREMY

Jeremy was a very stately and dignified gentleman in his seventies. While on the golf course at his winter home in Florida, he collapsed. Diagnosed with a brain tumor, he returned to his home in Ohio for surgery. Little could be done and his prognosis was very poor. He was referred to a hospice to help him, his wife and five adult children prepare for his death.

Jeremy had been a very astute businessman all his life and had always dealt with things systematically and academically. He had difficulty sharing his feelings. This sometimes frustrated his family, especially his oldest daughter, Sally, who was hoping to grow closer to her father by sharing their last days together. Despite her father's reluctance to share his feelings, Sally was a tremendous support to both her father and mother during this difficult time.

One day Jeremy shared with me that he had hopes of seeing his mother once again. We talked a bit about his relationship with his parents, his childhood and his mother's death some years before.

When I arrived for my next visit, I casually asked Jeremy if he had seen his mother. He looked at me with a frown and scrutinized me closely. "You know she's been dead for years?"

I nodded my head.

With almost a sly smile, Jeremy continued, "Well ... actually, I did go to heaven ... but I didn't see my mother." He seemed somewhat stressed, but went on to say, "But that's okay."

"It was?"

"Yes ... It wasn't time yet for me to stay in heaven. And besides, I was late getting there."

"What do you mean?" I asked, trying to recover from my shock and surprise. Jeremy had never been much of a talker and for him to share something so intimate was quite amazing. "Why were you late?"

"Well, I would have been on time, but your hospice chaplain ran late. So I stuck around to see him."

"Oh ..."

Jeremy seemed fairly mellow and subdued ... almost thoughtful. I decided to take a chance.

"And what did heaven look like?"

"About what I expected. Nothing real fancy. There was a nice white high-rise there that had pretty furnishings ... nothing elaborate ... just comfortable."

Without waiting for me to comment, Jeremy continued, "I rode on a gurney, you know a stretcher, it had golden wheels and I rode right down the street. The streets looked like they were paved with gold."

"Wow," I said, "sounds really beautiful."

"It was. Next time, I hope I can stay ... and then maybe I can see my mother."

Jeremy lived another two months. Much to my dismay and his daughter's, Jeremy never again spoke about his heavenly trip. I think his wife was secretly relieved.

Submitted by Susan Wohlfarth

## A WOMAN WITH LONG RED HAIR

When Jim Barnett was thirty, he was severely injured in an automobile accident. He hovered on the brink of death and lay in a coma for many days. As he lay unconscious, he had a remarkable vision.

"I was standing on the bank of a river in the middle of a green meadow. I could hear the water cascading over the rocks and was also aware of a gentle breeze blowing through my hair. From across the river, a young woman with long red hair approached me. She talked to me for a long time and told me I would survive my injuries and eventually be able to return home to my family."

Jim, in fact, did recover completely and rejoined his family. While he never completely forgot his vision, he didn't think about it for many years—until his wife, Marjorie, was near death.

His wife, Marjorie, had abdominal cancer. Her last request to her family was that she be allowed to die at home with her husband and four small children. Jim arranged her discharge from the hospital, hired a nurse to help with her care and brought his wife home.

He related the following:

"Right before my wife died, I was alone with Marjorie. We were just sitting together quietly. I was holding Marjorie's hand, when I noticed this young woman with red hair enter our bedroom. It was the same visitor I'd had years before. The three of us talked well into the night. She told us that Marjorie was soon going to die. The young lady said she would be waiting for Marjorie and that, eventually, I would be joining them, too. Both Marjorie and I felt very comforted by these words. Marjorie died very peacefully a few hours later."

He paused, "It didn't hit me until much later that night. I had a sister who died very young ... she had long red hair."

Submitted by Clarissa Crooks, R. N.

## THE WINDOW

One of my "duties" as a home care nurse is to go to the home after a patient of mine dies. I offer emotional support to the family, notify the coroner, prepare the body for "removal" and wait with the family for the funeral home directors to arrive.

While we wait, I usually talk to the family and allow them to share their feelings about their loved one's death. George was a new patient and I had not met his family prior to his death. After taking care of the "business" part of the job, I sat down with George's family. His wife and daughter were tearful but seemed at peace. As their story emerged, I understood why.

"It was dad's last wish to die at home," explained George's daughter. "So, on Sunday we told Dr. Justin that we wanted to bring Dad home. He contacted the hospice and you guys took it from there—arranging for the delivery of a hospital bed and a visit by one of your nurses. The nurse got Dad some pain medicine and that really seemed to ease his struggle."

The patient's wife picked up the story from there ... "I think George knew he'd finally come home. He seemed pretty comfortable and kept drifting in and out of awareness. His brother came and told him goodbye ... and that eased his struggle even more."

"But for some reason, Dad kept hanging on," his daughter said. "Mom and I had both said goodbye. I think we were both wondering why it was taking so long. By then Dad had slipped into a coma and his breathing was really slow. We thought each breath was going to be his last ... but still he hung on."

"And then this morning, the minister came. We all prayed together and were sitting here around the bed just as we are now. Suddenly the minister looked at me and said, 'You know what the problem is?'

'What?' I asked.

'You need to open a door or window so the angels can come in,' he said.

"Well, I never held much belief in that kind of thing— and I don't think Mom did either, but I opened the big window off the patio as the minister suggested. I was turning to come back to the bed when Dad took his last breath and died. Maybe it's my imagination, but I felt a rush of air go by me. I believe it was Dad leaving ...."

Submitted by Anne Wallace Sharp

## AUNT ELLEN

A bright, energetic little girl in shorts and a matching top bounced into the living room where I was talking with her mother. The child was introduced to me as Sally.

"Hi, Sally. My name is Tom."

# GIFTS

"Hi. I'm six years old. My Aunt Ellen just died and we went to the funeral. There were lots of people there. All my cousins came: Jamie, Freddie, Susie, and Paul. Paul came all the way from Texas. And there were pretty flowers and lots of music. Mommy cried. I did, too. Aunt Ellen is in heaven. Did you know that?"

I was just getting ready to respond to Sally's question, when she started speaking again.

"I'm not sad. Do you want to know why?"

I nodded my head, as Sally sat down beside me on the sofa.

"Cause I saw her, that's why."

"You did? When did you see her?"

"Before church. I was brushing my teeth. Mommy said I had to do that before we went to church. Aunt Ellen walked right into the bathroom. She looked so pretty, not like when she was sick. She was smiling and everything. Her dress was real pretty—white and soft. She had this magic wand in her hand with a sparkly star on the top. She stood beside me, smiled and told me to be a good girl. I'm always a good girl, aren't I, Mommy?" She paused to take a sip of orange juice and continued, "And you know what?"

"What?"

"Aunt Ellen told me she was going to live with Jesus in heaven. She said that heaven was a really pretty place. Someday, I'm going to go live there too. Did you know that? And guess what?"

"What?"

"Aunt Ellen was at church too."

"She was?"

"Oh, yes. She walked right down the middle aisle of the church and stood behind that brown box. Mommy told me that box is called a casket. Did you know that? And Aunt Ellen was right there. She looked real pretty. I told Mommy to look, but she didn't see her. But I did. Aunt Ellen smiled at me and I could tell she was real happy. That made me happy. But I was sad too. Mommy was crying and so was everybody else. Maybe they don't know that Jesus came to take her to heaven. But I told them. Aunt Ellen's with Jesus and she's happy and doesn't hurt anymore. Jesus made her all better."

Shortly after that, Sally went out to play and I spent a few minutes talking with her mother. "At first I thought Sally made all that up about seeing Ellen, but now I'm beginning to think she is telling the truth. I thought seeing Aunt Ellen might make Sally afraid, but if anything, it has made her less afraid. It must have seemed so natural to her—like Ellen was trying to tell her that everything was all right. Sally has cried a few times and talks about how much she misses her favorite aunt. But she also seems very much at peace. And I think what Sally saw has helped me too."

Submitted by Tom O'Neill

## HANNAH

When I met Hannah, she was dying and could no longer communicate. The following are several stories her "foster daughter" Barbara shared with me some of her favorite stories about her "mother."

Barbara's story:

*"Aunt Hannah" was my foster mother. My own mom died when I was thirteen and I went to live with my mother's brother. But it was Hannah who took on the mother role. We were not related by blood, but she became as close as any blood relative could be. I'd stop by her house everyday after school. I'd tell her about my day—my struggles with my lessons, my boy friends, my hopes for the future. She was always supportive and*

*loved me like I was her own daughter. We just adopted each other.*

*After I graduated from high school, I was married. Aunt Hannah was there in the front row, tears in her eyes, as I wed the love of my life. She helped with the raising of my own two children. I worked, but Aunt Hannah was there when they returned home from school. She listened to them as she had listened to me.*

*Our only quarrel was that Aunt Hannah didn't go to church. God was such an important part of my life. I had accepted Jesus while in high school. I wanted to share this part of my life with Aunt Hannah, but she resisted.*

*A few years ago when Aunt Hannah got sick, I took her into my home. When she moved in with me, she accepted Jesus. Her life, I think, began to change. She prayed everyday and there was a dramatic change in her attitude and beliefs. She'd be in her bed singing hymns of praise to God and it would fill my heart with joy just to hear her voice.*

*About a month ago, Aunt Hannah began to really weaken. She was by then confined to her bed. One afternoon, I heard Aunt Hannah talking to someone. I ran up the stairs thinking she might need something. As I walked into the bedroom, the conversation stopped. I asked her who she'd been talking to.*

*"I was just talking to my angel," she said*

*"You were?" I questioned*

*"Oh, yes. We talk all the time."*

*"What do you talk about?"*

*"Oh, I can't tell you that—but we sure do talk* about everything."

*I laughed. "You can't tell me what you talk about?"*

*"Oh, no, honey. You're not supposed to know ...* just yet."

*"Well, then, can you tell me what this angel looks like?"*

*"Oh, she's beautiful! And, honey, she's white."*

*"She is?"*

*"Oh, yes. She's white and she's so very beautiful!"*

# SHARP AND TERBAY

*"Well Aunt Hannah, I'm so glad you have someone to talk to, but I wish you could tell me what you talk about."*

*"I can't do that. But, I can tell you that she's not the only one who visits," Aunt Hannah said with a smile.*

*"She's not?"*

*"Oh, no. Sometimes the gentlemen come, too."*

*"The gentlemen?"*

*"Well, yes ... there's six of them. And they're all dressed up — so fine. Nice shiny black suits and ties. They're so handsome. Sometimes they just stand down there at the end of my bed — watching — and waiting."*

*"What are they waiting for?"*

*Hannah sighed loudly, as if I'd asked the most stupid question in the world. "Why, they're waiting to take me to Heaven", she said.*

*I was astounded at Aunt Hannah's revelations and felt very relieved. She seemed so peaceful and accepting. I'd be walking down the hall and hear her talking and I'd smile. One time, I entered the bedroom and she actually turned to her left, put her finger to her mouth and said, "Shhh!" She was telling her special angel to be quiet in front of me.*

*Another time, she woke up one morning and told me she was really tired because she hadn't slept all night. I was confused. "But, Aunt Hannah, I peeked in several times and you were snoring."*

*"Maybe I was, but I went to the VA last night. I spent hours out there talking to my brothers. We talked all night."*

*I thought she was confused or dreaming. But when I shared this story with Hannah's sister, I learned that Hannah's two brothers were, indeed, at the VA. They were both buried in the cemetery there.*

As I listened to these stories, I was touched by Hannah's faith and her extraordinary openness to her loving God. When she died a few days later, Barbara swore she heard singing com-

ing from her mother's room. I am sure the angels sang her home
to Heaven.

Submitted by Anne Wallace Sharp

## LOSING ONE OF OUR OWN

There are times when people outside my work place ask
me if I take death for granted. Do I become immune to its
effects? The answer to both questions is a resounding "No!" I
actually find that I take death more seriously and life becomes
more precious as the years go by.

A year ago, one of our home care nurses was diagnosed
with terminal pancreatic and liver cancer. The news of her illness
was devastating. All of us were affected and for most, the pain
was overwhelming.

This nurse was the epitome of the ideal Hospice nurse:
warm, caring and exuding love and humor, and always in touch
with her Creator and the needs of her patients. When the diagnosis was announced, I was angry, frustrated and so very, very
sad. These emotions were shared by most of the hospice staff.
We became caregivers and family for one another.

There was a box placed in the clinical area with Elaine's
name on it. It was be emptied at least once a week because it
would be overflowing with gifts, cards, prayers and letters—
expressions of our hopes and feelings for Elaine.

A part of us was dying and we couldn't stop it. As we so
often tell our families, death hurts, but you don't have to be
alone because others care and understand. As Elaine made her
journey, many tears were shed and expressions of love and care
were shared.

# SHARP AND TERBAY

On the evening of her death, the news spread through the building quickly. We comforted each other, but there was a real atmosphere of darkness that descended on the hospice.

Later that evening, I questioned God. What possible purpose was there in such a death? "You made a huge mistake, Lord," I wanted to scream. I knew in my heart that Elaine was no longer in pain and that her spirit was now celebrating its new life. However, I could make no sense of her death. Why? And why now?

I cried myself to sleep, in part because of Elaine's death, but more so, for the world's loss of such a gentle giving spirit. We so desperately need the Elaines of this world — and now she was gone.

The next morning, I awoke in my darkened room to the smell of flowers. I slept restlessly. My sleep was erratic; my dreams were strange — all involving funerals. Finally around five thirty in the morning, I smelled a candle burning and the flowers. I lay there making sure I was awake. I looked around to see if there was a logical reason for these fragrances. I thought of Elaine and asked her if she was stopping by. I remembered the prayer candle I had given her. But it was the smell of the flowers that astounded me. It was a fragrance I cannot even begin to describe. It lasted for about thirty minutes and then it was gone, as quickly as it arrived. I would like to believe that Elaine was there.

I stayed in my bed for a few more minutes thinking of Elaine and the new place in which she resided. Perhaps her work is now just beginning, for most certainly she is where we all want to be. Will she have the time and desire to help us in our weaknesses and touch us again with her strength and wisdom? She left us only a small fragment of herself while she was here. Are we capable of growing from that alone or can she gently coax more from us from her new home?

# GIFTS

The snow falling that morning was ever so gentle out-side—much like Elaine's presence. A smile creased my face as I spoke silently to Elaine, "I'm thinking of you, Elaine. My heart feels warm, my spirit strengthened and the air is filled with spring and new life. Thank you, my friend."

I wrote two poems to Elaine. The first was a poem of pain written when I heard of her diagnosis. My grief began when I learned the grim news. However her actual death was anti-climactic in comparison to this original pain.

The second poem was a poem of love written as Elaine began her final journey. The first reads:

> The air is heavy
> Sadness chokes my breath
> The spirit within me cries
> It cannot conceive a death.
>
> Where's the laughter?
> It seems so far away.
> Where's the music?
> There's no song today.
>
> The spirit wails within me
> The tears steadily flow
> Why can't these tears wash away
> The pain that continues to grow?
>
> Pain and sadness
> Overwhelms my being
> The sense of hope and tomorrows
> Seem all too quickly fleeing.
>
> My spirit mournfully aches
> Searching for inner peace

# SHARP AND TERBAY

What can be found
To make the crying cease?

During a moment of darkness
My spirit totally drained
A voice began to sing
A beautiful sweet refrain.

My spirit found its answer
In this lilting refrain
For only in true love
Can one experience true pain.

My spirit now accepts the pain
And allows the tears to flow
For out of all this sadness comes
A feeling that within me knows.

The words my spirit heard
From that enlightening refrain
Were just a simple phrase
I love you Elaine.

The second poem of love to my dear Elaine:

I thought of you today and
a smile creased my face.
Thoughts of you warm my heart and
Strengthen my soul
For never have I met one such as you,
Never again wil I encounter such a spirit.

# GIFTS

This evening as I lit my prayer candle,
My thoughts turned to you and
Even now I hear your voice
delight in your laughter and
can see you so plainly.
Never have I encountered such a spirit.

You see, Elaine, I have been very blest
to have met you, to have worked with you,
to have even experienced a small part of you
For I have never encountered such a spirit.

I pray for you often
my thoughts will wonder at times but
at least once a day my thoughts dwell on you
and a smile creases my face
my heart is warmed and my soul strengthened
for I have never encountered a spirit such as you.

I love you, Elaine
for the smiles
the warmth
the strength
but more than anything I love the spirit of you.

May God always hold you in His arms,
and gently kiss your face
for even God has never encountered such a spirit as you.

Love always,

Sue

# SHARP AND TERBAY

No—I never take death for granted. I am never immune from its pain. I don't want to be—for it is in death that I learn to live.

Submitted by Susan Handle Terbay

## THE CHARIOT

In the fifteen years I have worked as a hospice home care nurse, I have shared several stories that touch on the subject of spiritual reality. The following story is one that was told to me by another nurse.

One of her patients was a devout woman who was being cared for at home by family members. This woman shared with her hospice nurse that she was concerned because some members of her family did not share her belief in a personal, powerful, loving God.

She had been praying that God would give them an obvious sign of His presence. On the day this woman died, her hospice nurse was at her bedside, along with many members of the family. At the time of her dying, a rumbling noise was heard approaching the house. It grew louder and louder until the noise filled the room. The sound of large wheels turning echoed throughout the small house. The rumbling passed through the house and faded away as the woman took her last breath.

Her chariot had come for her and all in the room had heard it come and go.

Submitted by Clarissa Crooks

# GIFTS

## CHARLES

Patients die in many places — hospital rooms, bedrooms, easy chairs and the like. Charles opted for the chaise lounge chair on his backporch — a porch he and his son Kevin had built together many years before.

Charles had been "trying" to die for several days. Actually I think he was just waiting for all the "pieces" to fall into place. First of all, he waited for his son Jerry to fly home from Arizona. Secondly, he waited for the right time and place. He wanted the place to be his porch. He had hovered near death, semi-comatose for several days. Goodbyes had been said; prayers had been offered. Friends and family had waited, keeping watch and sharing special memories. But it seemed that just when everyone thought Charles was taking his last breath, he would rally and struggle on.

It was a Thursday morning. The sun rose bright and early and the sky was a brilliant blue. Charles, who had not spoken for days, suddenly decided to talk. "I want to go out on the porch," he said clearly. Everyone looked at each other in total amazement. But his wish was granted. His sons Kevin and Jerry carried him out to the porch and laid him on a padded chaise lounge chair. Gathered around him were his two sons, his daughter-in-law, a friend of the family and me (his hospice nurse and close friend).

It had been a long struggle for Charles. He had always been a "take-charge" person—totally in control of his life, regimented, a list maker, a logical thinker. His cancer had necessitated a lot of changes. He had to rely on others and he had to give up control. His son and daughter-in-law had moved in with him so they could take care of his daily needs. This had been difficult for all parties.

But on this last day of his life, all difficulties had been set aside. As Charles lay there on his porch, he returned to what he knew best—list-making and control. He began to go down his "list," thanking everyone present and some not present, for everything they had done. Individually, he recited the names and expressed his gratitude. His list completed, he closed his eyes and rested. His breathing came in deep, irregular gasps. Suddenly his voice shattered the silence. "I'm coming Pat, I'm coming." (Pat was his late wife.) His breathing became more labored, eventually ceasing.

Those of us sitting there on the porch knew we had witnessed a sacred reunion. No one spoke for a long time. We all knew we had received a gift of inestimable value.

Submitted by Anne Wallace Sharp

## HENRY

After doing my physical assessment and talking to Henry and his wife, I packed up my "bag" to leave their home. Henry was lying on the bed with his eyes closed, and his wife was sitting beside the bed. For some reason—and to this day, I'm not sure what made me ask the question—I asked Henry, "Have you been talking to the angels?"

Henry didn't open his eyes, but responded immediately, "Why, yes."

His wife seemed very surprised but didn't say anything.

"Can you tell us what the angels told you?" I asked.

"No."

"Did they show you Heaven?"

"Yes," Henry said softly and smiled.

"Was it beautiful?" I asked.

"It was gorgeous!" Henry said with great emphasis on every word. He still had his eyes shut, but the smile on his face that day will forever live with me in my memory.

When I attended Henry's funeral a few weeks later, I was surprised to hear the minister share this same story. "Isn't it wonderful," he said, "that Henry saw heaven, knew where he was going, and was able to give such comfort to his family and friends?"

Submitted by Debbie McMillan

## CARLA AND MR. BRANT

I was working on a surgical floor in a local hospital when the following incidents occurred. These stories have continued to impact my faith and work ...

Carla was an obstetric nurse who was fighting cancer. Despite her diagnosis and failing health, she continued to work stating, "When I can no longer work, I will die."

She was on my unit receiving chemotherapy. On Tuesday morning, her chemotherapy was finished and she was discharged. Everything had looked fine, but by the weekend, Carla was back and not doing well.

Over the course of the next two weeks, Carla received intravenous therapy, blood and platelets. All of her children were gathered together and a twenty-four hour vigil began at her bedside. Her pain was intense, until a morphine intravenous drip was ordered. As the days passed, she became increasingly swollen and yellow. She looked like she was going to explode. Her family had difficulty coping, traveling through the grief cycle like it was a roller coaster ride.

After two weeks at Carla's bedside, the family was exhausted and Carla was still unable to go home — or to die. At someone's suggestion, the family decided to go home. The last one left at one in the morning.

At three a.m., when I went to check on Carla, she was dead. She had a smile on her face and her eyes were looking up. She looked so peaceful. At that same moment, the call light went on in labor and delivery at the obstetric unit where Carla had worked. No one was there. I believe Carla was saying good-bye to her friends and co-workers.

Another story ...

I was working night shift on the the surgery floor when a gentleman in Room 104 put his light on. I answered his call. Mr. Brant told me he was afraid. "I saw them and they're coming to get me," he said. I asked who he was talking about and Mr. Brant responded, "Angels from heaven."

Mr. Brant was doing pretty well and I didn't think he was anywhere near death, so I reassured him that there was probably nothing to worry about. During the night, the patient across the hall, Room 106, died. In the morning, Mr. Brant put his call light on again. He questioned me about the events of the night. He told me he knew the patient across the hall had died.

" I thought the angels were coming for me — but I guess they were here to pick up the man across the hall."

Submitted by Lynn Cox

# GIFTS

## A LITTLE ANGEL

It was October of 1994. Little Nathan was a very active, healthy five-year-old. His mother and father were divorced and he lived with his mother. One of his stronger male role models was his maternal grandfather and Nathan relished the attention and love his grandfather gave him.

His mother had remarried and was expecting a new baby in the early spring. Nathan was excited about having a new baby brother or sister. He also enjoyed the attention and love of his new stepfather. Life seemed good.

It was in late October that things began to fall apart in young Nathan's life. His grandfather became very sick and within six weeks died of a rapidly progressing cancer.

Nathan, being the exceptional and sensitive child he was, sensed his mother's grief. He knew that his mother had loved Grandpa very much and that she missed him. Nathan missed him too. One day, while he was sitting at his little "school" desk in his playroom, he took out his crayons and scissors and made an angel. He presented this to his mother very solemnly and proudly, announcing, "This is your own special angel." He reassured her that this angel would watch over and take care of her now that "Papa" was gone. Nathan's mother carried the angel with her from that day forward.

That Christmas, Nathan decided to make another angel. This one was bigger—about eight inches tall. He was getting very good at making angels. Sadly, he knew his mother would need this angel, too.

In February, Nathan became ill. He showed signs of profound muscle weakness, became very tired and at times could barely lift up his arms to hug his mother. The family doctor was at a loss to understand what was going on and could not come up with a specific diagnosis.

# SHARP AND TERBAY

In March, Nathan seemed happy when a new baby brother was born. He proudly held the baby in his arms and had his picture taken. But Nathan was not doing well.

Test after test failed to show why he was so sick and weak. Finally, he was transferred to a children's speciality hospital some seventy miles away. Tests again proved inconclusive and the specialist suggested brain surgery as the only sure way to pinpoint a definite diagnosis. Desperate, Nathan's parents agreed. The surgery was successful in determining a cause for Nathan's problems but tragically left Nathan in a coma. His mother and father were devastated to learn that Nathan had a very rare brain disorder that was irreversible and would ultimately cause their son's death.

Nathan's family stayed by his bedside night and day, praying for a miracle. But time passed with no improvement. While he was in the hospital, Nathan's teacher from school brought in the large angel he had made. She had framed and matted the angel.

There was still no response from Nathan. His mother decided it was time to take him home where he belonged. The picture of his angel was lovingly placed over the head of his bed. His mother tenderly slipped her own special tiny angel in under the corner of the picture.

Nathan was home from mid-June until August 1995. Nathan was dying less than five months since the diagnosis. His family gathered around his bedside as he took his last breath. They all felt they had been blessed by a very special angel.

Submitted by Susan Wohlfarth

# GIFTS

## JOAN

As I listened to the music, scripture readings, and the priest's homily at Joan's funeral mass, my eyes were fixed on the casket and the family in the front pew—a husband, two sons, a daughter, and a mother. While I stared, memories floated in and out of my mind.

It was our children who first brought Joan and me together. Her second son, Richard, and my oldest daughter were the same age, attended the same school, and had become very good friends. Richard is a character, extremely hyperactive, but underneath the constant energy, a loving, warm young man. Of all of Joan's children, it was Richard that I knew (and loved) the best. In fact, at times I felt that he could have been one of my own children.

Joan and I saw each other at school, church social activities and teen groups. She was a quiet, pleasant woman, who always had a smile on her face. She was someone who kept busy, working diligently in the background. Her presence was always felt, but not necessarily noticed.

After our kids graduated from high school, Joan and I went our separate ways. My daughter went on to college, while Richard joined the military. Joan and I would come together occasionally at church functions, but our meetings became less and less frequent as time went by.

I heard through the church grapevine that Joan was ill and had been admitted to the hospital. After a series of tests, the doctors informed her that she had cancer and that the prognosis was very poor. When I heard this news I felt sad, but I also convinced myself that she would get better. After all, she was only my age. I needed to believe that there were still a lot of good years ahead for both of us.

Joan, however, didn't get better. In fact, she never went back home again. After a few weeks, the hospital called requesting a direct admission to the Hospice Center. I took the referral over the telephone. As I wrote down the necessary information, I couldn't believe what I was hearing. I was told Joan's prognosis was grave. The doctors did not expect her to live for more than a few days or weeks. This news devastated me.

I kept in touch with the admissions staff at the center so I would know the day and time of Joan's arrival, but I really didn't intend to meet her at the door. Yet, that is exactly what happened. I happened to be dropping something off at the front desk when the ambulance crew wheeled in the stretcher. A frail young woman wearing a floppy jean hat and holding a teddy bear was lying on the stretcher. When she saw me, a big smile spread across her face. She reached out her arms to me. I didn't know what to say. My mind kept stumbling over a pleasant greeting, but nothing verbalized. So, I returned the smile and took hold of her cool, frail hands. I told Joan that I would be down to her room to see her after she got settled. Joan had surprised me. I'm not sure what I had been expecting, but it certainly wasn't this smiling, up-beat person.

I stopped by the volunteer office to see if they had any flowers. Since a delivery had just been made, I was able to find a lovely rose which I took down to Joan. She seemed pleased with the gift, but looked tired. I kept my visit short. I asked her if she wanted me to bring her communion on a daily basis. "I'd love that, Sue," she said.

Joan was noticeably weaker and less vibrant the next morning when I stopped to visit. As I walked over to the bed, I noticed there were tears in her eyes. I asked her what was wrong.

"I fell last night, Sue," she explained. "I feel so embarrassed. It was such a humiliating experience. The nurses had to help me get up. I can't even go to the bathroom alone, without falling." Tears trickled down her cheeks.

# GIFTS

I felt very inadequate, but I tried to reassure her. I told her not to worry too much, then tried to lighten things up by reminding her what a klutz I am. "My God, I trip over my own feet all the time! I've gotten used to the humiliation—maybe you will too." Joking with her, I told her she was probably on too much of a sugar high and just needed to slow down. Finally, I saw the old familiar smile cross her face.

I was frequently drawn to Joan's room. I watched as she slowly began to lose her fight with the cancer. Some of the best visits I had with Joan occurred after all her other visitors had left. She seemed more open then and talked to me freely about her feelings. We talked a lot about our children, which was one of Joan's major concerns. She worried about them constantly— how they were dealing with her illness and how they would cope when she died. I told her what a fantastic job she had done as a mother and that her kids were terrific. I tried to tell her that she had nothing to fear, but she and I both knew that I was just trying to make her feel better. My words were just that—words, empty words.

Despite her constant struggle with the cancer and its accompanying pain, Joan never allowed herself to succumb to self pity. She kept her pain from her friends, wearing a mask and a smile. One day, when her mother had left the room to take a break, I happened to stop in. Joan was unusually agitated, pushing and tugging on her sheets. I called for the nurse, who in turn called the doctor, to obtain an order for stronger pain medication. While we were waiting for the medication to work, I held Joan's hand.

"I'm here," I told her. "Just hold on and listen to my voice. Maybe it will keep your mind off the pain." I kept talking. I have no idea what I talked about — perhaps, the kids, the church, the weather. It was one of the few times Joan allowed the agonizing pain to "show" itself. It hurt me deeply to see her struggle so, but I also felt blessed that she trusted me enough to take off the mask.

# SHARP AND TERBAY

Because Joan's condition was deteriorating so rapidly, the staff and family made arrangements for her son, Richard, to come home from his military assignment. I remembered my daughter's friend from high school. I was not prepared for the tall young man in full military uniform I saw standing outside Joan's room with tears rolling down his face. He smiled when he saw me and bent over to give me a big "bear" hug

Richard could not believe how quickly his mother's condition had changed since he had last seen her in the hospital a few weeks before. He was struggling with his mother's decision to receive only "comfort measures." As a paramedic, he was accustomed to doing everything humanly possible to save a life. Now he was being asked to do nothing. He questioned her desire only to be given hydration and food, and wanted to know if intravenous fluids and other procedures could be done. Gradually he accepted that these measures were not what his mother wanted.

Seeing Richard's struggle to come to terms with his mother's illness broke my heart. I tried to find the right words to say to him. He was going to have to learn to "let go." I told him that we were going to do everything we could to help his mother and his family, but that he needed to know that things weren't going to get any better. I encouraged him to just "be" with his mother. It took awhile but Richard accepted the inevitable.

Richard had met a lovely young woman while in military and they were engaged to be married. Joan had been working on the flower arrangements and other plans for the wedding before she became ill. Joan wanted to be at that wedding. As she became weaker, the family realized that this wasn't going to be possible. The young couple suggested changing the date of the ceremony and having the wedding in Joan's hospice room, but Joan would not hear of it. There was talk of video taping the ceremony, but it didn't look like Joan would live long enough to see the tape. Richard and his fiancee wanted Joan to be part of this very special moment in their lives and shared their feelings with one of the hospice chaplains.

# GIFTS

The chaplain suggested that the wedding rehearsal be held in Joan's room. After obtaining Joan's reluctant approval, plans were made for the elaborate dress rehearsal. Time was of the essence and within two hours everything was in place. The chaplain went through the entire ceremony with the wedding party in full dress uniform. In the room Joan witnessed her son's impending marriage and then gave the young couple her blessing. It was a very moving ceremony for everyone involved.

While Joan was in the hospital, she had expressed her fear of being alone. For this reason, her hospice room was constantly filled with people—family and friends were there with her around the clock. On one particular afternoon, there were five or six friends visiting when I stopped by. During my visit, I noticed that Joan was looking over to the side of her bed. "Oh, what beautiful blond hair you have," Joan said. One of the ladies laughed and said that she appreciated Joan's remark, but that her hair was gray. I knew that Joan wasn't talking about this woman, for Joan was looking past her. Joan had a very strange, yet peaceful look on her face. Joan had remarked about this beautiful young blonde girl several other times. I was envious—I wanted so much to see what Joan was seeing, because there was such a deep sense of serenity in Joan's expression when this special visitor was present.

I was also profoundly affected by an incident that occurred one day when I was giving Joan communion. I was standing by her bedside when Joan reached out and took my hand. She looked directly and deeply into my eyes and said, "I'm so happy, Sue." As I looked at her gaunt, balding, pale, frame, she was suddenly transformed into a radiant, beautiful, almost vibrant woman. Never have I experienced anything quite like that! It was one of the most joyful days Joan and I shared during her stay at the hospice. It left me with a feeling of peace ... and hope.

As Joan's body further weakened and death approached, her room became less crowded. Family became the main visitors. Perhaps, Joan's fears were beginning to subside. I continued to stop in, although she was no longer able to take communion. There was always some response from Joan, some awareness of my presence. One particular day, there was no response. Joan did not stir when I took her hand. Quietly I told her that I would see her in the morning, but, in my heart, I knew I wouldn't.

As I sat at the church and celebrated Joan's Mass of Resurrection, I looked around at all the familiar faces of her close friends and loving family. I realized that these people had known Joan far longer than I, and yet Joan once only an acquaintance, had became a very special friend to me in a matter of a few weeks. Her death had a tremendous impact on me and I think of her often. Sometimes I wish I had known her longer. However, I don't think time would have allowed me to know her better than sharing her last weeks of life.

Once in a while a patient's death reaches out and grabs at me, causing me to search within myself for the reason it affects me so deeply. Joan's did just that to me. I struggle even today as I remember her and her dying experience. The nearness of our ages, the fact that she died at the same age as my own mother, the very act of acknowledging my own mortality in her experience caused an inner conflict and torment as I witnessed her dying. Yet in the end, I found peace, not from anything I could control, in Joan's acceptance of the uncontrollable.

Submitted by Sue Handle Terbay

## IT IS SO BEAUTIFUL

Abigail and her family had a long standing tradition on the Fourth of July, a family reunion. This year was to be no exception.

# GIFTS

Abigail was nearing the end of her life and suffering tremendous pain associated with her cancer. However, she and her family were determined to go through with their holiday plans.

Her six grown children and their families gathered at Abigail's home for the family reunion. They all had the privilege of witnessing their mother, who had been heavily sedated with pain medication and in and out of consciousness, open her eyes. She smiled at them and said, "It is so beautiful." As she spoke these words, her breathing stopped. She died peacefully, free of pain, surrounded by her family's love and seeing the world to come.

Submitted by Clarissa Crooks

## TRUCK STOP

Irene's last request struck me as a little odd, but the family found it rather fitting.

Irene had suffered with breathing difficulties and pain, yet been joyful as she moved toward death. Each summer, Irene, her husband, and children would travel to Indiana for a camping vacation. They would stop at a small truck stop on the Indiana border for lunch. Irene would look at the menu, comment on the various sandwiches and soups, but always order the same thing —a pork tenderloin sandwich.

Her last request was that her ashes be taken to that Indiana campground and scattered. However, first her family had to stop at the truck stop and order her a pork tenderloin sandwich.

After Irene's death, I talked with Irene's daughter, JoAnn and I asked her if they had, indeed, stopped and fulfilled Irene's last request.

"Oh, yes," she laughed. "We walked into that truck stop carrying Mom's ashes, sat down at our regular table, and ordered the sandwich. In fact, we all had pork tenderloins. They were delicious. We laughed and cried. We had a great time and I'm sure Mom did too."

JoAnn continued. "And that's not all."

"What do you mean?" I asked.

"You know how Mom was struggling and yet so ready to die. She just couldn't stand to be fighting for every breath of air. She had said all her good-byes and I was ready to let her go. But still she hung on. I think it was for my brother, Mike. Mike was having such a hard time. When he finally was able to say good-bye, Mom died within ten minutes. I think she was waiting for Mike to be okay."

"Two days after we returned from Indiana, something strange happened. My daughter, Allie, was grieving and missing her Grandma. Allie woke me up and asked me to come to Grandma's old room. I did and as I walked in I could hear country music. We both stood there listening to the songs that my Mom used to love. Allie looked at me, I looked at her and we both shrugged our shoulders."

"Allie was so cute. She finally looked at my mom's picture and said, 'I think you're supposed to go to the light, Grandma.'"

"The music continued for the next few nights, and Allie kept repeating her instructions. It wasn't until my brother came over that we discovered where the music was coming from. We had left an old clock radio on in the basement—the electricity had gone off and the alarm had reset to midnight,which is when the music came on,"

I laughed, "So it wasn't really your mom ..."

"No, but she did come to Allie in a dream. Allie saw her in our old home, sewing. Her body was young again and she wasn't breathing hard. Allie knew that Grandma was okay and I knew after that dream that Allie would be okay too."

# *GIFTS*

JoAnn and her family continue to travel to Indiana for the summers. They still stop at their favorite truck stop and always order an extra pork tenderloin sandwich.

Submitted by Anne Wallace Sharp

## THE SEED

I introduced myself to Mrs. Thomas and explained that I was there to see how her husband was doing. Very matter-of-factly, she responded, "Oh, I think he's pretty close to dying."

I was startled by the calmness in her voice, but withheld further comment until after I had examined her husband. Mrs. Thomas was correct. Her husband was actively dying: his breathing came in short, irregular gasps; his skin color was gray and his face was gaunt and lifeless.

I confirmed her earlier appraisal and sat down to talk with her. "How are you doing, Mrs. Thomas?" I asked.

"Oh, I'm doing all right."

"You are?" I was frankly skeptical that anyone could be dealing with an impending death in such a calm manner.

"Well ... I'm sad ... naturally ... I mean we've been married for nearly forty years. And of course I'll miss Tom, but I know he'll come back to me and somehow put my mind at ease."

"What do you mean?"

"I mean that I know Tom will come back after he's died and let me know he's okay."

She paused. "I can see I need to explain. When I was younger, I didn't really believe in angels. I wasn't even really sure if I believed in God ... but that all changed when my father died ten years ago. You see, my father always worked in his garden.

He'd plant seeds each spring and then wait for the vegetables and flowers to bloom. Each year for his birthday, he'd ask for seed packets. Then for my birthday, he'd send flowers or vegetables that he himself grew. "

"When he got sick he couldn't work in his garden anymore, but he still loved to talk about all the things he'd grown. He died in early February ten years ago. I thought of him often as spring approached that year. And then ... one morning I was sitting here on this very sofa reading the newspaper. In fact, I was reading an article about gardening in the home section. As I was putting the paper away to go do something else ... I don't remember what ... but anyway, I felt something lumpy in the folds of my skirt. I reached my hands down and I found over a dozen seeds there."

"I knew right then and there that my father had sent those seeds to me ... and I knew he was all right."

Submitted by Anne Wallace Sharp

## I'VE BEEN BUSY

One of the patients I cared for was Michael a man in his mid-fifties with a lung ailment. He didn't talk much during my visits because he became very short of breath whenever he exerted himself. His wife, Mary, shared many things, however. She told me the story of their love affair.

Mary and Michael had been high school sweethearts. However, after graduation, each had gone his/her own way. They had each been married, but their marriages had both ended in divorce. They became re-acquainted through a mutual friend. Their previous love for each other was rekindled. They had been very happily married for ten years when he became ill. It was very painful for Mary to face losing her husband and dearest friend. I promised her that I would be available to support her during her grief.

Following his death, I shared with Mary the feelings she might expect to experience. I told her that a normal reaction to grief is the desire to have contact with the loved one who has died. I explained to her that sometimes strange phenomena do happen and that she should not be shocked if somehow he was able to find a way to get a message to her that would bring comfort her.

Months passed before I received a call from Mary. When I went to her home to visit, she thanked me for preparing her. She had made a habit of visiting Michael's grave frequently. On one of these occasions, she struck up a conversation with a man who was also visiting the cemetery. He had lost his wife. In their conversation, she learned that he had known and worked with her husband. The gentleman invited her to have a cup of coffee and she had accepted.

That same night, she went on to tell me, she was getting out of bed to go to the bathroom. She saw her husband standing in the doorway. He was smiling at her. She said the first thing that came to her mind was, "What took you so long?"

His response was, "I've been busy." He didn't stay long, but she felt his caring. She also knew he had no condemnation of her for having a conversation with another man. This eased the feelings of guilt she had been having all day long.

I assured her that I felt Michael was accepting and wanted only for her to be happy.

I have since pondered his remarks and find it thought provoking that "We are kept busy in our new life."

Submitted by Clarissa Crooks

# SHARP AND TERBAY

## LARRY

Larry was not a religious man and rarely talked about God or his faith. One day during a visit to his home, I casually asked, "Larry, have you seen any angels?"

Larry responded, very matter-of-factly, "Well, yes. In fact, there's one that sits right up there on the mantle above the fireplace."

"Really?"

"Oh, yes. He comes and goes all the time."

Larry went on to describe his visitor in detail. He seemed very comforted by the angel's presence and found this occurrence not at all unusual.

"Can you tell me what you talk about?"

"Oh, no. I'm not at liberty to share that information with you."

Submitted by Debbie McMillan

## NEW BEGINNING

In recent years, I cared for a woman in her nineties. Ethel had been an extremely active woman all her life. She possessed a creative talent for making crafts. For example, she had made out of painted wood, beads and hand-crochet Christmas ornaments for family members. These ornaments had become family treasures. When I visited her during the Christmas season, I noticed the family tree was covered with her handiwork. Her birthday happened to be on Christmas day, making the Christmas holidays one of her favorite seasons.

# GIFTS

Her daughter was a retired nursing instructor and provided excellent care. While she was very knowledgeable about the physical care required by her mother, she appreciated my insights into symbolic speech and the spiritual phenomena of dying.

One day when I arrived, Ethel's daughter told me her mother kept mentioning a man in white, who stood at the foot of her bed. When I examined Ethel, I asked her about this man. She calmly informed me that, at that very moment, he was standing at the foot of her bed. I asked her whether he was saying anything to her and she replied, "No."

I asked her if the man's presence made her afraid, and once again she replied in the negative. I shared with her my belief that he came from a spiritual realm and was here to provide her comfort. She accepted this and was able to enjoy the holiday season with her children and grandchildren, who had come from out of state to be with her.

After not eating for days, she was able to share a turkey dinner with them on Christmas day. During the meal, she had a vision. She told her family that she saw a letter written on the wall. She asked to be raised up so she could see who had signed it, but was unable to decipher the signature. Her daughter asked her if she could tell what the letter was about.

Ethel explained it was about "the beginning." This woman died peacefully the day after Christmas—with her family by her side. "The beginning" was a new life.

Submitted by Clarissa Crooks

# SHARP AND TERBAY

## WELCOME HOME

"I'm afraid I won't recognize Jesus when he comes and that I won't know what to do." Mark said to me one day shortly before his death.

His wife Brenda stood by my side with tears in her eyes as we tried to assure him that when the time came he would know what to do.

"He's always known exactly what to do. I hate to see him so concerned," Brenda told me later. I encouraged her to remind him of this at every opportunity. But I could see that both of them were anxious and afraid.

When I returned two days later I found Brenda and Mark more at ease. I asked her what had happened. She told me that a very close friend, who was also a priest, had visited Mark. The priest had led Mark in a meditation that would help him recognize Jesus and to know what to do.

"The remarkable thing," Brenda said, "is that since then Mark hasn't been afraid. He's not restless anymore. He seems to be at peace." Indeed, he did appear to be more calm and tranquil. Despite his ragged and shallow breathing, there was a serenity about him. When I left, I also felt less anxious.

Later that afternoon, Brenda called and told me that Mark had died. I rushed over to their house. Still crying, she met me at the door and we embraced. "You won't believe this," she stammered as she led me to the bedroom.

Mark was lying motionless, his face serene in the peace of death in the middle of their bed. As Brenda related the story of his dying, my own tears began. "We were all gathered, around the bed: the boys, myself, my sister and my best friend. It had been cloudy and dark all day, so I pushed back the curtains above the head of the bed. Suddenly, the sun broke out from behind the clouds and shone through the colored glass sign in the window that reads 'Welcome Home.' When the sun touched Mark, he took a breath. Twice more the sun did that, shining right down on him through that sign. Mark took his last breath as the sun receded the third time."

I was chilled and warmed simultaneously.

"I guess God made sure Mark could find his way home," Brenda stammered between tears.

"Welcome home Mark," we both said together, rejoicing in Mark's final victory.

Submitted by Anne Wallace Sharp

## ROBBIE AND MILLIE

Robbie was admitted to the hospice program for the second time. Six months previously, he had been discharged because his condition had improved and his doctors were hopeful that, if not cured, he was at least in temporary remission. When I saw Robbie again, it was a bittersweet reunion. It was good to see an old friend, but under these circumstances it meant that his lung cancer had come out of remission. His disease was now causing him severe pain in his right arm, as well as, difficulty breathing.

I was surprised when I saw Robbie again. When he had been discharged from the program, he had been almost bald, due to previous chemotherapy and radiation. The large man who met me at the door had a headful of dark curly hair. He looked far younger than his sixty years. He had gained some weight and looked better than I had anticipated. However, he soon began chemotherapy again, and it wasn't long before the curly dark hair was gone, to be replaced by his familiar Kojak-look.

Robbie was a "character." He came across as a gruff, abrasive and very private man. He didn't like needing other people and he cherished his independence. He wanted to do things his way or no way. His manner, at times, was very abrupt and his attitude often pushed people away. Those who "hung in" there with him gained his unspoken admiration and respect. I "hung in" there with Robbie partly out of my own stubbornness, but also because I grew to care about him a great deal.

When he was referred again to the hospice, he was still predominantly living alone. He had an "interesting," though strange relationship and arrangement with his wife, Millie. They lived several hundred miles apart. She had agreed to come stay with him for two weeks at a time to cook, clean and wash his clothes. She would then return to her home, to attend to her own home and needs. They had been married for over twenty years, but they seemed to get along best separated. This was confirmed by the bickering that cropped up between them when they were together. Both seemed to genuinely care about the other, but agreed they couldn't live together in harmony.

Millie was a sweet woman who never stopped talking. Her health began to fail shortly after Robbie's readmission to the hospice program. She was having severe pain in her left arm, and, at times, could barely use it. Despite her discomfort, she continued to cook, clean, and do his laundry. She was forced to return home early to see her own physician. While there, she took a misstep off the porch, breaking one of the bones in her left arm. She returned with her arm in a sling.

Robbie was mostly a loner. He was estranged from whatever siblings he had, but had resumed a relationship with his son, Joe, from a previous marriage. Joe brought much joy into Robbie's life by introducing him to his granddaughter of eighteen months. For a while, Joe was a bright spot in Robbie's lonely life. Unfortunately, Joe betrayed Robbie in a series of lies and questionable acts. Joe's betrayal was difficult for Robbie to overcome. Hospice volunteers took up the slack by buying groceries and transporting Robbie and Millie to appointments.

One day, Millie came home to find Robbie unable to move or get out of bed. She panicked and called 911. Robbie was admitted to one of the local hospitals. The cancer had spread and was now affecting his movement and strength. Despite Robbie's determination to walk again, the doctors did not feel that physical therapy would be beneficial. Plans were made to discharge him from the hospital. Because of his home situation and Millie's physical limitations, Robbie was transferred to the hospice center. His condition was quickly deteriorating and Robbie realized that he would never return home.

Tragically, at this same time, Millie was also diagnosed with terminal cancer. The arm fracture had been a pathological one, caused by metastasis to the bone. She was hospitalized. Neither Robbie nor Millie was in any kind of physical shape to visit the other. Now they were truly separated by a distance neither could overcome.

Robbie was now alone. His illness and weakness made him totally dependent on others. Unfortunately, there were very few people around for him to depend on. By this time in our relationship, he had learned to trust me. He turned to me for help, and in the process, allowed himself to be very open and vulnerable.

Robbie's number one concern was making funeral arrangements. Millie was physically unable to make them, so I volunteered. At Robbie's request, I began to make inquiries. Robbie had indicated his desire to be cremated. I called the funeral director that Robbie selected and made an appointment for him to meet with Robbie at the Hospice. As luck would have it, all the experienced funeral directors were at a convention and a very young mortician agreed to come talk to Robbie. I wasn't sure this was going to work, as the young man's knees shook throughout the interview. However, he did manage to complete all the necessary paperwork, despite profuse sweating and trembling hands.

Robbie seemed relieved that all the arrangements had been made. He appeared at peace, and ready to say his goodbyes. Millie's brother and his family came for what they knew would be their last visit. I called Joe, Robbie's son, but he never came. Millie was still in the hospital, so I made a long distance phone call. She and Robbie could, at least, share some special time—even if it was by telephone. It was a tearful phone call, as Robbie told his wife that all his funeral arrangements had been made. He suggested she have some kind of a memorial service for him when she got out of the hospital. They said their goodbyes to each other, amidst a roomful of tearful onlookers.

I felt burdened at times with the responsibility Robbie had given me, but I also felt blessed that he had come to trust me with his final arrangements and more importantly, his feelings. I worked with Robbie for a long time. He pushed me to the point of frustration many times, but I know that he also respected me and counted me among his friends.

A few days later, Robbie lapsed into a semi-comatose state. I was home doing laundry on a Sunday afternoon, when I suddenly had the distinct feeling that Robbie's spirit was with me in the room. I found out later that Robbie had died shortly after these feelings came to me. I felt comforted by Robbie's spirit. In my heart that he came to say goodbye and tell me that he was "okay." I rejoiced in his presence.

Goodbye, Robbie. I loved you, too.

Submitted by Marilyn Thomas

# 2

# Glimpses of Faith

*Many hospice professionals, as well as the two authors*
*contribute stories of their own, as well as patients',*
*spiritual faith.*

## A MESSENGER

In my personal faith, I believe that God sends us angels. Angels have different assignments. For example, the Angel Gabriel was a messenger to Mary. I believe we still have such messengers today. Their messages sometimes can be muffled in our hectic society, but if we look and listen, the angels are there. If we are open, their messages of love come across loud and clear.

In my heart, I will forever remember a fourteen-year-old Leukemia patient, who quietly and unassumingly delivered his message of love. For those of us who were open enough to discover this treasure, we will forever be blessed by what we found.

A social worker from Children's Medical Center called me regarding Terry. He was an inner city boy who lived under conditions "middle-class folks" only read about. To say this young man had already lived a life time in his fourteen years is an understatement. The social worker told me that Terry had asked not to go home to die, but that he wanted to come to the Hospice

Center. After talking with the center co-ordinator, arrangements were made for Terry to visit the Hospice Center. I was asked to give the tour.

The receptionist called me, announcing Terry's arrival. I approached the front desk and the social worker from the hospital greeted me. He introduced me to Terry's nurse, his mother and finally to Terry himself. He was a shy, quiet young man who had an incandescent smile and twinkling eyes. I began my usual litany of what the Center had to offer.

Every once in a while, I would glance at this young man and try to tell him something I thought he might want to hear. "You can eat anything you want—just let the kitchen staff know what your favorite foods are."

He responded, "I love pork chops."

"You've got it!" I told him, and once again that wonderful smile spread across his face.

It was obvious from the conversation between the social worker and Terry that they had a special relationship. This quiet young man was making adult decisions about the remainder of his brief life and I couldn't help but wonder, "what is he thinking?" How would I be reacting if I was forced to make some of these tough decisions?

After the tour, the four guests sat with the center co-ordinator to discuss the time of Terry's admission. The president and founder of the hospice told me later that day, "If we can't give this young man a place to live and provide him with all our knowledge and skills so his last days can be happy, then why are we in existence?"

A week later, Terry made his appearance. According to his physicians, Terry had approximately one month left to live. This was very difficult to accept, especially in light of how "healthy" he had looked when I gave him the tour. Except for his bald head—which, ironically, is in style—a "civilian" would never have guessed that this boy was so close to death.

# GIFTS

My interactions with Terry were different than other staff members. Our relationship began very slowly. I had hoped to play cards or other games with him. However, it took some time to get past his shyness, but once he relaxed and "let me in," I was hooked by the warm beautiful smile that always crossed his face when I walked in.

I began by stopping to see if he was okay. That didn't last long because Terry was often not in his room. He had a very busy "social schedule." His friends from the children's hospital would stop by and off they would go. He became quite the little "social butterfly."

One of the hospice nurses told Terry she would like to take him to a local amusement park. His face lit up. He told us he had never been to such a park and was excited at the thought. The planning began. The staff decided to take up a collection so Terry could have money to spend. We were quite surprised by his reaction. He wanted to work for the money—not just have it given to him. So the staff started finding him little "odd" jobs to do.

In my own department, there were four clinical secretaries who were eager to "mother" this young man. So we set up jobs for him on a daily basis. He kept track of his own hours, making up a "time card." He was an extremely good worker. In fact, we had to tell him repeatedly to slow down so he didn't make us look bad. He responded with a soft laugh. Soon he was turning away the volunteers "assigned" to play cards or video games with him so he could work. We, in turn, looked forward to his "visits."

Finally, it was time for his amusement park adventure. He talked about it incessantly. He rode every ride at least once—some, twice. Pictures of a happy, carefree boy were circulated through the office.

Shortly after this adventure, Terry's battle against cancer intensified. He wanted to come back and work in our area again, but the nurses asked me to discourage him; he was simply too weak. I told him he needed to rest and that we would hold the jobs for him.

One day when he was feeling pretty low, the "mothers," took up a collection and bought Terry a teddy bear. We took it down to his room. As we entered, we found him laying on his side. It was obvious, even from the doorway, that a lot of his spunk was gone. I gave him the teddy bear and told Terry if he needed a hug, that he could hug the bear and know that his "mothers" were hugging him in return.

We started to leave, but he tugged at my arm. He had received his report card from school that same day and he wanted me to read it. I picked it up from his side table and read aloud each subject and grade. Nothing was below a "C." It was a really fantastic report card, and I leaned down, kissed him, and told him how proud I was of him!

As I laid it back down and started to leave, a strong voice from the bed called out "Sue." I turned around, startled, and went to his side, "What is it, Terry?"

He said, in a quiet voice, "How much?"

"Excuse me. How much what?"

"How much you gonna pay me for such a good report card?"

I stood there, looking at that cherub face and began to laugh. "You little imp! I told you I was proud of you—even gave you a kiss. What more do you want?"

He just giggled.

"Okay," I said. "But it's only because I like you so much. I'll give you some money."

He grinned and told me the nurses out at the desk had an envelope there. The staff had taken up a collection for him. Talk about having his caretakers wrapped around his little finger!

In the days that followed Terry began rapidly losing his battle with Leukemia. All that was left for me to do was stop in, rub his little bald head, and kiss him good-bye.

# GIFTS

Other staff members, especially the nurses had become extremely close to Terry. His counselors became more acquainted with the little boy inside, and the ministers more in tune with his spirit.

Terry touched us all—at different levels, in different ways, at different times. He "provoked" us to love him, one of his ministers stated at his funeral, but even more he "evoked" love.

As Terry's death grew more imminent, the nurses explained to me how he would probably die. It was at this point that my tears started—he was really going to die. The day of his death, I felt drawn to his room. He never complained and continuously apologized for being such a cause for concern.

My final moments with Terry were spent rubbing his head. I told him how much he had taught me about love, laughter, and being a kid. He managed to give me one more beautiful smile. I kissed him and told him how much I really did love him. He nuzzled close to me. I reluctantly let him go and left.

He died that night in a peaceful sleep.

His funeral was attended by family, friends, neighbors, church members, and his extended family from Children's Hospital and the hospice. The service was a tribute to a special young man.

As he was dying, Terry had asked that a memorial brick be purchased with just his name on it. The staff at the hospice, as well as that at the children's hospital donated more than enough money to purchase this brick. The remainder was put towards the hospice's Children's Bereavement — a fund was started in his name. We believe that Terry would have liked that. He was worried constantly about his three younger siblings. So we knew in our hearts that Terry would want all children to have help with their grief issues.

There is a picture of Terry in the secretary's area where his "mothers" and all the staff can view it. We have it framed and on display in tribute to this remarkable young man—a messenger of love. He was only with us four weeks and one day, but his memory will stay with us for a lifetime.

Terry's message was love—unconditional, unselfish—freeing love. His message was that there is goodness in this world if we look for it, see it in each other and are open to its presence.

Our goal at the hospice was to attempt to make Terry's final days happy. We allowed Terry to be a kid again. In return, we met an angel.

The evening when Terry was dying, I was very troubled. I knew he would not survive the evening. I took a walk. I "talked" to his spirit. Later that night, I tossed and turned in a fretful sleep. The following morning, Terry "helped" me write the following poem. The words that flowed have not been changed. They came directly from my heart, directly from my spirit.


## MY CHILD


He's not my child.
I didn't give birth to him
I never nursed him,
or cradled him in my arms.

He's not my child.
I wasn't there to wipe the tears,
to play peek-a-boo,
to kiss his scratches.

He's not my child.
I wasn't present for his first words,
his first steps,
that wonderful first smile.

He's not my child.
I never taught him about life,

# GIFTS

Never held his hand crossing the street,
Never helped with his school work.

He's not my child.
We never talked about
his future,
his ambitions;
about girls and dating,
or about
the anguish of being a teenager.

He's not my child.
He's just a kid
And kids die every day.
Why should I care?
Why should I cry?


What could we possibly have had in common, a silver-
haired, forty-something, white, middle-class woman and a bald,
teenage, black, inner city boy?

Yet he was like my own child and had become a part of my
spirit. As the child reached deeper within me, my heart was
warmed by a profound presence.

He is my child.
Born of my spirit,
a part of me forever,
a son.

Submitted by Sue Handle Terbay

## THE TREE

Frank Turner, an eighty-eight year old African American, lived in a house which had no central heating. A cold draft, at ankle height, blew through out the dilapitated little cottage. His wife kept the oven on with its door open all the time in an effort to keep them warm.

Yet, this man owned several vacant lots up and down the street. When houses burned down or were condemned and wrecked, he bought the lots. He allowed his neighbors, who had even less than he did, to plant gardens on the property. He did not charge them for the use of his land.

His wife once complained, in my presence, that if he would only charge a little rent, they could make some much needed repairs to their own house. He replied that land and what it produces is a gift from God. "Only greedy people charge for things freely given by God," he said

During the weeks before his death, I saw many examples of his extraordinary character. I also witnessed and heard the admiration others felt for him. His adult grandsons, who were starting careers as electricians, came to him frequently for counsel. They wanted advice on how best to give fair estimates for their work and how to establish a position for themselves in the business community. His daughters-in-law vied for the honor of being the daughter who fixed food tasty enough to tempt him to eat a full meal. His pastor visited at least weekly and he received as much comfort, I think, as he gave.

I tried to describe this gentleman to my family and co-workers, but was never able to find words to convey adequately the quiet strength of the man—until I went to his funeral. I listened as his pastor spoke, " ... he was a tree planted by the rivers of water. He put deep roots into the earth and drew his food and his water from the source. He spread his boughs wide and offered shelter, peace and God's love to all he met ..."
Submitted by Maggie Bauer, R. N.

# GIFTS

## THE FAITH HEALER

Bob Ledford was a quiet man. He and his brother, Jim, had run a local business for years. People described Bob as a level-headed, no-nonsense businessman. He believed only in what he could see, touch and prove. His disease lung cancer changed all that.

I had been to see Bob several times and found he and his wife, Shirley, pleasant, likeable people. We had spent several visits out on their deck which overlooked the woods. We talked about Bob's disease, his love of hunting, and his struggle to come to grips with his failing health. As his lung cancer progressed, he was becoming weaker and more short of breath. However, he was determined not to give in. He wanted to keep fighting, looking for a way to get better.

In early October, I arrived for my scheduled visit to find Bob in wonderful spirits and looking better than I'd seen him in some time. I asked him the reason for this improvement.

Looking a little sheepish, he laughed. Then he proceeded to tell me in great detail what had occurred. For a man of few words, Bob spoke eloquently and animatedly. "I went to see a faith healer," he said.

"You did?"

"Yes and before you laugh, let me tell you what a phenomenal experience it was." He paused and continued, "His name is Daniel and he lives in Indiana. He's a Dunkard and has a farm about three and a half hours from here. I heard about him from my doctor. Apparently, he sees patients by appointment on Tuesdays and Wednesdays, but takes walk-ins on Monday. My brother drove me down. We left Sunday evening and arrived around midnight. Already there were cars lined up in Daniel's driveway. We pulled in behind a huge van and waited. I was pretty tired, so I laid down in the back of the truck."

"At about three or four in the morning, I was aroused by what I first thought was thunder. I sat up and looked out the window, just in time to see a magnificent black stallion gallop by at what seemed to be ninety miles an hour. He was pulling a black carriage with a tall, probably six-foot-four or so, dunkard driving. He was wearing a black coat, black hat and had a long white flowing beard."

"An hour later, another black horse and carriage passed. Each hour after that until the sun came up a carriage passed. Those horses were so close, I could have touched them."

"When it became light, I could see how many other cars were there. There must have been twenty cars, trucks, vans— even a motorcycle. My brother and I got out and talked to some of the folks. They were mostly from Ohio and Indiana, but one was there all the way from Arkansas."

"I was about tenth in line, so my brother and I waited. We watched a man enter vomiting. He had a brain tumor. He came out without a headache and no longer vomiting. A little girl entered also and seemed better when she came out."

"It was finally my turn. My brother and I were escorted into Daniel's house. A simple home with a few pieces of wooden furniture. Real plain. Daniel greeted us. He was amazing — maybe fifty years old, long with a white beard, clear blue eyes and wearing this funny little hat. His voice was so soft I could barely hear it. His hands were amazing. He talked to me of how the body wants to rid itself of disease and how I need to help my body do this. He prescribed some special bath salts which supposedly will rid my body of its impurities and poisons. He told me that I would expel my own cancer through the skin, but that first I would undergo much sickness, vomiting and weakness. I have to tell you I was cynical at first, but Daniel was convincing."

"He was helped by three or four young women. We all stood around in a circle, holding hands, I truly felt something— a lot of energy—power. I'm not exactly sure what it was, but something was happening inside me. Anyway, Daniel gave me a

# GIFTS

bunch of different herbs to take. I'm supposed to go back to see him in a month. Here's the clincher ... Daniel won't take any money—no gifts—no donations. He told me that his healing abilities are a gift and it would be wrong to take money for something that has been given as a gift. That convinced me."

"By the time we returned home, I was exhausted, but I felt good. I felt different. Maybe it's hope ..."

I listened to Bob's story with amazement, skepticism and hope.

Bob's condition did improve for a while. Physically, he was briefly better and mentally he was much improved. He began talking more, sharing more of his life's stories and expressing his feelings about his disease and death. His attitude remained positive. He believed that he would be healed. However, as his disease progressed, his focus shifted from physical healing to spiritual healing.

He was able to tell his family how much he loved them. He talked often about God. The night before he died, his wife sat up talking with him and holding his hand. She later told me she felt a strong sense of spirit in the room—a presence.

I said, "Maybe it was one of those black carriages coming for him with a huge stallion."

She teared up and nodded.

Bob died peacefully the next afternoon with his family around his bedside.

Submitted by Anne Wallace Sharp

Submitted by Anne Wallace Sharp

75

# SHARP AND TERBAY

## FRANK

An emergency request had been received from one of the local nursing homes. They asked if one of our hospice nurses could visit a patient who had been "actively" dying for several days. The nursing home staff felt that, for some reason unbeknownst to them, this patient was unable to "let go." They were concerned about the degree of his suffering and his agonizing struggle to die.

I agreed to visit the patient to see if I could help. When I arrived at the nursing home, I stopped by the director's office where I was introduced to the patient's family.

Everyone began talking at once. Two of the adult children voiced their anger at the nursing home. They felt the nurses were prolonging their father's life and making his death more difficult. Another family member insisted that her father be sent to the hospital. "I'm sure he'd get better, if he was transferred ..." she said. Her demand was met by scowls from the other family members.

I wanted to see the patient before I discussed anything further with the family, so I asked them if they objected to me visiting their father alone.

"As soon as I speak with him, I'll come out and talk with each of you," I said. They agreed.

When I entered the patient's room, I was surprised to see Frank, a man I had cared for when I was a public health nurse several years earlier. He was in severe respiratory distress, gasping for air with every breath. His eyes had the terrified look of an animal struggling to free itself from a trap.

I leaned over Frank, introduced myself, and asked him if he remembered me. He nodded his head to indicate that he did.

I moved a wooden chair closer to the bed and asked him what was wrong. He didn't respond—nor did he look at me. His eyes were focused intently on the bare wall. I asked him again, "Do you know what's happening?"

76

He turned toward me, and matter-of-factly stated, "I'm dying."

I reached out, touched his hand and said, "I know."

We sat there like that for a few moments, before I asked, "Are you afraid?"

His entire body shook with sobbing. "Well," I thought, "that's the problem. He is afraid of dying."

I tried to find out something about his belief system so I could help lessen his fears. Frank adamantly insisted that he had a strong faith in God and believed in an afterlife. "I'm not afraid of God," he stated firmly.

"Are you afraid of the pain?" He shook his head.

"Are you afraid for your children?" No, he wasn't, he assured me.

"Are you afraid of being alone?" Again, he shook his head.

I was running out of questions, when Frank finally blurted out, "I'm afraid of Margaret."

I remembered that Margaret was his wife. She had died eight years ago.

"Frank," I asked softly while I held his hand, "Can you tell me why you're afraid of Margaret?"

He began to sob again. The tears rolled down his face and his breathing became even more labored as he cried. Finally, he managed a few words. "I've been bad," he said.

I was really puzzled now. I didn't have the foggiest idea what he meant and I told him this.

"She's going to be angry with me," he explained in a gasping voice. The words came out with difficulty, and he paused frequently to catch his breath. "Margaret had such high standards.... Very moral.... Religious.... She won't like what I've done," he said. "I've had several girl friends," he confessed as the tears returned.

Several years earlier when Frank had severely cut his foot in a lawn mower accident his injury had required daily dressing changes, which were assigned to a home health aide. As his public health nurse, I had difficulty keeping the aides on Frank's case. When I questioned them about why they didn't want to return to his home, several of them had told me that Frank had made "passes" at them and gotten "fresh."

"I'm afraid to see Margaret," Frank continued, "I'm afraid she hates me for what I've done."

Frank and I talked for several more minutes. I told him that I believed when people died and were reunited with their loved ones, that all the negative emotions on earth were no longer felt. This seemed to reassure him.

He became even more peaceful when I said, "And besides, I believe that God has already forgiven you. I'm sure Margaret has too."

I suggested that he reflect back and try to remember a time when Margaret was extremely happy. He thought for a few moments and then smiled.

"It was when we were dating. I met her at a picnic and fell in love with her smile. And what a smile it was!" he reflected. He saddened as he continued, "Somewhere along the way, she lost that smile. I think it was trying to survive on our farm — struggling with all the kids. Somehow she turned all rigid and stern. But boy, I sure do remember that smile."

I asked him to concentrate on the image of his wife smiling and to keep this picture in his mind.

"I think Margaret will be very glad to see you, Frank. In fact, I believe she'll be so happy that she'll hold out her hands to you and welcome you home to heaven," I said reassuringly.

Frank visibly relaxed. We both sat quietly with this pleasant image of his wife. I hated to disturb this serenity, but I knew there was one more piece of unfinished business.

I told him that his daughter was having a really difficult struggle with the thought of him dying. He nodded his head, "I know, but, what can I do?"

"Maybe you need to tell her what's happening — that you're ready to die."

# GIFTS

One by one, the children were called into Frank's room, where they said their good-byes. His daughter came in last. Frank held her hand and comforted her as he told her that he was dying. She gradually accepted his words and was able to tearfully tell him that she would be all right.

Frank then gave them a list of possessions he wanted each of his grandchildren to have. By the time he finished, his breathing had eased.

I sat with Frank and his family for a few more minutes, then said my own goodbyes. I urged his family to stay close by.

"It won't be long, now. A few days at most," I said.

I turned to Frank, bent over, kissed him good-bye and said, "Hold onto that image." He nodded and smiled.

Frank died two hours later. I have never had to do so much work to help a patient "die" in such a short time frame. But never have such few moments brought such spirited satisfaction.

Submitted by Sandy Bonamassa


## AMAZING GRACE

Sylvia was a frail, dignified and very frightened woman. Her abdominal cancer had spread to the lungs and she was becoming increasingly short of breath. Walking from her bed to the bathroom exhausted her. I suggested oxygen. She repeatedly turned down the suggestion, saying she really didn't think she needed it.

Her shortness of breath finally became so severe that she was struggling to breathe all the time—talking or eating became a monumental task. I suggested oxygen again. She again began to deny her need for it but hesitated.

# SHARP AND TERBAY

"I'm really afraid of it—once I start it I won't be able to get off it. I'm afraid I'll grow dependent on it," she confessed.

I explained that she could use it when she needed it, but didn't have to wear it all the time unless she wanted to. She reluctantly agreed to try. I underestimated her hesitation and her fear.

When Tom from the oxygen home care company delivered the oxygen, he found my patient literally terrified of the tubing and the concentrator unit. Sitting in a large recliner chair in the family room, Sylvia expressed her fear and told him that she had changed her mind.

Tom began talking to her and explained very patiently how the oxygen would help her conserve her strength. Sylvia still balked at the idea. Tom could see that Sylvia's fear was only making her more short of breath.

He noticed an old piano sitting against the wall and asked Sylvia if she played. She responded that before she got sick, she used to play the organ and piano at church.

Tom smiled, "My father was a minister and I grew up playing piano and the organ too."

"Really? Can you still play?" Sylvia asked.

"I'm a little rusty, but I'll see what I can do," Tom said as he pulled out the piano bench. He fingered the keys and launched into a beautiful rendition of "Amazing Grace."

Sylvia closed her eyes and relaxed as the music filled the room. When he finished his recitation Sylvia opened her eyes and smiled, "I guess I could try that oxygen, after all."

Submitted by Anne Wallace Sharp

# GIFTS

## CALVIN

Sometimes, we in the medical profession don't have much to offer a patient. Calvin was ninety-five when he discovered he had pancreatic cancer. Due to his age, the doctors recommended no active treatment. That was fine with Calvin. As he saw it, a daily dose of prayer and sun (by sitting on his front porch) was all he needed. Calvin lived two more years with a sense of well-being and a strong faith. Maybe Calvin knew something the rest of us didn't.

Submitted by Kim Vesey

## SPIRITUAL CARE

When attending to the spiritual needs of a patient, it is not always possible for the chaplain to know how effective his words or presence has been. There is no agenda for our visits. Sometimes a visit can be significant and other times it is not. Often we may not be aware of the many dynamics which affect a particular patient during a visit, unless it is pointed out by someone who was there at the time. The following is a copy of a letter which was written after a visit from one of the hospice chaplains:

I was sore—sick with pain and suffering and a man came in. He comforted me and gripped my hand. As the tears and suffering continued, he offered a prayer to God to ease the suffering and pain.

As the nurses ministered to me, he comforted me and I gripped his hand. He didn't flinch, but let me grip with all my strength.

He stayed until the hurting diminished and then he left.

I scarcely saw him come and didn't see him going. He'll never know how timely he came and the comfort that flowed to me.

God bless him, may the Lord make him aware of the great blessing I felt.

Submitted by V. "Pete" Hood, Chaplain

## KATHERINE

Katherine, a delightful, petite woman in her mid-seventies, greeted me with twinkling eyes and a sweet smile. She had requested daily Eucharist and I was given the privilege of walking yet another spiritual journey with one of the hospice patients.

As we visited, I found out that Katherine was a member of my church. We were able to share a little more during my visits, than I did with other patients because we knew many of the same people and shared common interests. I noticed her room was always full of roses. When I spotted a statue of St. Theresa, "The Little Flower," on her table, the roses began to make sense. I found out that Katherine had a deep love and devotion to St. Theresa. Over the years, I also had developed a devotion to this young saint. (For those unfamiliar with the story of St. Theresa, it is said that when you ask her to intercede to God in your name, she will answer you with roses.) Katherine and I shared some special memories regarding our favorite saint.

One day she revealed that St. Theresa would have an answer for her soon. I asked Katherine if she would tell me what it was. She smiled that sweet smile and, with a twinkle in her eye, said she most definitely would.

On the day before her death, I stopped by with a rose for Katherine. She was surrounded by family, so I did not get a chance to see or talk to her. I left the rose on the table and quietly left the room. I returned to my desk and placed another rose that I had picked up for myself in a vase.

That Friday was very busy and I had stayed late at work. Before going home, I thought I would stop in to see Katherine since I had missed our time together earlier. As I was turning off my light, I noticed the rose on my desk was wilting, but I was too tired to take the time to throw it away. It could wait until I returned on Monday.

As I entered Katherine's room, the only light came from a small lamp on the corner table. It was very quiet and empty and the room reminded me of a chapel. I walked over to Katherine's bed, gently brushed her hair off her forehead and whispered her name. To my surprise, she raised up her hands, jerkingly, and cried softly, "Don't touch me!"

Startled, I apologized and told her I would never hurt her. She looked at me and just as quickly, quietly said, "Sue, it's okay —you can."

She gave me a very tired, sweet smile again. I asked her if she had prayed to St. Theresa lately and she stated again that she had been told something was going to happen. Once again, she promised to let me know what it was. I asked her if she had seen the rose I brought to her. She said no and asked me to bring it over to her. As I showed her the still radiant rose, a beautiful smile crossed her face and then she closed her eyes. After placing the rose back on the table, I leaned down and kissed her good-bye.

That was the last time I saw Katherine.

Katherine was on my mind off and on all weekend. I wondered if her death had brought the answer for which she had been looking for. I wondered also how she would let me know the message she had received from St. Theresa.

# SHARP AND TERBAY

The following Monday when I arrived at my desk, the wilted rose I had left on Friday was perfectly preserved— totally dried. I have dried roses myself before but never one which remained in such perfect form. I felt this was Katherine's answer. Even though the rose had died, it was still beautiful. Only now it was in a different form. Katherine, though she had died, is similar to the dried rose. She is more beautiful in a different form.

Submitted by Susan Handle Terbay

## AMEN

One of my patients, Robert Todd was a real family man with four grown children. One of them was in the merchant marines and travelled extensively. He was able to get leave to come home when it became evident that his father's condition had become critical.

Mr. Todd continued deteriorating. One night as I arrived to check on my patient, I found him to be actively dying. His breathing was irregular and shallow, and I knew his time was short. His wife, son and one daughter were present at his bedside. His other two daughters had gone out shopping and there was no way to reach them.

I talked to him, believing that he could still hear me, even though he appeared to be in a coma. I told him we had called his minister, and he would be coming shortly. I also told him that we had attempted to reach his other two daughters but had been unsuccessful. I encouraged him to "hang on" until they returned home, if this was his wish.

# GIFTS

The minister arrived and comforted the family. Prayers were said, but I could see the patient was slipping away. We had finally been able to reach the two other girls and we told him that they were on their way home. His breathing continued to grow worse and he was close to death when his daughters arrived at his bedside.

Together the family formed a circle around his bed. They each said good-bye to him and then began to sing some of his favorite hymns. The minister led the family in the Lord's Prayer, while the family all held hands in a circle around the bed. His wife held one of her husband's hands, while another family member held the other. Thus the circle was complete. As the prayer came to an end, Mr Todd's breathing stopped. As the Amen was spoken, he slipped away, encircled by his loving family

Submitted by Clarissa Crooks

## WHERE DO YOU WANT ME, LORD?

One cold evening in December 1990, I was out walking and praying, "Where do you want me, Lord?" Several ideas came to mind and were dismissed immediately. Then I thought, "Hospice," and knew that was the answer I had been searching for. I had prayed for a job that would give me a challenge and an opportunity to use my gifts. The whole process of applying, interviewing and hiring fell into place, I have never had a doubt that I am where I belong.

I am often asked: "How do you do it?" and "Isn't it depressing?" I don't think being a hospice nurse is depressing. Yes, it is sad, but, not depressing. I don't believe we can run away from the emotional pain suffering causes. We all experience it in our lives. To avoid it only delays the growth that can result from the struggles we face.

I believe God is in control and nothing can happen to me without his permission. It may not be His will, but He allows it. Whatever God gives me is a gift and all His gifts are perfect. So I thank Him for the perfect gift. Then I pray that God will help me learn from the gift, that He will be given the glory, and that it will bless everyone around me. One of the blessings that has come out of my difficulties is a more sensitive awareness of the hurting all around me.

While I am caring for the patients to whom I am assigned, I also try to comfort the friends and families that visit the patients. Frequently, their pain in some ways, becomes mine and I pray for us when I am at home. I have learned from my work at the hospice that death is a gift from God. It is a rebirth. The loss and grief is for those left behind. We want to hold on to our bodies because it is all we know, we want to hold on to our loved ones because we can't imagine life without them.

I believe that suffering is not only an inevitable part of being human, but also of becoming like Christ. One way God helps us become more Christ-like is to make us feel responsible for relieving other's sufferings. This increases our empathy, makes us less critical and decreases self-pity. Then when we compare our lives to others, ours becomes easier.

I have great respect for the staff at the hospice. They are skilled, knowledgeable, and compassionate. They genuinely care for those who hurt. As patients work through their grief, they often share their thoughts with the staff. Intimate relationships are formed and we are touched by the influence we make in each other's lives.

Let me tell you about John. John, an attorney, was a very private man who liked to be in charge and in control. At times it seemed he was deliberately difficult, deciding which medication he would take, and when and how he would take it. I decided he needed to be in control of his "treatment" so I tried to save some extra time for him each day. I always greeted him with a hug, which he accepted with a smile, but never returned. He didn't like to talk much, partly because it hurt his throat. So he would often say, "Talk to me, Gretchen." I would tell him about my prayers and the answers I received. His interest grew as I shared my life with him. But when I offered a chaplain to pray with him or myself, he declined with a wave of his hand.

Time went by and one day as I was leaving his room, he asked, "Aren't you forgetting something?"

I looked at his face and knew the answer as I asked, "Do you want a hug?"

"Yes," he said as he slowly and laboriously, walked to me and hugged me.

"I need your spiritual guidance," he said. "I can't do this by myself." Then he asked me to pray for him there in his room.

As his condition deteriorated, he requested prayer again and pointed at his throat. I asked if he wanted me to pray that he would be able to swallow food more comfortably and he nodded. After I returned from a weekend off, I heard that he was swallowing more easily and eating again. I reminded him that our prayers were answered. He nodded in agreement and appeared deep in thought.

After John died, I told his daughter about our conversations. She said, "I'm so glad you could reach him. We never were able to, nor would he allow a priest to visit except when he was dying."

I believe God uses everyone to reach someone at their point of need. A hospice isn't just a place to die. It is a place where people resolve the past and grow to accept the future.

Not only death takes place, but also closure and rebirth. The people left behind often experience a renewal as they reminisce, review, resolve and say goodbye. It is humbling to be given the experience of sharing such a private and sacred journey.

# SHARP AND TERBAY

We all experience pain. We can't always eliminate it, but we can share it. We often make it easier to bear just by being there and listening as we treat the symptoms of the disease.

To put it simply: a child who heard her friend's tricycle was broken went to help. When she returned home, her mother asked her if she had fixed it? The child replied, "Oh, I couldn't do that. I just helped her cry."

Submitted by Gretchen Borne Root


## CHARLIE

"Dad is a stubborn, grumpy war veteran," his daughter warned me, apologizing in advance. I thanked her for the warning and said I felt sure I could handle him.

The first words Charlie Gardner said to me were, "Don't let the door hit you in the butt on your way out." Touche.

Charlie was definitely a challenge for me. We traded jabs, jokes, fears and tears. He had had a tough life. He was blind in one eye, had cataract in the other, was a bilateral amputee, had a tracheotomy (with voice amplifier), and was receiving intermittent tube feedings—just to name a few of what he called "my little inconveniences." His devoted daughter provided his daily care and I provided his weekly supply of "pleasant aggravation."

Over time, his condition deteriorated and his daughter was unable to manage his care at home. We both knew his death was rapidly approaching, so we transferred him to a hospice.

Charlie became very isolated and withdrawn. He and I spent time each day talking. He hated the way he looked, the way he had to live, and his lack of independence. Yet, he demanded every possible treatment. He was started on intravenous fluids and had blood drawn with increasing regularity.

One afternoon, while I was sitting by his bed, I asked him if he was afraid.

"No," he gruffly responded, "Not of dying, anyway."

With further questioning, he eventually identified that his fear revolved around his lack of faith in God and his fear that God might not forgive him.

"I've not always done it right," he admitted.

The hospice chaplain and I spent much time with him exploring his feelings and beliefs about God and forgiveness. Charlie "worked" very hard. One day he was able to ask God for forgiveness—he died comfortably, relaxed and at peace four hours later.

Submitted by Kim Vesey

## PERSHA'S STORY

Grief is a many-sided emotion. Working at a hospice has shown me a cross-section of the reactions both patients and loved ones experience in facing death.

From my first visit to the in-patient facility to the present time, the strongest feeling I sense is one of peace. This is partially due to the physical surroundings, but more because of the caring, loving attitude of the staff.

As a volunteer care-giver I have the time to talk, and more importantly, listen to the patients and family members. I am truly impressed by the devotion of family members who are physically and emotionally drained by their long bedside vigil. Many say that they could not have gone through this ordeal without support from the hospice.

There are many light-hearted moments, too. Like the joy we share in bird watching or in seeing a family of ducks waddle up the window. Or seeing an up-'til-now faithful husband casting an eye about for someone he hopes will take his wife's place.

When I tell people that the Hospice facility is not a place of gloom and doom, but one of peace and even joy, they do not always understand. And when I say that anyone is fortunate to end his days at Hospice I may get a look of incredulity. But we at the hospice understand!

Submitted by Persha Price

*During the course of collecting material for this book, a hospice nurse I know was diagnosed with pancreatic cancer. News of her illness sent shock waves through the organization. The following is an excerpt from a daily journal written by Lynn Gitzinger, chaplain and bereavement counselor:*

## REFLECTIONS ON FAITH — WHY LORD?

August 23, 1994

The question continually comes to mind — "Do we have a mistake here? Has the universe finally lost its balance? How could God have screwed up so badly?"

My desperate need to make sense of a situation which everyone knows makes no sense is wearing me down. Do we think if we can make sense of it, then there's the possibility of exercising some kind of control or do something productive to make it better?

# GIFTS

Everything in me cries out no, no, no! This isn't really happening. It can't be happening. This dream better end soon because it hurts too much to be true.

Okay ... so that's the initial reaction ... after the shock and numbness.

So now let's talk it out. What is the realness of the situation? What makes me fight against the reality that Elaine has the worst possible cancer?

Well, I need to start with who is Elaine? She is a nurse, a church woman, a friend; she is a wife, a mother, a daughter and a sister.

None of the above descriptions are reason enough for Elaine not to have cancer, and not to die. So, I'll go on!

I knew Elaine best as a friend and a nurse. Of all the nurses I know, and there are quite a few, Elaine is the most holistic, because of her deep grounding in her God. She has a spirituality that understands (in her heart) what life on this earth is about and where this life should eventually lead us. She realizes the finite nature of the physical body and that this body merely houses the spirit or essence of something infinite. Yet, she knows the beauty of the human body as a real work of art through which the spirit works out it's life on this planet. Elaine grasps deeply the delicate balance and interconnectedness of body and spirit. Because of this recognition, Elaine is the best (spirit) her body could have. She maintains that balance between body and spirit, thus honoring this earthly dwelling through good nourishment, healthy tension and a balance between restfulness and wakefulness.

Because Elaine understands all of this and has taken care of herself, done all the "right" things so to speak—cancer should not happen to Elaine.

I tell others "don't 'should' on yourself." We do this all the time. Somehow or other we adopt the attitude that if we do all the "right" things then life should go "right."

# SHARP AND TERBAY

I tell myself: Stop right there, Lynn! There is your answer. "Life should go right!"

Life as we experience it is life on this planet earth. All earthly life—be it vegetable or animal—has a certain life span. Life on earth was meant to come into physical existence and go out of physical existence. All growing things, all creation comes and goes. There is no definite time line for any living thing. Our difficulty as humans is that we have decided we can improve the life of this planet. We have fallen into the egotistical trap of thinking we can make this life better—perhaps perfect—plants that grow bigger and better, animals that become splendid creatures, and of course, human beings that can live longer and healthier lives. Can we for a minute stop and think that maybe we are corrupting something by changing it's very purpose; by trying to make it be better than is it's nature?

Whether Elaine is fifty—seventy—or one-hundred—or even two-hundred, we would never be ready for her as a physical person to stop expressing herself through her physical body. Because all the beautiful things I mentioned about her, making her a good nurse, as well as, a good church woman, friend, wife, mother, daughter and sister—all these various aspects of her life really flow from her essence, her spirit. She is going to be a beautiful woman in all ways, because she is first a beautiful spirit, which happens to be housed in a physical form we all have come to recognize as Elaine. But Elaine's physical form is just that— physical—with no more right to a longer life span than any other life form. Her physical house is subject to the frailties that all material things are subject to: destruction, disease, decay.

Deep in our heart we know there are no answers to why tornadoes, hurricanes, fires, floods, disease, violence happen the way they do. We cry out in anger against such disasters— but they happen.

In Elaine's case, I don't want her to die. The good and beauty that emanates from her are characteristics that are desperately needed in our world, our cities, our neighborhoods, our families, our hospice. It scares me to think of working at the hospice without her presence, her force (life-force), her being. I draw courage, strength, support, understanding, and hope from Elaine. But if I'm honest, if I speak from a level of truth and understanding that I've arrived at slowly over the years, then I have to admit that Elaine has accomplished what I think this life is about. I believe she arrived at the truth that life on this earth needs peace, harmony and balance, rather than excess. These characteristics breathe life into all levels. She has been the spiritual midwife for so many spirits as they labored to re-birth. She helped their physical bodies to arrive at comfort to the degree possible so that their spirit could emerge with peace. She helped them to grasp that this transition we call death is the most natural act for the body to undergo. The body has served it's usefulness and now releases it's life form; it's essence is to merge with the universal essence. And now after helping so many others to come to that point, it is her turn.

I ask myself (if I really focus) am I ready to let go of this physical form? No. I want to be able to go on talking, sharing, laughing and giving and receiving hugs. I want to continue to deepen my connection, my unity with her essence/her spirit. I think I have always been connected to her on this deeper level. Something intangible has always drawn me to her.

When needing a hospice nurse to walk the journey with Mom (Author's note: Lynn's mother died of cancer at a hospice program), I knew without hesitation I wanted Elaine. I went to one of the team leaders and asked if that would be possible. Elaine agreed and so, it happened. What a blessing Elaine was, not only to Mom and me, but to my sisters as well. Elaine's spirit draws out the best in each of us, be it patients, family, co-workers or others.

At this point, I feel I have come full circle. Life on this earth in these bodies is about relationship and the giving of and receiving of life. It only begins here (as far as our physical awareness is concerned), but continues on until spiritual unity—unity of essences is complete.

August 30, 1994

Unfortunately during most of our lives, our time, attention and energy goes into that which makes up our material, physical life and world. Yet, that is only a part of who we are. We are first and foremost spiritual beings, who are on this planet, having physical experiences. But because the spiritual side of us, in fact our very essence, is (for most of us) beyond our senses, (beyond being seen with eyes, heard with ears, touched by hands, lips or any other part of our body),we don't pay attention to it—we seldom focus on it. Our various religions and organized churches, for the most part have missed the main point as well. There is much said about the relationship between God and, prayer, vocal and internal. Our religions have put God out there—or up there—or in some Church—and then given Him all the attributes of our physical bodies. God will hear you or see you.

The union of our God and humankind is much, much deeper than that. Unfortunately we only have human words to use and human examples to draw from. Perhaps the most understandable example is the "union of spirits" spoken of in a marriage relationship. The sexual union of the bodies is only an outward physical sign (and oftentimes in our modern time has ceased to be that) of the meeting of spirits — of essences of two individuals. The sexual act lasts only so many moments in time, yet the deeper union of two people who deeply love bridges more than time and space.

I believe it is this union of spirits, of essence, that is possible for all people to share. We do it all the time without being aware. Perhaps a better word to describe the union of spirits is sharing one another's energy (life force). Why is it that people you know and care about suddenly "pop" into your mind? Could their life force be sending their energy to you? Why does a mother "experience" in her heart, so to speak, when a child of hers is in need? Is it a sharing of energy—of life force? As we live life, getting more and more in touch with what really matters, are we really simply becoming more in touch with one another's energy?

Could Jesus be the one person who most deeply learned how to be in touch with the energy or life force of others—or Mohammed or Gandhi or Moses or Mother Theresa? When you consider any of these people and measure them according to the world's standards of success, they seem total failures. Yet, why do they stand apart? What makes them different?

Getting back to Elaine—is it her presence, something that is given off by her person that touches others. Is it her energy, her aura (as it's been called)? Is it because she is in touch with the origin of essence, the origin of presence, that others can sense something different about her?

Earlier, I referred to Elaine as being the most holistic person I know. Her physical life, her physical beauty is evident because she is in touch with the source of it all. She allows the spiritual essence to touch in all ways the physical world she is living in. Once again, who would want to let go of this person?

Now consider the depth of each one's relationship with Elaine—family, husband, son, daughter, mom, dad, brother, etc. and add to that depth the pain of, the shock of, the anger against, the absoluteness of wanting Elaine to be part of their life forever. If we focus on Elaine in the physical form, this cannot happen. If we focus on union of spirits—of essence — then this is the time to deepen that union. We need to focus on the bigger picture of what we are about as spirits. There will never be, need never be, a cessation of the union of our spirits. We all come from the same source and always have been and always will be united. Let us take the time now to unite our energies, our spirits.

Submitted by Lynn Gitzinger

# SHARP AND TERBAY

## JOHN

John had an unusual request and at first glance, it appeared that there was no way to fulfill his wish. John was completely bedfast, close to death, and very depressed. His wish? To go fishing one last time.

John's nurse came to me, her nursing supervisor, with this dilemma. We put our heads together and began to problem solve. The first obstacle was how to get John out of his home. He couldn't sit in a wheelchair, so somehow we needed to find access to a stretcher.

This obstacle was quickly overcome. We called the ambulance company that the Hospice regularly uses and crossed our fingers. To our surprise they literally jumped at the opportunity to transport someone for "fun." They were so used to dealing with people in crisis, patients dying, and life and death situations, that the thought of taking somebody fishing was very appealing.

Okay. So we had the transportation situation solved. Now where could we find a "fishing hole" that would be accessible for a patient on a stretcher. We both had terrifying visions of a runaway stretcher, speeding towards the water's edge. We needed a place with level ground—preferably, close to the road. Obviously pushing a stretcher across miles of grass and dirt was out of the question. Finally, one of the staff suggested a small lake nearby which was surrounded by trees, but most important, easily accessible.

What a joy it was to tell John that he was going to be able to fulfill his wish! His gaunt, ashen face was transformed by the huge smile that stretched from ear to ear. John's nurse accompanied him on his fishing adventure. They shared a picnic lunch under an oak tree, overlooking the water, and then spent several restful hours fishing. I'd like to tell you that John caught a "whopper,' but unfortunately the biggest catch was measured in ounces. I'm not sure the size of the fish really mattered. It was

# GIFTS

the sun, water, fresh air and the very act of having a fishing pole in his hand that truly counted.

John returned to his home tired, but happy. He had said goodbye to an important part of his life. His depression lifted and was replaced with a peaceful acceptance.

It continues to amaze me what people can do if they want it badly enough. I guess everything is possible.

Submitted by Sandy Bonamassa


### THE JOURNEY

I am on a journey
My goal is perfect peace
Along the way I have the
support of my friends....
I have come through anger, fear and pain...
The change has helped me search...
The change has helped me grow...
The change has helped me appreciate my friends..
And at the end of the journey we will all
BE ONE ...
Submitted by Team One


## SUSAN

I met Susan and her husband, Bill, three days before her death. Susan was forty-six years old and a registered nurse. She had cancer of the kidney and, as Bill put it, "fought hard and gallantly."

On my first visit, I found her lethargic and unable to swallow food or fluids. Bill was obviously worried that she might become dehydrated. We spent a long time that afternoon discussing comfort issues, including the pros and cons of using intravenous fluids for hydration. Susan was too tired and weak to help make the decision. After much thought, Bill decided he couldn't let Susan suffer any more. He asked that she not have intravenous therapy. I instructed him in comfort measures and promised to re-assess her the next day.

During my visit the second day, it was increasingly clear that Susan was near death. We reviewed again, the issue of hydration and comfort. Bill wanted to stand by his decision, because "she seemed so peaceful." I spent time preparing him on what to expect and how to provide comfort. I again promised to visit the next day.

Upon my arrival, Susan was restless and "actively" dying. We crushed her pain medication and administered it under her tongue for quick absorption. She was sweating profusely, so we turned her to gently wash her back. When we rolled her back over, her eyes (which were her only means of communicating at this point) met Bill's. She followed his every movement. I encouraged him to touch her, talk to her and spend a few private moments together.

I left them alone. Suddenly, the door swung open. Bill was crying.

"I think she's gone," he said. I entered the room, as Susan took another long, deep, isolated breath. I quickly called Bill, their sons, and Susan's twin brother into the room. She was still with us—barely. I gently massaged her head. Bill held her hand and sweetly told her it was okay to let go.

I asked their sons if she had any special or favorite music. They said she loved Christmas music. Even though it was July, I encouraged them to bring in a tape player so we could put some music on for their mother. Where there's a will; there's a way. They moved in a massive stereo system with two large speakers.

# GIFTS

In a moment, we were listening to "Jingle Bells." It was festive and we all gave a slight chuckle. This song was followed by "Silent Night." The part of the song which says, "...sleep in heavenly peace..." came on. Susan took her last breath as the phrase repeated, "...sleep in heavenly peace."

What a beautiful experience! I will never forget it. Every time I listen to that Christmas song, I will always remember Susan and the heavenly peace of that moment!

Submitted by Kim Vesey

## HIGHER POWER

Dick Stoddard was a hospice patient with lung cancer that had metastasized to other vital organs. He lived in a modest home on the edge of farmland. His vast collection of hurricane lamps added great warmth to his cozy home. He and his wife were recovering alcoholics and had been "dry" for several years. They had one daughter still living at home.

Dick did not belong to any particular denomination, but he was a very spiritual person. He spoke often of the "higher power" he accepted as a part of AA's "twelve step" program. His "higher power," God, was always with him.

Before leaving after each visit, we always closed with prayer. Dick made sure that everyone in the house was invited to join in on the praying.

The night Dick was dying, his wife asked me to come out and to be there with them. It was one of the most touching nights of my life.

Dick was partially alert. He knew who I was and seemed glad to have me there with him. His homecare nurse was also present and, at first, there were a lot of hugs and reassurances by everyone that this evening was very special. We shared some scripture. Dick especially loved the Twenty-Third Psalm and I read this out loud. Then Mrs. Stoddard asked me to read some special prayers from their Alcoholic Anonymous book. They knew them almost by heart. The Third Step prayer:

"God, I offer myself to Thee—to build with me and to do with me as Thou wilt. Relieve me of the bondage of self, that I may better do Thy will. Take away my difficulties, that victory over them may bear witness to those I would help of Thy power, Thy love, and Thy way of life. May I do Thy will always!"

The Seventh Step prayer:

"My Creator, I am now willing that You should have all of me, good and bad. I pray that You now remove from me every single defect of character which stands in the way of my usefulness to You and my fellows. Grant me strength, as I go out from here to do your bidding."

Following these prayers, I had the privilege of being present as Mrs. Stoddard said a very special good-bye. She sat at the bed, holding his hand and then did some of what we call life review with him. She recounted how they had come together and the very special circumstances around the conception of each of their children. She reassured him of how special their lives were together and the unending love that would always be theirs. They both thanked God for their lives and the many struggles and joys they had shared together. There were lots of tears shed—tears of love and tears of joy for what they had shared, tears of sadness at the coming separation and tears of emotional turmoil at the beauty and holiness of this time together. Not long after, D.S. died peacefully.

# GIFTS

Their Higher Power had surrounded them with peace, courage, strength and love.

Submitted by Chaplain V. "Pete" Hood

## HOLIDAYS

I began working at a hospice of in March 1985. I was awed by the challenges that patients and their families faced on a daily basis. As the holidays rolled around, Thanksgiving took on a whole new meaning for me. I was thankful for being given the opportunity to meet and care for so many incredible people. I was also grateful that I had a beautiful, healthy, loving family at home.

As Christmas neared, I found that I was unusually depressed—this was not normal for me. I couldn't imagine celebrating Christmas while my patients were experiencing such bittersweet feelings. They were grateful to be able to spend Christmas with their families, yet they knew it would probably be their last Christmas.

A wise person offered me insight and reminded me that none of us really know when we will have our last Christmas with our families. Reframing how I looked at Christmas helped me to be especially thankful that I had the opportunity to spend another Christmas with my family.

I make the most of each one ... for no one knows when it will be our final celebration together.

Submitted by Kim Vesey

# GIFTS

## MY FIRST HOSPICE DEATH

I have never forgotten my first hospice death. I can still remember how scared I was when I got the call from the on-call nurse that I needed to go see my patient who was "actively" dying.

Ellen was a new patient who had only been in the program a day or two. I had never had the opportunity to meet her before the call came that she was dying. I had only been with the hospice a few short weeks and had not yet experienced a home death. Would I be able to remember what I needed to do? Would I be able to cope with this family, especially since this was a young mother with small children and parents who were still living? (I had small children and could too easily relate.)

I should not have worried. When I arrived at the home, I found a family who was coping very well with a death which, though it may have been untimely, was not unexpected. I was sure that much of the credit for the coping skills the family showed was due to the expert help given to the family throughout the night by the on-call nurse. Ellen was definitely in the last stages of her disease, but lingered on.

Because of the young age of the patient and her small children, I stayed with the family until late in the afternoon, thinking Ellen would die at any moment. I thought each breath would be her last, but she hung on. Finally, I decided I had to leave to see to other patients. As it happened, I had just left the home when the Ellen died and I was paged to return.

After I completed all the details pertaining to Ellen's death I sat down to talk with her family. It was during this talk that I learned how much control a person has over their own time of death. I learned that Ellen was a very private person and didn't like to have strangers around. But more importantly I learned that Ellen had been very close to her father. Her father had recently moved and the family had difficulty reaching him.  In fact, they did not reach him to let him know his daughter was dying until he arrived at his job.  Ellen was told when her father was finally reached and at that point, she was still responding enough that the family was sure she had heard.  Ellen actually died one hour before her father arrived.  As it turned out, he had taken one hour to go home and pack a few things before coming to his daughter's side.  She had been on time—unfortunately, he wasn't.

Submitted by Kathy Skarzynski

## AN INSTRUMENT OF HEALING

To Caregivers:
    To be an instrument of healing:
      Remember:
    You are the only song your patient may hear!
      Tune Yourself!
    Work out the  Disharmony within you
                Anger
                Fear
                Anxiety, etc.
    Pull into perfect pitch the sounds of
                Love
                Forgiveness
                Grace
                Peace, etc.
      Let yourself be played
                A melody of Strength
                A melody of Confidence
                A melody of Courage
                A melody of Hope

# GIFTS

A melody of that touches the soul!
For you are an instrument of healing,
Wholeness and life!

Submitted by Chaplin V. "Pete" Hood


## HEALING

Many religious people believe that God will cure their disease ... and if God doesn't it's only because they didn't deserve it or because their faith wasn't strong enough.

A colleague shared the following perspective with me. I have used it often:

"God heals in two ways. He can remove the disease from the body—"cure." Or He can remove the body from the disease —"death."

Either way, God won't let us down.

Submitted by Kim Vesey, R. N.

# 3

# Glimpses of Acceptance

*The hospice professionals and the authors*
*contribute stories illustrating reconciliation with fate.*

## ARLENE

In the course of more than twenty years in nursing, I have encountered many different kinds of patients. I have witnessed profound courage in the face of overwhelming odds. I have seen tragedies that brought out the best and worst in people. I have felt the despair of watching helplessly as men, women and children struggled and died. I have shared many intimate moments with patients and families. I have been an honored "guest" at the "birth" of many souls as people have made their passage from life to death. I have rejoiced in miracles, despaired at senseless tragedies, marvelled at the indestructibility of the human spirit, and mourned the loss of many special people, who in the brief time we shared together, became my friends. And I have learned and grown, as both a nurse and a human being, because of my interaction with these individuals.

# SHARP AND TERBAY

I have also had my share of "difficult" patients—those individuals who made me utilize every ounce of nursing skill I possessed. These "problem" patients also stretched and challenged me personally. I find it ironic that I have probably benefitted most, professionally and personally, from those individuals whose behavior and attitudes—indeed, whose very being—pushed me to the limits of my patience and understanding. I have learned much about myself, my attitudes, judgments, fears, and my own journey toward self-awareness, as I struggled to deal with these "problem" patients.

Arlene was such a patient. Manipulative, demanding and negative, she was an extremely difficult patient to care for. During the few months I knew Arlene, she brought me frequently to the point of frustration, anger and alienation. Often I didn't like her behavior, and at times, I didn't like *her*. And yet, lurking behind this problem behavior, there existed a unique individual who had very human needs, feelings, fears and hopes. She also had a very profound lesson to teach me.

I first met Arlene in May of 1993, after her physician had made a referral to the hospice program. Arriving at her suburban home for my first visit, I had no reason to suspect that the next few months would be so tumultuous and frustrating for both Arlene and myself and for many of the other health care professionals who assisted in her care.

The door was opened by an amazingly energetic woman who looked far younger than her seventy-five years. She began talking as we seated ourselves in her immaculate living room area. There was not a speck of dust nor an item out of place. She was wearing a bright blue robe and her blondish hair was perfectly in place. Not exactly what I had expected for a woman who had just had major surgery two weeks before, and who had been diagnosed with extensive ovarian cancer and liver metastasis.

# *GIFTS*

Arlene told me of her fifteen month struggle to pinpoint the cause of her abdominal pain and diarrhea. She recounted countless visits to a succession of doctors, all of whom told her that nothing was wrong. She sounded extremely (and justifiably) bitter and angry. She became very tearful when she mentioned the pain she had been enduring for such a long time. She also sounded very angry as she talked about her three daughters.

"They said they'd be here to help take care of me—but do you see them anywhere?"

The tears started again as she continued, "They just can't accept that I have cancer and that I'm going to die. They think I should be out running around, going to concerts and doing things like that. I mean, the cancer is in my liver and I know what that means. When it's in the liver, it's all over."

Arlene and I talked some more and decided to address what she said was her biggest problem—the physical pain. I contacted her physician and obtained an order for a stronger narcotic. Arlene seemed satisfied but skeptical. "I've been in pain for fifteen months. I'm not sure I know what it would be like not to have pain, but you can try."

Over the course of the next few weeks, I visited Arlene several times. She continued to verbalize that the pain was her primary problem, so with the physicians' concurrence we adjusted the dosage of her narcotic accordingly. The increase in medication was not effective.

During this period of time, she also underwent one course of chemotherapy. As she put it, "I don't want to, but I have no choice. My daughters and my doctor think I should do it."

She continued to voice bitterness and confusion over her relationships with her daughters, stating, "They're never here when I need them."

Conversations with her daughters revealed concern and confusion on their part as well. "We offer to come over and she doesn't want us there. We come over and try to help but we're not doing it right. We can't seem to please her," they said, confused. I was beginning to feel confused as well. What was going on? I was also frustrated that I didn't seem to be making any headway in helping Arlene with her physical pain.

After three weeks of unsuccessful pain management at home, Arlene and I decided that an admission to the Hospice Inpatient Unit might be advisable. I also referred Arlene to the Bereavement Department to help her deal with her feelings about her diagnosis, her relationship with her daughters and her death.

During her twelve day stay in the Inpatient Unit, various combinations of pain medications were prescribed with varying degrees of success. By the time she was discharged home, Arlene reported that "the pain is finally gone."

Arlene continued to be very open and verbal about her feelings for her daughters. "They think I should do more, take physical therapy, walk, get out. What's the point? I'm going to die."

She also continued to express bitterness, saying, "I did so much for them and now they're not there for me, but I don't want them there hanging around trying to make me do things I don't want to do."

Her daughters vocalized increasing frustration with their mother's negative attitude. I found myself agreeing with them. Arlene's physical condition was still remarkable for a woman of her age and her diagnosis. Yet she seemed to have given up. She simply didn't appear to want to live any longer. Every time I saw her, I was frustrated with her "I'm just going to lie here and wait for death" attitude. Many visits to her home were spent watching Arlene lie on the couch with her eyes closed and her hands folded over her chest. I mentioned this to one of Arlene's daughters, who said, "Mom's practicing—that's her casket pose."

One day she informed me that her pain was remarkably better, that she had decided not to pursue further chemotherapy, and that she was going to cut down on her pain medication because she felt fine. I cautioned her about changing her medicine, reminding her that the medication had ended the pain. She promised not to adjust anything and then voiced the first of many concerns about being home alone again. We talked about hiring someone to stay with her and also about future admission to our the hospice Residential Living Unit. She assured me that she would give it some thought, and would let me know what her decision was.

Arlene called me several days later and told me she had had a horrible "attack." She described her symptoms: heart racing, shortness of breath and feeling very frightened. I explained that her symptoms may have been the result of a panic attack and might be related to her fear of being alone. She insisted her symptoms had nothing to do with fear, panic or being alone. She informed me the problem was all the medication she was taking.

"So I've stopped taking it," she said. "The morphine patches make me feel funny so I took them off. I hate the taste of the liquid morphine."

I offered to obtain a different prescription and warned her that the pain might escalate. She rejected my offer and said she would be fine, that she would continue to take the small pain tablets.

When I saw Arlene a few days later, her pain was back with a vengeance, as I had suspected it would be. Arlene's first comment to me as I walked in her home was, "What can we do about this pain? Can you fix it?"

Not only was I frustrated; I was angry. All the hard work in the Inpatient Unit to control her pain had been undone by Arlene's decision to stop her medication. Now she was asking *me* to "fix it." I took a deep breath and reminded Arlene that for the medication to be effective she had to take it on a regular basis. After talking with her doctor, we readjusted Arlene's pain medications again. I wrote out a schedule for her to follow. She promised me she would closely adhere to the prescribed medication.

Over the next two weeks my frustration mounted as Arlene became once again non-compliant with all of her medications. She did not take her pain pills, and in addition, stopped taking her stool softeners. She complained bitterly about constipation, but refused to follow any suggestion I made. An antibiotic that had been ordered for an upper respiratory infection was also stopped after three doses, "because it's not doing me any good. I'm still coughing." When her doctor ordered an antidepressant for her to take at bedtime, Arlene took one dose and then stopped it as well because, "It makes me feel funny and certainly didn't help me sleep."

My patience was wearing very thin. I wanted to scream at her, "What is it that you want? How can I help you if you don't let me?" I felt angry, manipulated, and at a loss to really understand her behavior. All I could see was her negativity and I didn't like it. She was being very difficult. No, she was being impossible, and I was ready to tear my hair out.

As the Fourth of July weekend approached, Arlene's pain escalated. She talked constantly about how tired she was of being in pain and how she just wanted to die.

"The pain is unbearable. It reminds me that I'm dying, and at the same time, reminds me I'm still alive," she said. After a discussion with her physician, yet another narcotic was prescribed. As I was leaving, Arlene walked me to the door. I told her I thought she was looking a little better, a little stronger, a little more relaxed. Remarks like this were intended to help her focus on the quality of life she could have. However, Arlene responded with derision and anger. She became nearly irate and then began crying, "You don't really appreciate how sick I am." Previous efforts to cheer her up had also failed repeatedly.

"I'm not any better, naturally. I'm a lot sicker than you think I am."

The next morning Arlene called me and told me she had been awake all night and didn't see how she could possibly get through the long holiday weekend. After much soul searching, I decided to suggest another Inpatient Unit admission. Arlene responded positively to my suggestion.

"I really would rather stay here, but if you think I need to come in, I suppose I should. I probably do need to be in the hospital, since I'm so sick. I'm just too sick to stay at home, I guess," she said.

My first thought was that Arlene got exactly what she had wanted—an admission to the hospital and a recognition of how really sick she was. There was no question of her being sick and she did, after all, have terminal cancer. But why couldn't she just admit this need? I believed I had been manipulated, but I also felt relieved. I decided to let someone else deal with Arlene for a while, because I needed the rest. Maybe someone else could find a solution to Arlene's pain. I felt helpless to understand it and I wasn't convinced that the pain was as intense as Arlene described it. Having watched her jump up to answer the door, talk animatedly on the telephone when nobody was watching, and dash to the bathroom seemed incongruent with the pain level she described. Yet, I also knew the pain was real. Why wouldn't she listen and follow my suggestions? I believed that the pain could be controlled and this fostered a real sense of failure on my part.

I began to have lengthy conversations with the bereavement counselor who had been assigned to Arlene's case. Donna was doing her mental health practicum at the hospice for the summer. She was an extremely intuitive and energetic person who offered an incredible amount of insight into Arlene and her problem. Donna and I talked almost daily about how we could best help Arlene deal with both her physical and emotional problems. It was clearly obvious that the physical and emotional problems could not be separated. Was Arlene's pain physical — or emotional—or a combination of both? Did she really want to die? Was she angry, despite her protestations that being angry served no useful purpose? Could the relationship with her daughters be salvaged? How could we help Arlene and her daughters prepare for the end of Arlene's life? Why was I struggling so much? Why was I feeling so much confusion, frustration and ambivalence? What was going on within me?

I have taken care of hundreds of terminally ill patients and have frequently felt frustrated when, despite my best efforts, I was unable to alleviate pain, anxiety and fear. But never had I been so obsessed with any one patient. What was my struggle all about? What lesson was I supposed to learn? What was I missing?

During the course of Arlene's stay in the Inpatient Unit, various combinations of narcotics were tried, once again with varying degrees of success. And yet despite complaints of excruciating pain, Arlene often refused to take her pain medication with any regularity.

I continued to visit Arlene in the Inpatient Unit, but my visits became shorter and less frequent. Her negativity and manipulation continued to anger me. I found myself avoiding her. I visited out of a sense of duty and responsibility, but rejoiced and breathed a sigh of relief when I found her sleeping and I could slip out unnoticed.

Donna, began to visit Arlene more often and described some very positive times spent talking with her. They reminisced about Arlene's childhood, her marriage, her divorce, her daughters, her likes and dislikes, and her feelings about the past, present and the future. Donna reported a growing friendship with Arlene that I found frankly surprising. I wondered if Donna saw the negativity and the manipulation. She reported her awareness of all these behaviors, but also said there was something else lurking beneath the surface—a lonely, frightened woman who wanted very much to be liked and accepted.

Had I been so "hooked" on the negativity and manipulation that I had failed to see the loneliness?

No, I knew being alone was a very significant issue with Arlene.

Had I been so keyed into "fixing" the physical problems, treating the pain, that I had overlooked Arlene's need to be liked and accepted?

Possibly. I was certainly struggling. I didn't like this woman—and I felt guilty because I didn't like her.

# GIFTS

Had I accepted her?

No. I was still trying to "fix" her—trying to "turn her around," end the negativity and make her stop being so manipulative. I was trying to make her acknowledge her fears and feelings.

I tried to overlook these behaviors. I'd walk into her room determined not to let her behavior bother me, but I repeatedly failed. Her behavior did bother me and she knew it.

So I tried another approach. I began asking her what she needed from me—what she wanted. Her response invariably was, "Why am I still alive? Why can't I just die?" I tried to answer her questions, quoting all the "right" responses about the dying process. I explained to her that both body and spirit needed to be ready before death could occur. I'd tell her that it wouldn't be long now. I'd report all the signs I could see that her physical condition was deteriorating. But the truth was I had no idea why she was still alive, why she couldn't die?

Physically, her condition was deteriorating. She had virtually stopped eating because of her fear of having a bowel obstruction. She was so thin that one could count and feel each individual rib and vertebra. And yet she remained alert, mobile and very much alive.

I continued to talk with Donna and other staff members about my feelings for Arlene and my frustrations. Despite my dislike for this woman, I did want to help her. From the initial visit on, she had verbalized that she wanted to die. I mentioned this to Donna.

"What's keeping Arlene from dying?" I asked. Everyone, including her daughters had given Arlene "permission" to die. Arlene indicated her readiness to be done with the struggle and pain as well. Donna suggested that while Arlene was not afraid to die, she was afraid of the dying process because she didn't know what to expect. Donna and I agreed that perhaps I could help Arlene by discussing the actual dying process.

"Okay," I thought, "that's something I can do." During my next visit with Arlene, I broached the subject. I asked her if it would help alleviate her fears if she knew what to expect. Arlene responded affirmatively and I began explaining what might happen. I reassured her that the hospice staff would be present, that every effort would be made to keep her free from pain, and that every measure would be taken to keep her from suffering. Midway through what I thought was an open, honest and productive discussion, Arlene abruptly changed the subject. She began criticizing one of the other nurses who cared for her. End of discussion. So much for Plan A.

I returned to Donna and reported the plan had failed. Back to square one, I thought. "*Why won't she die? What's holding her back?*" I was astonished at Donna's reply.

"Maybe we're focusing on the wrong thing," she said. "Everyone is telling her it's okay to die. Maybe somebody needs to tell her it's okay to live." Whew!

The next few days were significant. Arlene's manipulative behavior continued as her fear mounted. She began to have frightening dreams of being pursued by dark figures. She also had vivid and horrifying hallucinations of people standing in her room, threatening to harm her. She was so vocal about these nightmares that she frightened her roommate and was moved to another room.

A chance remark by another nurse took me by surprise and caused me to reconsider my own feelings about Arlene. Her comment that Arlene was the nastiest woman she ever met and that she didn't care if she is dying and that there was no excuse for her behavior echoed some of my own feelings. However, hearing this other nurse make these statements infuriated me. I couldn't believe that I was angry.. Here I was defending a woman I disliked intensely. I heatedly reminded this nurse that Arlene had a tremendous amount of fear and unresolved grief, and while this didn't excuse her behavior, we, as nurses, needed to be more compassionate and understanding. As I listened to myself talk about Arlene's life, her pain, her struggles and her fears, I realized with astonishment that while I still didn't like this woman very much, I had come to accept her and respect her.

I went downstairs to the Inpatient Unit thrilled that now I could approach Arlene with a different, more positive attitude. I found Arlene in her new room—a bright, cheerful lounge with an abundance of windows opening to the beautiful rose gardens outside. An idyllic spot. But Arlene was furious. She didn't use this word, but looking at her face, it was obvious she was tremendously upset. I asked her what was wrong.

"I'm being punished," she proclaimed. I asked her to explain.

"They told me I had to be moved. The other lady in the room was sicker than me—that's what they said. I'm dying, but she's sicker than me. So I had to move." During her stay with us, Arlene had many delusions about her care and what was being said about her, but I suspected this time she was right on target. She probably was being punished.

I apologized for the insensitivity of the other staff and tried to refocus her attention on how much nicer this particular room was. And it was a beautiful room. But not to Arlene.

"Look how light it is. You know how I hate the light. I want darkness," she remarked, as she pulled the sheet up over her head. I told her I would see what I could do about making the room a little darker and, as I was leaving she spoke again.

"It's bad enough that I'm dying, but do I have to be constantly reminded by looking at that EXIT sign?" And sure enough, there by the door was a large bright red sign with the letters EXIT lit up and screaming at her. I repeated that I would see what I could do about getting her moved to a more appropriate room and headed for the nurse's station.

In the meantime, Donna had stopped by to visit. When I rejoined Arlene thirty minutes later, she and Donna were laughing. Arlene was lying flat on her back with a towel over her face. She peeked out to see who had entered. Donna smiled at me and said, "Arlene's trying to figure out a way to keep the light out." Noticing a yellow plastic bath basin nearby, Donna suggested using this as a covering. Arlene promptly grabbed it and placed the basin over her face and began laughing.

"I must look pretty weird and I really can't breathe with this over my face," she said. As I joined in the laughter, I realized that this was a side of Arlene I hadn't seen. She then requested that we both sit by her bed, and she reached out to hold our hands. This, too, was a new experience. Arlene had never asked me to hold her hand or been in any way demonstrative of her feelings with me. Previous attempts on my part to hold her hand had been met by her pulling away. The three of us sat quietly like that for a few moments. I noticed that Arlene was looking at Donna and smiling.

"What?" I asked. "You two look like you have a secret."

Still looking at Donna, Arlene said very quietly. "It took awhile, didn't it? But she finally came around."

I knew exactly what she meant. I had finally accepted her, looked past the manipulative behavior, and recognized her need to do it her way.

I did not see Arlene again for several days. In fact, the next time I saw her was on the last day of her life. I was called down to Arlene's bedside by the inpatient unit nurse. The nurse told me that Arlene was in an incredible amount of pain and was struggling miserably. Maybe I could have a calming effect. The nurse informed me, that she thought Arlene was dying.

She was. I walked into Arlene's room to find her writhing in pain and moaning as the struggle to die consumed her entire body. She recognized me, grabbed my hand and in a surprisingly strong, clear voice, asked, "Why does it hurt so much?" I didn't have an answer and didn't try to give one. Perhaps that was what she needed from me—to stop trying to "figure it" out, to stop trying to "fix it." Perhaps, there was no answer. Death was just full of so much pain, so much sadness, so much grief. I sat by her side for almost two hours, holding

her hand and stroking her forehead and hair. I realized sometime during that two hours that I was no longer Anne, the nurse,
and that she was no longer Arlene, the patient. We were just
there together. There was little verbal communication. However,
she did tell me she had made peace with her daughters and said
good-bye. Despite the lack of verbal communication, we met
each other at another level. We did speak eloquently from our
hearts and souls to one another. My struggle to help her die
eased. It was my presence, acceptance, love and comfort that
helped her. Her struggle eased also as I sat with her, tears rolling
down my cheeks. I watched her body and breathing relax. Her
pain finally receded and she closed her eyes. She withdrew her
hand from mine and placed both hands on her abdomen. I knew
it was time for me to go, that this final stage was one she wanted
to finish alone. I leaned over, kissed her on the forehead, said
good-bye and told her I loved her, would miss her. She acknowledged with a small smile. I knew that she was finally at peace and
I left. Her fear was gone and her struggle was ending. While I
didn't completely understand what had happened between us, I
also felt at peace. I wondered why I was chosen to be at the bedside with her? I had asked if she wanted the girls there and she
had said no. Had she waited for me? And yet I knew intuitively
that *it* was right. I was supposed to be there.

Arlene died very peacefully ninety minutes later. She was
alone, lying in exactly the position I had left her in. She did it
her way. I believe ... no, I *know*, she wanted it that way.

One of the primary goals of hospice care is to help the
patient achieve physical and emotional comfort so they can focus
on the quality of life. I'm not sure that we, as a hospice team,
accomplished this goal with Arlene. And yet, I'm not so sure we
didn't. Maybe with Arlene, as with other patients, it is not a goal
that we at hospice can achieve. It is the patient's goal to achieve;
their choice to make; their death to "accomplish." As with life,
each patient makes his or her own journey and decisions. The

patient must direct the course of their own care. Arlene chose to die her way. This was a difficult decision for me to accept because of my own preconceived ideas, judgments, and opinions about how it could be, should be, or how I wanted it to be.

Perhaps I focused too intently on Arlene's physical pain, but the physical pain was something I could see—something I could treat—something I could try to alleviate. I was not successful in alleviating it. Why?

I believe that Arlene chose to keep her pain. In part because her fixation on the physical pain enabled her to focus on the physical symptoms, and ignore the underlying emotional issues. The physical pain also made her disease and the severity of her condition more real to Arlene, her family and the staff. Perhaps the pain made her more acceptable.

How could pain make her more acceptable? I'm not sure. Arlene had a very difficult childhood. She talked often of the lack of love and closeness in her own family. She spoke of "not knowing what love looks like." I know from my own experience of growing up in an abusive family that children raised in pain often learn to trust what is painful. Growing up without love, perhaps Arlene thought the staff and her daughters would love her because of her pain— or at the very least we would take care of her. The pain enabled her to get her needs met. She needed to connect with others, but she seemed so uncomfortable with her emotions—her feelings of grief, sadness and anger. The pain, for Arlene was more acceptable if it was physical. The pain made her "special"—deserving of time and attention. It made her real.

Finally, I think Arlene chose to keep the pain because it was hers—something that no one could take away unless she made the decision for it to be gone. I learned from Arlene that a patient's pain is not mine to take away. It is their pain to do with as they choose. I have come to realize that sometimes pain serves a very valid and positive purpose. It is a very personal thing—a possession that should sometimes be guarded, cherished and kept.

Arlene also taught me to trust the process—the patient's process. As a health care professional, I could help by being present to, by listening and by caring. However, I could not control or direct her death. Just as the pain was not mine to take, neither was her dying process. It is also a precious personal possession.

Each patient must live and die their own way. It is my purpose, my gift to the patient, to allow that process to occur; to keep *my* agenda, *my* beliefs, *my* assumptions, *my* hopes separate from theirs.

I found myself caught up in Arlene's behavior. All I could see for a long time, was her negative attitude and manipulative personality. My own childhood had been full of both negative behavior and manipulation which triggered a response on my part that got in the way of accepting Arlene. When I was finally able to separate my issues from Arlene's, I was able to accept her and care for her in a way that benefitted both of us.

Arlene fought a good fight, she had the courage to face her fears and work through her personal struggles and the conflict with her daughters, to find the peace she craved. She lived with the pain until she was ready to let it go. She gave me the courage to look at some of my own fears, to acknowledge my own pain and showed me also how I use physical pain to sometimes distract from emotional issues. She taught me that often struggle is necessary. For without the struggle, one cannot truly appreciate the peace one finds when the struggle is over.

Arlene, with Donna's help, also helped me realize that sometimes a hospice nurse can get so caught up in helping patients die, that we forget to give them permission to live.

I didn't like Arlene for a very long time. I detested her manipulation and was infuriated by her negativity. I was frustrated with her noncompliance, her unwillingness to let me help her, her failure to listen and her passivity. I disliked her demanding ways, her critical nature and her hidden agenda. Yet, during our struggle together we came to a mutual respect and acceptance of one another. She accepted me long before I accepted her. On that last morning together, I realized that I had come to love this woman as well— that I could forgive all her faults—that they just weren't important anymore. I forgave myself for my negative feelings towards her. I understood that she gave what she could and accepted what she was able to accept. I understood that I, too, had done the best I could. She gave me the gift of sharing the last few hours of her life. I gave her the gift of being there with her—unconditionally.

Submitted by Anne Wallace Sharp


## REFLECTIONS ON MY MOTHER'S DEATH


My mother's recent death from a brain tumor led me to reflect on my life and my experiences as a hospice nurse. It was with amazement that I realized, even as a child, I was ministering to the terminally ill. I treated my first hospice patient, my grand-mother, when I was eight years old.

It was the summer of 1956. I remember riding to my grandmother's home, with my mother in her 1948 black Ford. Mother and I made this trip each week to help take care of my grandmother. Grandma had suffered a series of strokes and was bedfast, requiring twenty-four hour care. Iva, my mother's sister, returned home and was grandma's live-in care giver. The remaining daughters—Frances, Emma and my mother Charlotte, would make weekly trips to help assist with grand-mother's care.

What are my memories of Grandmother? She stayed in a small bare room that had one large window off the parlor. The light from the window made the room very bright and helped focus attention on the large hospital bed in the center of the room.

My grandmother had long gray and white hair that flowed to her waist. When she was well, she wore it braided and wrapped around her head. Now that she was sick, her daughters braided it very simply and allowed it to fall down her back or over her shoulder.

I remember my visits quite clearly. When we arrived I would climb up into bed with my grandmother and sit next to her. My grandma was always a quiet woman, never saying much, just holding me. I enjoyed unbraiding her hair and brushing it for her and grandmother seemed to like that too. When she smiled at me, I had a wonderful, warm feeling. I also cleaned her fingernails and toenails and applied lotion to her hands and feet.

When my grandmother died in October of that year, the family had the viewing at the house—in the parlor. Our family drove to her house. It was raining that day and I wore a blue raincoat and hat. I remember getting out of my father's car and running into the house. There was my grandmother in the parlor in this huge casket. Flowers filled the room. I remember walking up to the casket, but I was too little to see grandmother. A relative lifted me up for a closer inspection and I looked her over from head to toe. She wore a beautiful pink dressing gown with slippers to match. I touched her foot. But the one thing that was so shocking was my grandmother's hair. The funeral director had cut it off! Her hair lay in soft white ringlets over her head. It didn't even look like my grandmother.

Today as a hospice nurse I am the one who trims the patient's nails. One of the nurses on the unit even bought me my own special trimmers. I still enjoy applying lotion, soaking and trimming nails. Maybe it's my way of remembering my grandmother.

But how did I come to nursing and to the hospice?

In January, 1989, I returned to college at age forty to complete an associate degree in nursing. In high school, I was a member of the nursing club, but when it came time to enroll in college, I had entered the teaching profession. Now, over twenty years later, I was ready to pursue my dream of becoming a nurse. In June 1991, I graduated and worked for two years as a medical surgical nurse. I learned my skills and quickly advanced to the position of resource nurse. I took training in chemotherapy and became interested in cancer patients.

The longer I worked the more frustrated I became. I soon realized the special needs of the terminally ill patients were not being met in this general hospital setting. I saw patients die in pain. I saw patients' families go home at night when they wanted to stay. I saw dying patients fed continuous tube feedings and drown in their own fluids. I became more and more uncomfortable with my job. I was appalled when an elderly emphysema patient was resuscitated and winced as I heard his ribs break during our efforts to "save" his life. I began to encourage patients to take responsibility for their own medical care. I also encouraged them to ask their physicians questions and to take charge of their own lives.

At the same time my discontent was growing. Anne Sharp, a friend who I had met through a divorced group, encouraged me to apply at the local hospice. Anne worked in home care and seemed to find hospice nursing a real ministry of love and care. She encouraged me to apply for a job in the hospice In-Patient Unit. In the fall of 1993, I submitted my application.

I had to overcome a big obstacle—my discomfort with driving to the hospice—a thirty minute trip down the busy interstate near my home. This drive had always been a problem for me. I was afraid and intimidated. I had developed more confidence while driving my daughter to college in Michigan. But heading south still made the hair on my neck stand up. However, I was determined and decided that I really wanted to change the focus of my nursing career. Driving on the interstate was not going to stop me.

# GIFTS

On the day of my interview I allowed an hour extra. I got lost three times. I asked God if He was trying to tell me something. I took His silence as a "No." Several weeks later, I was hired. I gave my two weeks notice at the hospital and took a week's vacation. During my vacation, I practiced driving to the hospice with my daughter. Today, I think my blue Honda could get there without me. I just have to point it in the right direction.

The hospice is where I'm supposed to be. It is part of God's plan for me. I feel privileged to care for the dying and to minister to their families. Working for the hospice also helped prepare me to deal with my own mother's death.

On Mother's Day 1995, my parents arrived at my home in the middle of the afternoon. I knew something was wrong the moment I saw my mother. The right side of her body was impaired, her face drooped and her speech was slurred. She was dressed appropriately, but her hair was in disarray—not at all like my mother. She seemed "flat" and her thought process was delayed and slow. I was sure my mother had suffered a stroke.

A week later my mother was diagnosed with a brain tumor. When the neurologist told her she had three to six months to live, she just listened. Later she told a close friend that she had six weeks. My mother was right ... she lived exactly six weeks.

Mother remained at home for four weeks. My father cared for her physical needs until she could or would no longer eat, then he withdrew. I became her nurse and primary caregiver, with my family and my brother helping out when they could. Each week, I could see a big change in mother's condition; and after her seventy-fifth birthday, her decline was very rapid. I was assisting mother with her morning bath one morning, when my father had an anxiety attack. He suffered chest pain and shortness of breath. I called 911, but when they arrived, he refused to go to the hospital. I called Anne—Mom's hospice nurse and my friend. I had asked Anne to take care of Mom. Subconsciously, I was asking her to take care of me. She graciously agreed.

Anne drove up to Piqua immediately. After talking to me and my father, she walked into the dining room where the hospital bed stood. Anne gently told my mother that our family needed to regroup. Mother agreed to go to the hospice.

That afternoon, my mother was admitted to the Hospice Center so my father and I could rest. Feelings of despair and sadness washed over me. I walked onto my parents' front porch and cried. I realized now how families must feel when they walk through the hospice doors where I work. I felt moving her was the beginning of the end.

I was working the night shift (11 p.m. to 7 a.m.). After work, I would stop by my mother's room and feed her breakfast. Two things occurred at the hospice that I did not expect. My father, who had been my mother's constant companion, only visited a few hours a day. He refused to stay the night. And my mother did not like the center. She barely tolerated her stay. I could not understand this for she was in one of the biggest and nicest rooms. She had a lounge with a view of the surrounding grounds and gardens. I was perplexed and our family had to decide what to do next.

My father, my brother, and I were all of the opinion that Mother should stay at the hospice. We all agreed that was the best choice—for Mother and for us. On Friday morning, I talked to Anne and asked her to go downstairs and ask Mother what she wanted to do. I knew Mother would be honest with Anne. Whereas, she'd tell me only what she thought I wanted to hear. I did not want my mother to return to her home. In only one short month, I was exhausted. I could not continue to care for my mother in the morning and evening, sleep during the day, and work all night. If mother insisted on coming home, she would have to come stay with my family in Troy, because Dad was too exhausted. I knew, with my family's help, I could take good care of my Mother.

# GIFTS

Anne explained the situation to my mother and she chose to come home with me. Mother's stay at the hospice was extended over the weekend in order to prepare the house for my her arrival.

Over the weekend I brought home all the supplies I would need from the hospice. The hospital bed was delivered Monday morning. A twin bed was moved downstairs so my father could sleep in the same room with Mother.

Nursing assistants would come daily to bathe Mother, while my family would take care of her other needs. And so, Mother came to my house. Within hours her condition changed—more pain, less response and more difficulty breathing. I was reluctant to go to work that night however, after calling the family to come to the house, I decided to work anyway. I stayed in contact by phone with my family. All through the night and the next morning my Mother's medications were changed to provide more comfort.

That week I continued to work at night, while my family stayed and took care of my mother. This afforded them an opportunity to spend some quality time with her and to provide hands on care. On one of the evenings before I left for work, my three daughters and I stood together at Mother's bedside. Morgan, my three-year-old granddaughter, was present also. The five of us changed Mother's gown, applied lotion to her body, performed her oral care, and put balm on her feet, knees, elbows and hips. I looked around the room at my girls. I was so thankful for this opportunity for all of us to care for my mother in her final days. I knew in my heart that this was one of the greatest gifts we could give to her.

On Friday morning, I left the hospice and told the staff I would not be returning until after Mother's death. It was my time now to be with her!

I walked in the house and I could see and hear the changes immediately. My mother's lungs were filling up with fluid. The medications we were giving her were not effective. I called Anne and she offered to drive up. I also requested a visit from the hospice chaplain who would offer my father some much needed support.

Anne drove up and assessed my mother. We agreed that Mother's condition was deteriorating and that she didn't have long to live. The congestion she was experiencing was not acceptable to me. Anne called the doctor and obtained an order for a different medication, which fortunately proved effective.

The chaplain spent the morning with my father. My father told the chaplain that my mother would die the next day (Saturday). I asked him if mother had told him this. My father shook his head and told me he had had a premonition earlier in the week.

My mother did, indeed, die on Saturday—six short weeks after being diagnosed with a brain tumor. I rejoice in the fact that her death was peaceful and that her final days were spent surrounded by those she loved. The timing of her death was truly phenomenal and convinces me how much in charge she really was. I suspected that my mother would live to see her seventy-fifth birthday, but I wasn't sure about her presence at my wedding.

I was remarrying my former spouse. After six years of being divorced, Chuck and I had not so much reconciled as developed a new, stronger relationship with each other. Mother knew of our plans to be married on July 9, but I believe she considered us married already. She didn't feel she needed to be present at the ceremony. I believe she had her own time table. She wanted to be "dead and buried" before my wedding. That way, she knew I would have time to make wedding arrangements and honeymoon plans. She died on June 24, giving me two weeks to "grieve" and prepare.

I never realized the value of funerals until my own mother's death. My mother had requested that there be a closed casket and no calling hours. After Mother's death, the family met at the funeral home in Piqua to finalize the arrangements. An oak casket with brass trim and an ivory lining was

# *GIFTS*

chosen. I had wanted to bury my mother in a pink dressing gown like my grandmothers, but I was unable to find one. Instead I chose the pale pink suit dress my mother wore to her fiftieth wedding anniversary party several years earlier.

My father insisted upon no calling, that is no public viewing. The family would view my mother privately Monday evening. On Sunday, I gathered Mother's clothes together to drop off at the funeral home—her dress, slip, ivory hose and pink shoes. My father did not want my mother buried with any of her good jewelry. So I picked some pearl earrings that Morgan, my mother's first great grandchild, had worn to my daughter's wedding. I sent a matching pearl necklace one of my daughters had worn. I also took Mother's favorite pink fingernail polish and a picture of my mother at their fiftieth anniversary party.

Monday morning, I felt something was missing I wasn't sure what it was. I drove to my parents home in Piqua and collected mother's favorite purse. I filled her purse with items that told the story of her life and her family.

There were family pictures, a letter from my father written to my mother while he was serving his country during World War II, my mother's make-up and the glasses that she so dearly loved. Also included were bridge tally sheets with her friends names on them from her bridge club, a deck of cards, a pocket Bible and a card she had sent me. My daughter Heather's tassel from her college graduation just a few weeks before, a picture of Chuck in his sheriff's uniform, my certificate from Ginghamsburg Church where I had just become a member (my finding a church had meant a lot to my mother) and a poem Anne had given me a few years before about courage and strength were also placed among her treasures. The list went on and on, but the important thing for me was the joy I felt at compiling this collection of memories. It provided great healing for me.

# SHARP AND TERBAY

That evening the entire family met at the funeral home. My mother looked beautiful. Until that moment, I had never understood the value of the ritual of viewing the dead. I had always thought it strange when I heard people say, "Don't they look nice." Now, I understood. I needed to see my mother look nice again.

I brought her a corsage of pale pink roses. As I walked up to the casket, I lifted the blanket to see my mother, just as I had done forty years ago when my grandmother died. There on my mother's little finger was her gold finger nail. I could remember when she bought the solid gold pinkie fingernails years ago—she had loved them.

I placed some of the papers we had gathered under mother's pillow and I sat her favorite gold purse beside her in the casket.

As I looked at my mother, I realized what an extraordinary person she was. She had accepted her disease, but found the loss of independence and control intolerable. She had set her timetable and stuck to it. She had told her friend six weeks and six weeks it was. The power of her mind and spirit was unbelievable!

On July 9, I stood beside Chuck as we made our wedding vows. I was wearing my mother's diamond cluster ring. I also had a large white pillar candle burning. This was the same candle that had been present at her funeral. (I also burned that candle the night of Chuck's re-election to the sheriff's office in March 1996.)

Submitted by Lynn Cox

# GIFTS

## ANDREW

When I first met Andrew, he struck me as an angry, self-absorbed and bitter man. My initial impression was correct. He did mellow—but not without a struggle.

My fourth visit was the turning point in our relationship. The three previous ones had been brief. I took his vital signs, talked with him a few moments and then was told I could leave if I didn't need anything else. I scheduled the fourth visit on a Thursday. He wrote it on his calendar and said he would see me then.

As I knocked on the door to his apartment at the appropriate time, I was ushered in by Thelma, a hired nurse's aide who was living with him. I could hear Andrew's voice coming from the bathroom.

"Who is that, Thelma?"

"The hospice nurse."

"How dare she! Who does she think she is coming out here without calling or asking? She's got a lot of nerve!" He was screaming as he was wheeled into the room from the bathroom.

I began, "We had an appointment ..."

"No, we didn't. You never called. Just barged right in. Who do you think you are?" His face reddened as he yelled. "You're terrible. You just think you can walk right in here whenever you want!"

I'd already had a long day and I'd had enough. I picked up my bag and headed for the door.

"Where do you think you're going?" he yelled.

"I'm leaving. You, sir, are rude. And I refuse to sit here with you yelling at me."

His mouth dropped open. I doubt anyone had ever said anything like this to him before. And this time, when he spoke, his voice was calmer and lower. "No. Wait ..."

Thus, our relationship developed out of what, I suspect, although he never said, was respect for me. I had stood up to him and had not allowed him to bully me.

Andrew's daughter, Audrey, later told me that he had been a bully all his life. He had run the family with an iron fist and demonstrated little love. His wife had devoted herself to his every beck and call, literally dropping everything to meet his needs. He had been emotionally abusive to all his children. He was a stern and unyielding parent and man.

"There were never any hugs. As long as I can remember, he has never once said 'I love you' to anyone—not even Mom."

What a sad, lonely and bitter man he had become. He believed that money could buy anything—respect, friendship, love and even health. But money had failed him because it could not cure his cancer. This frustrated and angered him greatly.

The one shining light in the last few months of his life was his nurse Thelma. His daughter had found Thelma through a local nursing agency. She showed him unconditional love and acceptance. She refused to be bullied and demanded his respect. He came to depend on her for all his physical and emotional needs. Although he never said it, I believe he came to love Thelma deeply.

Andrew's struggle with death was a long one. For over a month, he lingered on restless, confused, and hallucinating the edge of death. He could not rest. He spoke of businesses he still needed to create and work that remained to be done. He frequently burst into angry and irrational tirades. At times, he was virtually impossible to be around.

But, Andrew also began to listen, slowly, and reluctantly, The words of the home care staff began to sink in. We talked to him about death, about a forgiving God, about his work on earth being done and about going home to heaven to be with his wife and about letting go. I believe he heard — and finally relaxed.

# GIFTS

I encouraged his family to affirm him to let him know that they cared, would miss him and forgave him. They could not do these things. Nor could he. There were no "I love yous," no hugs, no closure on their relationship. He repeatedly told the staff how proud he was of his family and that he loved them. However, he could not verbalize these things to his children.

Andrew's last few weeks were filled with music—the one true love of his life. Volunteers came to play the piano and his raspy shaking voice could be heard weakly singing along.

As I said good-bye to Andrew, I commented on his love of music and on how he had grown since I'd met him. I spoke of Thelma—his dependence on her and his feelings for her. I told him that I knew it had been difficult for him. I praised his willingness to finally talk about his death. I told him he was leaving behind a legacy of music and four successful happy children. Tears formed in his eyes.

"Soon you'll be going to a place where your body will once again be whole—where you will be reunited with your wife and where you will be at peace," I said.

"I wish I could believe that," he said, softly, tears rolling down his face. I kissed his cheek and said good-bye.

He died two days later in his apartment holding the hand of his one true friend — Thelma. Her tears fell freely.

His children arrived later.

I do believe that Andrew is in a better place. Perhaps he has finally found that great sense of inner peace which he never attained here on earth.

Submitted by Anne Wallace Sharp

# SHARP AND TERBAY

## REBECCA AND BETHANY

Roger had liver cancer. He also had two very young children—Rebecca, six and Bethany, four. They needed to be prepared for their father's impending death.

Roger's condition had rapidly deteriorated when I was called to his home early Labor Day morning. The events of that day helped me to understand that a child's interpretation of death is different than an adult's and usually cannot be anticipated.

Roger took his last breath around ten in the morning with his wife at his side. Once she regained her composure, I accompanied her to the kitchen so she could tell the children that their father had died. The four-year-old looked intensely at her mother and then quickly returned to the picture she was coloring. Rebecca, responded more vocally. She was upset! That she was supposed to march in the local Labor Day parade at 11 a.m. and might be late.

The girls' response was very stressful for Roger's wife. She couldn't understand how her daughters could be so unaffected by the death of their father. I tried to explain to her that children's grief is unique and that the process of grieving might come in spurts. I told her that children need to be allowed to express their grief in whatever manner they feel comfortable. I assured her that their seeming lack of acute grief—that we, as adults, reveal by crying, etc.—did not reflect a lack of true love for the person who had just died. With time, Roger's wife understood this.

She later told me that the girls had opened up to her. When they were alone and talking quietly, Bethany and Rebecca spoke often of how much they missed their daddy.

Submitted by Kim Vesey

# GIFTS

## SONG OF A DYING YOUTH

In lieu of charitable donations,
Remember me with exotic flower arrangements.
Lay me to rest in a gold plated casket.
Celebrate my youth with good wine,
espresso and a movie premier,
that's all about me.

Have a fund raiser
to lift me to the heavens
in a hot air balloon.

If I can't stay and
grace the world with my wit,
humor and charm;
If I must move on at such a tender age,
contribute what it takes
to send me off in great style —
enough to disarm all who'd be fool
enough to believe
that it's best since I'm so ill
that I must leave.

For when I do,
I take with me all that
I could have given to you,
and you,
and you.

Submitted by Jan Jessen

## ROBBIE

I found Robbie hard to like and hard to help. He tended to push people away, testing their endurance and their commitment to him. He reminded me too much of my father—an abusive, angry man.

My first few visits were filled with tension as we sparred back and forth. We were both struggling with what to say, how to act. He had little patience with me—taunting, teasing, challenging and angrily accusing me of not caring and understanding. He was right. I didn't understand and I was having a difficult time caring. I dreaded my visits with him and couldn't wait to leave.

After much bickering back and forth, Robbie and I finally reached a "cease fire." One day he pushed and I pushed back. I told him that I was very sorry he had cancer and that I knew he was desperately trying to cope with his failing health, but that this didn't give him any right to take his anger out on me. I told him either I would step aside and find him another nurse he might like better or he could respect me and we would try to work this out together.

I expected him to become even more angry, but he surprised me.

"I don't want another nurse. You're fine," he said.

Our relationship improved from that day on. I think his respect for me increased because I had confronted him and not allowed him to brow beat me. We began talking of his past and his memories of the days when he was a young carpenter. He had worked on many structures during the days when the city was growing and expanding. I found many of his stories fascinating and I enjoyed hearing him talk about his "better days."

I also enjoyed watching him interact with his "best friend," a small, scruffy dog named Chili. Robbie loved that dog with all his heart and the feelings were definitely returned. Chili weighed, at most, fifteen pounds, but believed in his canine heart that he was a mighty German shepherd. He was devoted to his master. I enjoyed Chili and this seemed to "win" a lot of points with Robbie.

Our visits together were still somewhat tense, but we were both trying and working at it. Surprisingly, at one point Robbie's condition improved. Chemotherapy and radiation seemed to have arrested the spread of his disease. After conferring with his physician, it was decided that Robbie no longer had need of the hospice services. The smile on Robbie's face when he heard this news lit up the entire hospice.

He shook my hand as I left and said, "Now don't you take this the wrong way, but don't come back! I don't want to ever see you again." I laughed, said good-bye to Chili, and wished Robbie well.

Six months later, I returned to work after a weekend off, to find a new patient referral in my mailbox. Robbie was back. I thought a lot about being Robbie's nurse again. However, that particular time, I had an extremely heavy and demanding caseload. I wasn't sure I had the necessary energy to adequately care for Robbie. Even when he and I "got along," it was still a struggle for both of us. His constant testing, pushing, manipulating required a lot of patience. I wasn't sure I could handle it. Regretfully, I decided that Robbie would benefit by having another nurse. I believed then and still do, that this was the right decision for me and for Robbie.

However, I kept "tabs" on him, by talking with the nurse and social worker who were assigned to his care. They told me of his failing health and the deterioration in his physical strength.

I learned that he had been admitted to the hospice center. Something drew me downstairs. I hadn't seen Robbie for over six months and I wasn't sure how he would receive me or how I would feel. But I felt compelled to stop in and say hello.

I barely recognized Robbie when I opened the door of his hospice room. The big, burly man I said good-bye to six months earlier had disappeared. This man I saw before me was weak and dying.

As I walked in, Robbie opened his eyes. He smiled and the blue eyes that used to challenge me began to tear up and twinkle simultaneously. I smiled back, approached the bed and took his hand in mine. He squeezed and weakly said, "I'm glad to see you."

"Me, too," I said, as tears formed in my own eyes. No other words were spoken. I stayed with Robbie for a few minutes, holding his hand. Whatever problems we had in the past were no longer important. This time there was no tension and no difficulty communicating. Those few moments together were very meaningful.

I will forever be thankful I had the chance to say goodbye to Robbie.

Submitted by Anne Wallace Sharp

## JUDY

Judy was a proud, dignified, eighty-five-year-old widow. Her husband had died twenty years earlier. One year after his death, she was diagnosed with bilateral breast cancer. She subsequently had a double mastectomy. As her age advanced, she decided to move in order to live near her niece. When I first met Judy, she had freshly teased hair, newly manicured nails and precisely applied make-up. She lived in a senior citizen apartment complex and was used to taking care of herself. In her mind, she believed she would remain independent until the end. "Then," she told me, "I want to go to bed one night and just not wake up in the morning." Unfortunately, things didn't work out as Judy hoped.

# GIFTS

One day when I arrived for our visit, Judy did not respond to the security intercom. This was very unusual. I summoned the building manager who let me into the building. Together, we rode the elevator to the third floor. I became keenly aware of my increasing anxiety and pounding heart. I wasn't sure what we would find.

We arrived to find Judy's apartment door locked. Another bad sign. The manager unlocked the door and pushed it opened. I was calling Judy's name when I spied her slippered feet under the table. She was on the floor. She reported she had fallen the night before on her way to bed and had been unable to get up. She had laid on the floor for approximately fifteen hours, unable to telephone for help.

After assisting her to the couch, she and I began to talk about what was going to happen. She sadly acknowledged that she could no longer manage at home by herself. By mid-afternoon, Judy had decided to go to our the hospice care facility until other plans could be made. She had made the choice herself, but as the ambulance crew wheeled her out of her apartment, I saw the sparkle and pride go out of her face and body.

Once she arrived at the unit I worked at, plans for nursing home placement were initiated. I visited her on a Friday and told her she would be transferred early the following week. Her physical status revealed no significant change. As I got ready to leave, she grabbed my hand, and pulled me gently back to her side. "Good-bye ... I love you ... Thanks for all your help." That was Judy's final good-bye.

She died less than twenty-four hours later. I truly believe that once Judy realized she could no longer live independently, she chose not to live at all. In reality, I guess her belief that she would live independently and then die in her sleep ultimately came true.

Submitted by Kim Vesey

# SHARP AND TERBAY

## FAVORITE DOGS

I'm a dog person. I have two of my own. They are part of my family and an important component of my life. When I have company, my dogs seem to have the mistaken perception that these visitors to my home are actually coming to see them. Their tails start to wag, they begin to prance around, they show off and they are eager to make everyone feel welcome by licking and nuzzling. They also often jump up onto laps for the caresses and attention they feel they so richly deserve.

When I visit a patient, I am very aware of pets and what an important role they play in family life. I always go out of my way to greet a pet. After all, they believe I am really there to see them. Who am I to argue with this canine or feline logic?

Patients and families seem to warm to the attention I offer their pets. Often I am more quickly welcomed into their confidences. I can almost read their minds, "Well, she likes the dog. And the dog seems to like her. She must be okay."

I have met some interesting people and some fascinating animals during the years I have worked at the hospice.

Lady was a black miniature poodle who perched on the back of the sofa watching diligently for the mailman to come. She hated the mailman and barked at him ferociously. However, she seemed to enjoy my visits. She had belonged to Elinor for ten years. They were devoted to one another. If Elinor had pumpkin pie for dessert, so did Lady. If Elinor took a bath, so did Lady. As Elinor's disease progressed, she began to put her affairs in order. She said her good-byes to friends and family and was ready to let go. But what to do with Lady? It was all she talked about for days—who would provide the best home for Lady? Finally, a cousin offered Lady a home in the country. Elinor thought this was a fine idea. Lady would have the run of the house and would enjoy chasing after the chickens, pigs and sheep outside. With her last task accomplished satisfactorily, Elinor died with Lady nuzzled in by her side.

When I knocked on the door of Martin's home, I heard a deep bark. As the door opened I was greeted by a thin gentleman and an immensely overweight Bassett Hound.

"Hi, I'm Martin," the patient said, "And this is Flash."

I couldn't help myself. I began to laugh.

Martin smiled, "I know—he doesn't look like a Flash, but it seems to fit."

Flash was a delight. As I talked with Martin, I found out about Martin's disease and Flash's medical problems. Flash was diabetic and had just been put on a rather severe diet.

During the months that I visited Martin, Flash lost thirty-eight pounds.

"He's got a new lease on life," Martin said to me one day. "He's like a pup again—playing and running."

As Martin's disease progressed, Flash's health deteriorated also. Flash began to lose his eyesight. Martin and his wife seemed more concerned about Flash's problems than their own. And for the next few weeks, Martin's failing health was matched by Flash's deterioration.

I would guess that as Martin nears the end of his life, that Flash may also.

Logan was a large, noble looking Russian wolfhound, that came up to my waist. He was also very inquisitive and curious. He enjoyed roaming the neighborhood and stopping by to visit neighbors. When he was done with his visiting, the neighbors would call his family and tell them they were sending Logan home. He would show up on the doorstep minutes later, looking a little sheepish, but obviously fulfilled. The second time I visited Logan's family, I pulled up in the driveway, opened the back door of my car to get my briefcase and Logan jumped into the back seat and wouldn't get out. He was ready to go for a drive. Nothing I could say or do would deter him. Fortunately, he was hungry . The promise of a great milk bone lured him out of my automobile.

I have on frequent occasions posed for pictures with the family dog—not the patient, but the family dog. I have gotten down on the floor, cavorted and played with a pooch or three or four. My dogs go nearly ballistic when I finally return home with the scent of several strange creatures saturating my clothing. They are extremely jealous, but tolerant. They somehow set aside their feelings of betrayal to warmly welcome me home.

I have seen countless dogs lie calmly in their master's or mistress' bed as death comes. They mourn. One family had to literally physically restrain a small mixed terrier from taking an enormous bite out of the leg of the funeral director who had come to remove the patient from the home.

As I visit my patients I have enjoyed all the dogs I've met —Flash, Lady, Chili, Ginger, Penny, Freckles, Duffy and Logan and countless others. Each had a unique personality. Each welcomed me openly and warmly into their home. Each mourned the loss of their master. Each impacted my life and the life of their family.

I thank them all for their unconditional love
and acceptance.

Submitted by Anne Wallace Sharp

## MEG AND DON

It was my very first hospice visit. My supervisor and I approached the door and knocked. An elderly man answered and stepped out on the porch. He pulled back his jacket to reveal a small handgun.

He spoke low and intently, "Meg doesn't know she has cancer and she won't know ... Understand?"

I timidly responded, "I won't bring it up, but if she asks I would have to be honest." I held my breath, waiting for his response, but he seemed to accept my answer and led me into the house. The rest of the visit proceeded without incident.

Meg's cancer had spread to her bones and caused a serious spinal cord compression. She was bed-bound with only minimal use of her arms and no use of her legs.

Three months later, Meg asked, "Why can't I walk? Why aren't I getting any better?"

Her husband was in the next room, watching and listening. I could see him glaring at me, as if to say, "Don't you dare."

I asked her to trust me and told her that if I was able to come back the following week, I would answer all her questions. She said she trusted me and would wait.

I spoke politely but firmly to her husband, Don. Meg was asking, she had the right to know, and he didn't have the right to keep this information from her.

"I made a promise to Meg. I told her I would answer her questions if I came back next week. Now, you can tell me not to come back, but ..." He reluctantly agreed that I could return.

At my next visit, I pulled a chair up beside the bed and gently held her hand.

"Do you remember my promise last week?" I asked.

"Yes ... tell me what's wrong with me," she replied.

I had advocated for honesty and truth and now the big "C" word seemed stuck in my throat. I explained that she had cancer and that the disease had caused the collapse of her spinal column resulting in her inability to use her legs.

She took a deep breath, briefly looked away, then squeezed my hand, "I knew it ... I've suspected it all along. Thanks for being honest ... and for trusting my ability to deal with it," she said.

# SHARP AND TERBAY

Honesty is best. She knew it all the time. I mourned the fact that she and Don had lost so much valuable time together, that they hadn't been more open and honest with each other and that they had spent so much time trying to "protect" each other. Don never admitted it, but I believe he was very relieved to have "it" out in the open.

(Authors' note: This is not an uncommon scenario. Family members believe they are protecting a loved one by not telling them they have a terminal disease. I have found that almost most of the time the patient "knows." The tragedy is that no one can really talk about feelings. I have also seen patients who did not know and who struggled fearfully to understand why they were so sick. I have had patients on the verge of death who still seemingly didn't have a clue to what was happening. Their lack of information haunts me. Yet, even then, some family members insist on keeping the truth from the patient. Honest, forthright, open communication—while painful—allows for a resolution of grief for both family and patient.)

Submitted by Kim Vesey

# 4

# Glimpses of Love

*The authors and other professionals explore what love means in the face of loss, in more tales from hospices.*

## A COMMUNITY OF FRIENDS

"This is going to be a difficult case," the assessment nurse told me. "Your patient is abusing his pain medication—maybe even selling it to his friends."

I took a deep breath, filed the information away, and called Troy to schedule my first visit. He sounded weak on the phone and requested a visit as soon as possible.

"My pain is really out of control," he said.

As I arrived at the small white frame house in one of the older sections of town, I was nervous and unsure what awaited me. The door was opened by a middle-aged man in faded jeans and a Harley Davidson T-shirt. He had long blond hair and an unruly beard.

"Hi, I'm Troy. Come on in."

Troy was obviously in pain. His movements were slow, deliberate and accompanied by facial grimacing and occasional moans. Troy sat down in an old rocker and introduced me to his friend. "This is my friend, Earl. He's helping to take care of me," he said.

Earl was also middle-aged and dressed similarly. "I'm glad to meet you. I hope you can do something to make Troy more comfortable," he said as he extended his hand warmly and shook mine firmly.

After checking Troy's blood pressure and other vital signs, I asked him about his pain medication. He was taking Vicodin which is a moderately effective synthetic codeine used for mild to moderate pain. It wasn't doing the job.

"How much of this are you taking?" I asked.

"Two tablets every three hours, but it doesn't even dull the pain."

I told Troy I would call his doctor and obtain a stronger medication.

"Good luck," Troy said. "He won't give you anything. He thinks I'm a drug addict and that I'm selling my pills to my friends."

Earl supported his friend saying, "Because Troy is a cyclist and looks the way he does, everyone assumes he's an addict—or worse. The fact is that Troy has been sober and off drugs for twelve years. He's the only reason I'm sober today. The man saved my life."

Despite what the assessment nurse had told me, I found Troy completely honest. I didn't think he had a drug abuse problem. This man was in pain and needed help.

I called his doctor and received the answer Troy had anticipated.

"We won't give him anything stronger."

My anger began to escalate.

"Now listen here. This man is in pain. He needs something" I said.

"He's putting you on," the doctor told me.

"I know pain when I see it. He can barely walk and the Vicodin just isn't cutting it."

"The answer is still no," the doctor said.

I felt like I was banging my head against a stone wall. I tried desperately to think of other options.

"How about if we admit Troy to the hospice unit for pain control?" I asked the doctor.

"He won't agree to that," the doctor replied. "He just wants the drugs."

I turned to Troy and asked him if he'd agree to a hospice admission.

"Anything. I'll do anything to get rid of this pain," he said.

I informed the doctor that Troy had agreed to the admission. Twenty-four hours later the doctor apologized to Troy. It had taken massive doses of morphine to control the pain and ultimately, an epidural catheter was inserted to deliver the morphine directly into Troy's blood stream. Finally, with his pain controlled, Troy was able to return home.

There were always visitors at Troy's house. Fellow bikers stopped by daily to offer support and prayers. Most of them repeated Earl's comment. "He's the reason I'm sober."

When Troy died his friends were there. And when Troy was laid to rest, his friends escorted him to the gravesite on their motorcycles, in full colors and gear.

The assessment nurse was right and wrong. It was a difficult case, but not for the reasons she gave me. I was angry that Troy and his friends were stereotyped as drunks or addicts. I refused to let Troy be labeled. With his pain finally controlled, Troy was able to relax, sleep and finally die in peace.

His "community" was different from mine, but similar in many ways, too. They looked different—came from different backgrounds—lived a different lifestyle—but in the end his comrades offered support, friendship and love. What more could anyone ask from a community of friends?

Submitted by Anne Wallace Sharp

## MELODY

I will remember Melody forever because she significantly touched my life.

She was born in the spring to Mike and Alicia, a young couple who already had a three-year-old child. She looked like a beautiful, healthy baby girl. However, she only had a few months to live. Melody was born with a rare genetic disease and the doctors told her parents she had the grim sentence of less than six months.

Whenever a child is referred to hospice, the staff is affected by the child's impending death. Of all the referrals taken, the ones involving children are the toughest to accept. Melody was less than a month old when the referral was made by her physician.

Since birth, Melody had required intensive care at the hospital. She lived there in a tangle of tubes, wires and machines. Her mother and father saw her only from a distance.

The word came that little Melody would be coming to the hospice. This was an unusual event. We had young people on a few occasions at the center, but never a baby. As one of the clinical secretaries, I was asked to call around to find a crib. It was amazing how many people responded to my requests. Within a few hours we had a crib.

An adult patient room was turned into a small nursery. The large bed in the room was covered with blankets, diapers and baby clothes. The crib had a baby seat inside it because Melody was so small that she needed the security of the blanketed seat around her.

Her tiny body looked so vulnerable. Because the nurses and doctors all feared infection, the nursing staff placed a sign on her door restricting visitors. I was one of the first to be given the privilege of seeing her. Unsure of what to expect, I walked over to the crib and peered down at the little sleeping form. My heart reached out to the tiny baby girl. As I stood there she began to squirm and cry. I looked out at the one of the nurses and swore that I had not pinched her. I was given permission to pick her up, but first I had to wash my hands, remove any pins and wear a gown. I accomplished all three tasks in a matter of seconds. It had been twelve years since I had held my sixth child, as a new born, in my arms. I wanted to hold and cuddle this precious baby.

A rocking chair had been placed in the room and as I sat down and cradled this child, I looked her over like a new mother does, checking fingers and toes. She was so perfectly formed. Were they sure she was dying? Gently I wrapped her in a blanket and lifted her up to my shoulder. With her little head on my shoulder, I gently touched my cheek to her and kissed her. Her tiny mouth broke into a smile. As I cuddled her, I rubbed her back and she responded by snuggling ever so close, as if to reach even further inside me. I hummed the same Irish lullabies I had to my own babies. Slowly Melody responded by tugging at my heart, as only a baby can. I gave way to a baby's trusting love.

I found myself drawn to her room daily. Despite the fact that the nurses told me she was blind and could not hear, I knew that Melody could hear and see in her own way. She was a great listener, not with her ears, but with her body. Sometimes we talked about the weather, or about the day's events. We even became deeply theological at times. I would ask her what she thought of the world situations and she responded by loving me. She never moved her head a lot, but she often nuzzled in the crook of my neck.

From the beginning it became obvious that feeding Melody would be the major focus of her care. It was so difficult to watch these gentle nurses place the small tubing down her tiny nose, all the while rubbing her belly and soothingly talking to her as she fought the procedure. After taking about an ounce or two, the next step was getting her to burp. Part of her sickness involved digestion problems. It was imperative that she relieve the gas and rest comfortably. It was a constant and frustrating challenge.

# SHARP AND TERBAY

It seemed the only time Melody was really comfortable was when she was in an upright position. Because of their busy schedule, the nursing staff was not able to constantly hold the baby, so the office staff was asked to help out—we jumped at the opportunity. I helped to formulate a schedule whereby every half hour someone would check in and hold Melody. This was done to help the nursing staff develop a routine for her. After several days, it was no longer necessary for the staff to come every day. Individuals only needed to be available when a "rocker" was needed.

Melody's mother, who was recuperating from both emotional and physical problems, had gone back to the hospital. She had been admitted for depression—a fact that surprised no one. We took pictures of Melody to her and she seemed very happy that so many people were caring for her baby. They were the first pictures she had seen of her baby without the tangle of tubes and wires. Melody's father, Mike, faithfully visited on his lunch break so he could spend the evening with his three-year-old son. It was a sad situation for a young family to endure.

The office staff was "warned" from the beginning that we were opening ourselves up to being hurt if we became too closely involved with Melody. Once I held her in my arms, I was hooked. I gave permission for the hurt to come in, because I felt it was worth the risk. If I couldn't allow myself to love, then what is the point in living?

Melody was taught to suck and with great relief, the tube feedings were stopped. As I watched over her, it became obvious to me that she was not developing like other babies. She was not growing properly.

After her release from the hospital, Melody's mother began making visits to see her baby. At first they were just visits, but then she was able to take Melody home for short periods of time during the day. The stays at home became longer and finally Melody was able to remain at home with her family for good. I experienced a mixture of emotions. More than anything I wanted Melody to be with her family. But a part of me wept quietly as I watched Melody leave. She had been with us for a month. Even though we no longer were called upon to rock her on a routine basis, it had become a habit to stop in to give her a kiss, touch her little hand or just whisper loving words.

At the hospice, I find myself dealing day in and day out with dying and trying to come to an acceptance of death. Yet deep down, I felt a hope that maybe this time the doctors were wrong—that Melody would live.

But she did not. Melody died shortly before her four month birthday. She died at home in her mother's arms. The news spread through the hospice quickly and all of her surrogate mothers grieved. She had touched all of us in different ways. While we were all saddened that she had died, we were also thankful that her pain and struggle were over.

A picture of Melody sits in a gold frame at the nurse's station. It is a picture of a beautiful little gift a picture etched in our hearts forever. That picture is a constant reminder of the love Melody gave and received. Life is so precious no matter how short or how long.

Submitted by Sue Handle Terbay


## HAPPY BIRTHDAY, GRANDPA


Sherry and Brad had been deeply affected by their grandfather's death. Because their mother worked, the two children spent most of the day at Grandpa's house. Sherry (seven) and Brad (nine) had watched as Grandpa got sicker and sicker. They had heard Grandma talk about him not getting better and both knew that he was going to die. They felt very helpless, frustrated and sad that Grandpa wasn't going to get well. They watched their mother cry and knew that she was very upset about losing her father. They had also watched Grandma who was especially sad. The children felt badly that they couldn't make her happy like she used to be.

Grandma had talked to both of them about saying good-bye to Grandpa. This had been difficult. However, Brad and Sherry had both told Grandpa how much they loved him and had said good-bye as best they could.

When Grandpa died they were very sad. They would miss him. He had been a very important person in their young lives. They felt especially sad that he had missed his birthday. He had died one week before his seventieth.

They decided that Grandpa's birthday should not go unnoticed or uncelebrated. They talked to their mother about doing something special, but she didn't think it was such a good idea. Not to be denied, Brad and Sherry approached their grandmother. She was thrilled and thought it was a wonderful idea.

Brad and Sherry helped Grandma bake a special birthday cake with chocolate icing (Grandpa's favorite) the night before his birthday. The next day the three of them planned to go to the cemetery for a special party.

When the children awoke the next morning, they were disappointed to see the rain outside. It was pouring. They both wondered if the party would have to wait. But Grandma decided they should go anyway. The three of them drove to the cemetery in the driving rain. Needless to say, the cemetery was deserted.

With umbrellas in hand, Brad, Sherry and Grandma walked solemnly to the gravesite. They stood by the grave and all three began singing "Happy Birthday" to Grandpa. They lit the candles on the cake, but the rain kept putting them out. They were not to be deterred, however. Grandma cut four slices of cake and they placed the extra slice on the ground. They knew that Grandpa couldn't eat it, but decided the birds and squirrels would enjoy the treat. Grandma lit her cigarette lighter, and they all three blew out the light, making a wish as they blew.

The strange little threesome stood in the rain, eating their cake and talking about how much they missed Grandpa. They spoke of the special things they had done together. Grandma cried. So did Brad and Sherry.

After spending this special time with Grandpa on his birthday, they got back in the car and Grandma drove home, feeling content and at peace. Grandpa had his special birthday party after all.

Submitted by Tom O'Neill

## SYLVIA

Sylvia had come to spend her last few months of life at the hospice. A fiercely independent woman, she had struggled and fought the aggressive cancer that quickly was consuming her body. Determined to take care of herself, she had managed to stay home far longer than friends and family had ever imagined. Finally, the physical and emotional pain were too much for her to bear and she requested an admission to the Hospice facility. It was a hard decision for her, but one that she made with dignity. Family and friends had been supportive and caring, but could not adequately provide the amount of care that Sylvia now needed.

Her needs were many. Severe pain necessitated ever-increasing amounts of narcotics. The intensity of her emotions frightened her, but she found comfort in the words and presence of the hospice staff. Her questions about the dying process, God, heaven and spirits challenged the staff who talked with her. She struggled to find meaning and answers for her own burning issues, particularly the severe disfigurement that accompanied her disease. She was determined to find peace so she could complete her journey.

She made friends quickly at the hospice—among both the staff and other patients. She talked frequently with others, sharing stories and feelings. It was not uncommon to pass a patient's room and find Sylvia there in her wheelchair talking intently, laughing, or sometimes crying with a new-found friend.

Several weeks into her stay, she learned from one of the nurses that one of her new friends, Millie, was close to death. The nurse seemed particularly distraught because the patient's family couldn't be reached. Sylvia asked for her wheelchair. With the help of the nurse, Sylvia made her way to her friend's bedside. She sat at Millie's side, holding her hand, stroking her arm, laughing, crying, and reminiscing about their brief, memorable friendship. Sylvia stayed with Millie until Millie's family arrived and then quietly departed. One of the nurses commented to Sylvia about the tremendous gift that she had given.

Sylvia replied, "No one should die alone."

Sylvia's battle with her own disease finally ended three months later. Her journey those last three months was a difficult one. She struggled continuously with pain—physical, emotional and spiritual. But, as death approached, her struggle eased and she reached the end of her journey.

Her family and friends sat at Sylvia's bedside all through the night—a long vigil of tears, stories, memories, music, prayers, sadness and rejoicing. Sylvia's struggle was over. She was at peace, surrounded by so much love. Sylvia was right ... no one should die alone.

Submitted by Elaine Wheaton

# GIFTS

This is not a "real" hospice story. It involves a patient cared for prior to coming to hospice. This woman and the love we shared played a large part in my decision to become a hospice nurse.

## IRISH EYES

"We're sending you a patient," the emergency room nurse told me, and proceeded to give me report on the woman who would soon be occupying Room 536, Bed A. A fairly ordinary beginning for such an extraordinary relationship. The patient's name was Ellen. She had a seizure, and was being admitted for further evaluation and testing. I greeted my new patient as the attendants were transferring her to the ward bed and I introduced myself. I was immediately enthralled by her clear blue eyes, her smile that seemed to light up her entire face, and her warm and open manner. I liked her the moment I met her. I came to love her.

The diagnostic workup showed lung cancer which had already spread to her brain, causing the seizure. The doctors recommended chemotherapy and radiation, and she optimistically pursued both treatments. She was determined to fight the malignancy as best she could, but remained realistic, knowing that the treatment offered no cure. She was discharged home after a ten day hospital stay. I promised her I'd keep in touch.

As the days and months passed, amid my busy duties I failed to keep my promise, but I thought of her often. As I went about my tasks in the hospital she came to mind, but I just never seemed to make the time to get around to calling her. One evening towards the end of my shift, I just couldn't get thoughts of her to stop. It had been six months and I wondered how she was doing. I picked up the telephone, dialed her number and hoped she would remember me. Her daughter Mary answered and seemed pleased to hear from me. When I asked how her mother was doing, Mary hesitated for a moment.

"Not so good," she said. "She's had a bad few days. And an awful lot of pain. The doctors put her on Methadone and now she's sleeping so much we can't get her awake long enough to talk to us. And when she is awake she's so doped up she doesn't make any sense."

I offered to stop by and see Ellen after work.

"That would be terrific. Maybe you can get a better idea of what's going on. I'm wondering if she's getting too much medication," Mary said, genuinely appreciative of my interest and my offer.

As I drove to Ellen's house after work my mind was busy trying to anticipate what I would find. It had been six months since I'd seen her. Would I find the same woman I'd come to like so much in the hospital or would she be a shadow of her former self? Had the chemo and radiation been effective? What about the side effects?

I knocked on the door and was ushered in by Mary and her husband, Jim.

"We just tried to wake her up and she didn't respond at all. We're wondering whether we need to take her to the emergency room," Mary said with concern.

Their anxiety was contagious. As they led the way back to the bedroom, I prepared myself for the worst. Jim turned on the light and I approached the bed. As I did so, Ellen opened her eyes, saw me and popped out of bed like a jack-in-the-box.

"God love you," she said as clear as a bell. "Let's party!" And we proceeded to do just that. We talked, ate, and drank coffee and soda all through the night. As I drove home the sun was coming up and I knew in my heart that this time I would keep in touch as promised.

As Ellen's disease progressed she moved into her daughter Carol's apartment. The chemo and radiation had briefly arrested the disease, but had now stopped being effective. Ellen chose to discontinue the treatment. The doctors told her it was just a matter of time. I spent more and more of my free hours with her. I was now calling her Granny like the rest of the family did. Everyday before going to work I'd stop by Carol's apartment and spend several hours alone with Granny. I told myself it was because Granny needed me, but the truth of the matter was that I needed her too. She'd become a surrogate mother. I found myself talking to her like I had never been able to talk to my own mother. I shared my feelings, fears, concerns and hopes. She listened with unconditional love and acceptance.

I was enchanted by this courageous Irish woman who, no matter how badly she felt, had a smile on her face whenever I walked in. Her famous "God love you" warmed my heart every time I heard it. I was accepted as one of the family, celebrating birthdays and holidays with this extraordinary woman and her family.

During this time I was hospitalized with an irregular heart beat. I will never forget the Saturday afternoon that my hospital door opened and in walked Granny and her daughter. I couldn't keep the tears from falling. She could barely walk, and she had come to cheer me up. I felt and acknowledged the love we shared.

Other memories of Granny live with me still. I remember the time we had dinner at my house and Granny fell and broke her arm. She accused me with a glint in her eye of deliberately making the carpet too thick. I recall celebrating when she was able to have a bowel movement after five days without one—the sound of the plop of that stool was like music to our ears. I also fondly recall driving to Mansfield with her to surprise her daughter Sharon for her fortieth birthday. We listened to the Statler Brothers and sang together one song after another. Granny and I talked until all hours of the night and morning. I will always remember laughing, sharing meals and other special moments together, watching Elen's body weaken while her spirit grew stronger, seeing her blue eyes twinkling even through the pain and talking about her fear, faith and love.

# SHARP AND TERBAY

As her death approached we all gathered around her bed. She had slipped into a coma after a long struggle. We kept our vigil through three long days and nights, talking together, laughing, crying and playing Statler Brother records over and over again. Toward the end, she seemed to rouse slightly. She opened her eyes, smiled and said just aloud the name of her dead husband. She seemed to relax before our eyes and stopped struggling. There was no doubt in my mind where she was going or what she had seen. She died peacefully a few hours later as we all held her hands, cried together and said good-bye to Granny.

At her graveside three days later, the same group joined together with the other mourners and sang "When Irish Eyes Are Smiling." There wasn't a dry eye in the crowd.

After thirteen years I still miss her. She was an extraordinary woman—a gift to all who knew her. And, yes, I believe those Irish Eyes are still smiling—smiling down on all who loved her.

Submitted by Anne Wallace Sharp

## THE WAKE

Some of our briefest encounters are our most memorable. My association with one particular patient, Eleanor, had been very short and yet, I was profoundly touched by her death and her family's response to it.

I was called to her home to do the official pronouncement and prepare her body for removal to the funeral home. I knew in advance that there was to be no funeral, no viewing. At Eleanor's request, she was to be cremated.

# GIFTS

When I arrived there, I found Eleanor lying peacefully in her bed. I was startled momentarily and then realized what the family was doing. They were having their own private viewing.

Her daughter had applied just the right amount of make-up—her cheeks were rosy, her eyes lightly shadowed and her lips were tinted a dusty pink. Her hair had been brushed and softly framed her thin, now peaceful face. A funeral director could not have done a better job.

A small bouquet of flowers had been placed in her hands. She was dressed in her favorite nightgown, a soft pink color and the family had provided matching earrings. The family gathered around her bedside to quietly say good-bye. I felt like an intruder, but they welcomed me and continued their eulogy.

Eleanor's mother, a delightful vibrant woman in her eighties was reminiscing. As she told the story of her daughter's birth, I thought that this was truly a case of things coming "full circle." Several generations stood gathered, honoring this special woman who had been daughter, wife, mother and friend. As the mother finished her words, Eleanor's husband leaned over his wife.

"Do you have one last kiss for an old man?" he said quietly and gently kissed his wife good-bye.

I have witnessed many deaths, attended many funerals and memorial services, but none quite so intimate and moving as this very special one.

Submitted by Sonia Kreider

## OLD CRONIES

Joe lived in a run down trailer with his cat, Ralph. I liked Joe the moment I met him. He had a delightful sense of humor and was always glad to see me. We talked about his disease, his family, his life and his frustrations with being "cooped up" in his trailer.

After I had been visiting Joe for several weeks, he confided in me that he desperately wanted to visit the bar he used to frequent prior to his illness.

"I just want to see the old place one last time and say goodbye to my friends," he said. He explained that he had discouraged them from visiting, because he didn't want the other men to see how he lived and how sick he really was.

"I miss those guys—I need to see them one more time."

I offered to take him in his wheelchair. Despite his weakness, he refused to consider the wheelchair. He was a very proud man and told me that he would either walk in or he wouldn't go. He grudgingly admitted that he would need some help getting in and out of the bar, but he was adamant about walking in under his own power. He wanted to sit on his favorite bar stool not in a "rickety old wheelchair!"

I suggested that he rest for a few days, conserve his strength and then call me when he felt strong enough for the outing. About a week later, Joe called and proclaimed that he was, "as ready as I'll ever be."

I picked Joe up at his trailer. He had dressed for the occasion, wearing a clean tee-shirt, and baseball cap and a pair of jeans which were too baggy for his deteriorated frame. We drove to the bar and I escorted Joe inside, where we found a seat off in a corner.

Joe's face lit up as he looked around the bar. One by one, his old drinking buddies wandered over. It was obvious to everyone that Joe was very ill, but every time someone brought up this

# GIFTS

topic, Joe promptly changed the subject. He was determined to talk about the "old days," not what was happening now.

Joe and his cronies reminisced about the times they shared, and even managed to get in a few well placed "digs" about local politics and politicians. Joe sipped his soft drink as he and his friends laughed and talked.

Joe had not come empty handed. He had "gifts" for his friends. He had thoughtfully gathered up many of his prized possessions and now came the moment for their distribution. He gave a favorite pipe to one man; a torn picture to another; and an old coin to yet another. It was a special moment for me to watch Joe give away what little he had, and to note the graciousness of wise old men who received them. For Joe and his friends, these gifts were invaluable treasures!

Saying his good-byes was difficult, but he managed to do so, and finally was ready to leave. He walked out, his back straight, under his own power.

I saw Joe's buddies at his funeral several weeks later and they smiled. They gathered around me after the service and we chatted for a few moments. As they were leaving, one of them turned back and grinned at me.

"We're heading back to the bar—gonna have a beer or two —for Joe!"

I smiled, too—that would have made Joe very happy!

Submitted by Sandy Bonamassa


## THE LAST GOOD-BYE*

Thursday dawned bright and clear. April can be cold, but this day brought with it a hint of spring and a promise of warmer weather. Clear blue skies, bright sunshine, a gentle breeze and

*Originally appeared in *Nursing 95* as "What I Didn't Tell Bob." Reprinted with permission of Springhouse Corporation.

temperatures in the high sixties greeted me as I rolled down the window in my car. I drove to not only my last visit of the day, but my last one before a week's vacation.

Bob was a favorite of mine. We had hit if off from the first visit, kidding each other in a warm, comfortable, friendly way as if we had known each other for years. He had pulmonary fibrosis, a chronic obstructive lung disease, that was progressively robbing him of both his breath and his life. He was on continuous oxygen, delivered through a small hole in his trachea (a special procedure had created an opening so that oxygen could be delivered directly into his lungs.) Even with the oxygen, his breathing was labored, his color was poor, and he was constantly fighting an upper respiratory infection that further complicated his breathing.

Despite his shortness of breath, Bob was always talking. He loved to tell stories, to laugh and to joke. He liked to entertain and it was obvious to me that he was good at it. He enjoyed people and people enjoyed his company. I always felt welcome in his home, like a member of the family or an old friend. I looked forward to seeing him.

As I pulled my car into the driveway, Bob was waiting outside for me. He was sitting in a lawn chair in front of his garage, his oxygen tubing stretched across the lawn, still providing him with the much needed air. As I exited the car, I noticed the baseball cap on his head and the huge grin on his face.

"Rubbing it in, aren't you?" I accused him, as I read the word Arkansas across the front of the hat.

"I couldn't resist," he grinned. The previous week we had kidded back and forth about the upcoming NCAA basketball Final Four championship game. Being from North Carolina, my favorite team was Duke. Bob's favorite team was Arkansas, the victors of the close, well fought game and Bob was making sure I knew it. We both laughed and settled into an easy conversation that jumped from topic to topic like a skipping stone—restaurants, movies, news, headlines, his family, etc.

# GIFTS

Eventually, the conversation turned to his health and how he was feeling. He said he was feeling a little better, that the infection finally seemed to be clearing up and that he was looking forward to the warm weather and being outside a little more. That made me feel better, because of my vacation I wouldn't be seeing him for over a week.

I told him this and he grimaced, "You mean I have to get used to another nurse?"

"I know—such a burden for you, but try to be nice and behave yourself. I'll be back a week from Monday. You'll just appreciate me more when I return," I said.

He laughed, wished me well and told me to have fun. I told him to keep feeling better and that I would see him soon.

Unfortunately, Bob died suddenly while I was gone.

I happened to see his name in the obituary section of the newspaper several days later and I was both shocked and heart-broken. He had died one week after that sunny Thursday. I felt cheated because I hadn't said good-bye, and I felt guilty because I hadn't been there when he needed me.

I knew I needed to put some closure on my relationship with Bob and that I also needed to see the family, so I attended the funeral home visitation. I walked in and the first person I saw was Bob's daughter, Barbara. She rushed over to me, tears streaming down her face and threw her arms around me.

"Dad loved you so much!" she said.

My tears joined hers as I said, "And I loved him."

Later as I cried again with his wife, Lorraine, I told her, "Bob was more than just a patient. He was my friend. I'll miss him a lot."

I do miss him. Watching a patient die can be a very hard, frustrating, and helpless experience. Sometimes all we can do is sit by, watch the struggle and try to ease the pain. But being there is also a blessing. It is a gift to share with someone their last journey on earth and to witness the peace and serenity that comes as the struggle ends.

# SHARP AND TERBAY

Though I cannot be with him, I carry with me the image of my friend sitting in his driveway, with an Arkansas cap on his head, and a grin on his face. I have a feeling he's still grinning.

Submitted by Anne Wallace Sharp

## HEAVENLY GIFTS

Ralph was a challenging patient. He was a forty-nine year old gentleman with cirrhosis of the liver, brought on by years of alcohol abuse. His biggest frustration was that he had "lost control." His life was lying shattered about him and there wasn't anything he could do to make it better. He was lovingly cared for by his girl friend of many years. They had little money.

Ralph died in April of 1995.

Just before the following Christmas, I received a package in the mail. Inside was a note from Ralph's girl friend, which read, "Debbie, this is a present from heaven."

I opened the package and there was a beautiful sweatshirt with bears and flowers on the front. The wording read "Love Bears All Things."

I continued reading the note, "When Ralph saw this shirt, he told me that you needed it. He told me to wait and mail it to you at Christmas. This is Ralph's gift to you from heaven."

Submitted by Debbie McMillan

# GIFTS

## UNFINISHED SYMPHONY

Mommies are dying
Leaving behind so much undone.
An impossible task, dear God,
so much to ask.
Children are growing and
asking questions, so many will
be left unanswered, indeed,
unheard, and even, unspoken,
swirling around in their minds.
Husbands are struggling to answer
the questions, holding on to the
woman so loved
keep the pieces together
and still they fall apart, leaving
a broken heart.
Or two or three or more
because the family is just beginning
and the wallpaper's not all hung yet,
the music lesson incomplete,
the songs not all sung.
Life is such a bitter sweet mix,
seize the moment,
seize the day
keep the little things in motion
before it all fades away.
Mommies are dying,
Husbands are trying to hold it
all together
And children are laughing
and then they are crying,
"Why all this stormy weather?"
God grant them peace

# SHARP AND TERBAY

and love,
and acceptance.
Help them through this reckless,
crazy, painful dance.
Make them ready for good byes,
put it all in place,
give them a sense of safeness
about their destination.
But for mommies, acceptance
and sometimes peace,
just never comes.
So much in their lives is unfinished,
so much to leave undone.
The best they can do is rest
their weary heads and
softly slip off to God
with trusting resignation.

Submitted by Jan Jessen, R. N.

## A MOTHER'S LOVE

I am frequently overwhelmed and inspired by the strength and love of the patients we serve. One who vividly displayed such traits was Gail a thirty-four year old mother with cervical cancer who, although barely able to sit up, prepared meals for her sons each evening and continued to do the laundry. It was her hope to protect her sons by not dying while they were home. She wanted to spare them that memory.

# GIFTS

On the day she died, I visited early in the morning to see how her weekend had gone. I was met at the door by the patient's mother, who said Gail was not doing well. I entered the bedroom and saw very vivid signs of imminent death. Gail asked me if she was going to die that day, "Yes, I think so," I replied.

Then I went across the road to use a neighbor's phone to order oxygen and to call Gail's husband to come home. When I got back to her house, Gail was sitting in the kitchen bravely trying to eat a bowl of Fruit Loops.

She spent much time with her husband that day, telling him how much she loved him. When he called me to come again later, I witnessed a beautiful death with completed good-byes and a great sense of peace. Her final gift? She spared her sons by dying ten minutes before the school bus came home.

Submitted by Roberta Erwin

## RESOLUTION

Often death provides an opportunity for healing of strained relationships. This was true for Grace Patterson and her daughter, Julie.

Grace was, by her own admission, a stubborn, independent and private woman. After her husband died, she lived briefly with her sister. Following her diagnosis of cancer, Grace moved to be closer to Julie.

She lived alone in an apartment for nine months until her condition further deteriorated, at which time a nurse's aide was hired to stay with Grace. Grace was adamant about maintaining her independence and keeping her own residence. She refused to allow anyone to stay at night, promising us that once in bed she would stay there until the aide arrived in the morning—a promise she kept.

Although Grace rarely volunteered information, she openly admitted there was strain in the relationship she had with her daughter. She alluded to a difficult childhood, a less than satisfying marriage, and admitted that she had never been a very demonstrative person.

Yet when I could get her talking, Grace shared fascinating stories about her German relatives, her husband's job as a Detroit policeman, and her own experiences working in an automobile factory. As I was leaving one day, I told Grace how much I enjoyed visiting her, and that I liked her very much.

"You do?" she questioned. "I'm not sure anyone has ever said that to me." I thought that it was sad she was dying and felt so unloved and unappreciated. I wondered what was going on between this mother and her daughter.

My only conversations with Grace's daughter Julie usually centered around symptom management and updates on Grace's condition and Julie's comments on how the nurse's aide was doing. In eight months of visiting Grace, this was the only time I saw Julie. When I asked Grace if Julie visited, Grace responded, "Sometimes."

As Grace's condition deteriorated, there was a coinciding problem with the nurse's aide. Rather than hiring another aide, Julie decided that Grace should move in with her. I was frankly skeptical and voiced my concern to Julie.

"I'm not sure you know what you're getting into. Your mom requires a lot of care," I said.

"That's okay," Julie said. "I'm taking a leave of absence from work and I want Mom here."

It was a magical, mysterious move and it worked! Grace told me that, for the first time in years, she felt that her daughter cared about her. She and Julie talked about the strain in their relationship and apparently made peace.

Grace died two weeks after moving to her

daughter's home.

Julie later told me, "Mom told me that Jesus was coming to take her home. But she also told me that she loved me. I don't think she ever said that to me—even as a child. What a wonderful gift."

Submitted by Anne Wallace Sharp

## MIKE

"May I please have a wheelchair for my mother?" The young boy standing in front of me couldn't have been more than ten years old, but his words and demeanor showed a maturity far beyond his years. I provided the wheelchair and he returned moments later with his mother seated comfortably on the cushioned seat. The rest of the family followed behind him as he wheeled her into the hospice center.

Introductions were made. I explained that I would be giving them the tour of the hospice they had requested and urged them to ask questions. The young man's name was Mike and for the moment, he was "in charge." Mike's mother Gloria was in her mid-thirties and was expected to live only a few more months. Gloria knew her time was short and had requested to see the center. The decision had already been made that during the final stages of her disease, she would be admitted there. So this, I knew, was an important tour. Gloria wanted the family to see the center and make sure that it would meet all their needs.

As we exited the elevator, Mike took charge again. He pushed his mother's wheelchair down the carpeted hallway and began his questions. What do the rooms look like? How's the food here? Can my mom have visitors? How long can we stay?

Can our dog visit? And on and on. The answers were very important to this young man.

We went outside to view the beautiful grounds and gardens, stopping momentarily just to enjoy the setting. Mike disappeared suddenly and returned moments later with a huge grin on his face.

"There's a great pond here, Mom! I can go fishing," he said. His mother seemed as delighted with this news as Mike was, and I learned later that Mike was a real fishing enthusiast.

Gloria's shy husband Richard occasionally asked a question, and Mike's siblings made a few comments, but it was obvious that Mike was "in charge." He was the one doing most of the talking and the questioning. As we continued our tour, we strolled down the memory walkway, which is comprised of bricks bought by family members and/or friends and inscribed with the names of the deceased. Mike wanted to know about the bricks and what they cost. He never took his eyes off his Mom and periodically would ask her if she was doing okay.

As the family departed, Mike thanked me for the visit. Gloria smiled and told me how pleased they all were at the facility. I thought, *What a neat family.* A week later, I was surprised to see Mike standing at the reception desk. I smiled and asked him if I could help him. "I want to buy one of those bricks," he said. I escorted him to the marketing department and introduced him.

I learned later that he had made a down payment on one of the large bricks (which sell for $500). He had proudly handed over a ten dollar bill and stated that he would bring in his allowance every week until he had paid for it. He told the marketing representative that he wanted a very special brick for his mother and he wanted it to be a big one. Mike never missed a week, bringing in his ten dollars every Friday afternoon.

A few months later, Mike's mom was admitted to the center. Her condition had significantly deteriorated and her time was short. I would catch frequent glimpses of them from the upstairs windows sitting on one of the benches under the trees, their dog laying by Gloria's feet.

She died in the center, surrounded by her family. A large brick commemorates her life and death. With the help of his uncle, Mike purchased the brick and arranged for the inscription. The family also purchased a bench in her memory. The bench sits under the trees not far from the special brick. Oftentimes when I sit there, I remember Gloria, a beautiful young woman and her family—especially her son, Mike.

Submitted by Sue Handle Terbay

## JACK

He was not supposed to be my patient, but things have a way of turning out the best, I believed, for all concerned. I saw Jack for the first time on a day I was "covering" for another nurse. Jack and I hit it off so well that he asked me to continue with him. I was more than happy to do this, for I too had felt that we had connected.

Jack was an engineer—a logical, rational, intelligent man who usually had a list of questions for me which I struggled to answer as honestly as I could. He had questions about his disease, his medications, his physical condition, but, refused to discuss his impending death.

"I cannot give up hope," he said and I agreed.

Unfortunately, his doctor was not being totally honest with Jack. Or perhaps, Jack just wasn't listening to what his doctor was saying. The disease was spreading. Palliative chemotherapy had helped for a short while, but the potent drugs were now causing more harm than good.

I tried to broach the subject of quality time versus quantity, but Jack refused to discuss this issue. He wanted both. Ultimately Jack decided on his own to opt for quality and stop his chemotherapy.

As time went by, we talked of Jack's fears. Nights were horrendous. He felt "out of control" and fearful that his wife wouldn't hear him call. She was an excellent caregiver, but Jack worried that she wouldn't respond quickly enough or wake up and hear him. A nurse's aide was hired to stay at night. He came to rely on her to meet his needs and slept soundly when she was there.

I could see Jack deteriorating before my eyes. His weight was dropping steadily; his pain was escalating; he was becoming weaker by the day—but still he wouldn't talk of his impending death. I accepted this decision, and often just sat with him talking about safe subjects such as his family, his travels, his hopes and his dreams.

One afternoon, I made a joint visit with his social worker. (We use the team approach at our hospice, utilizing nurses, social workers, chaplains, bereavement counselors and volunteers to offer the patient and family the optimum in holistic health care.) The social worker was out on the porch talking with Mary, Jack's wife. I was alone with Jack. He looked at me and before I could speak, his eyes welled up with tears. I was somewhat surprised that my own eyes also became filled with tears. As we gazed into each other's eyes, I walked over and took his hand in mine.

"Why are you crying?" he asked me.

"Because you're dying and I care very much about you."

"Thank you," he said.

I sat by his side, holding his hand, while we both cried.

"I never cry," he said.

"I don't usually either," I said, "But I do love you."

"You do?"

"Yes."

"Wow," he said, and cried some more. "I don't want to die."

"I know."

"But I am, aren't I?"

"Yes."

"I need to hold onto my hope, though. Maybe it's not hope of getting well anymore, but it's still hope," Jack said.

"No one wants to take your hope away," I responded.

"I wish I could do this with Mary," Jack finally said. And, at that moment as coincidence or fate often has it, Mary and the social worker walked in.

I told Mary what Jack had just said. She came over, took my place by his side, held his hand, and told him how much she loved him. "I love you, too, Mary," he responded.

One week later, with Mary by his side, Jack died in the same chair he had "lived" in for the past three months.

I would have to say that Jack's last few months were ones of quality. Not long enough, I'm sure, but nonetheless, meaningful and important. As I waited for the funeral home to come, I held Jack's hand one last time, kissed him on the forehead, and reflected back on our first visit. Yes, I was supposed to be his nurse, and he was supposed to be my friend. It was good to journey together, even if just briefly.

Submitted by Anne Wallace Sharp

## DAVID

David was a challenging case. The thirty-seven year old man had gone to his doctor because of abdominal pain and swelling. Much to his dismay, the diagnosis was metastatic gastric cancer. He spent five weeks in the hospital. Carolyn, his wife, was in disbelief. She vowed to take care of him.

# SHARP AND TERBAY

How would Carolyn tell their children? The kids were eighteen months, four, six and nine years old. Would they understand? Would they remember their father when he was dead?

David came home late on a Monday afternoon. Carolyn and I spent time talking about his care. I demonstrated each of his various treatments and we discussed the fact that death appeared near. In fact, David had come home to die. She and I spent time with the three older children and individually tried to prepare them for his impending death.

When I went in to visit with David, he was visibly weak and tired. We spoke about his fears and his goals. His greatest fear was that his children were too young to remember him. Would they remember his voice? His ideas and thoughts? We decided, if he had the energy, he could make a personal, private tape for each child. He could include feelings, thoughts, and love —most of all, he would leave the gift of his voice.

He was anxious to get started as he also knew his death was nearing. His family obtained a tape recorder and labeled a tape for each child. David spent several hours that last night making each of his children a tape.

I received a call to inform me of his death at six the next morning. I got chills as I walked in his room and saw the tapes at his bedside. I'm sure it took most of his energy, but what a beautiful, loving gift to give a young child — something to treasure forever!

Submitted by Kim Vesey

## FOR ANGIE FROM KELLY

(This is a poem written by Jan Jessen on behalf of one of her patients. The poem is for the patient's daughter, as if written by the patient.)

My dear Angie,

# GIFTS

My heart is saddened that my earthly life is closing
Just as your childhood is now unfolding.
My ailing body is tired and I must let it rest
I want you to remember how very much I love you
I tried to stay, I gave it my best.

I know as you read this
I'm gone from your sight
You can't touch me or hug me
Or hear what I have to say.

Close your eyes, Angie
And you'll feel I'm near
When it snows, I am dancing along with the snowflakes.
And the rain carries my tears to wash away your heartaches.

Through the wind, feel my kisses upon your face.
In the spring, I'm a butterfly, I'm every place.
For I'm not my ailing body
That's gone from this place.

I am my heart and my soul
And God has set me free.
There's an angel on your shoulder, dear daughter, always
And that angel is me.

Love,
Mom

Submitted by Jan Jessen

## PEGGY'S GIFTS

Roger was transferred to the hospice center to die. He had been in one of the local hospitals for two weeks due to a deterioration in his health. His cancer had caused his right lung to collapse and efforts to re-expand it had largely failed. His wife, Peggy, did not feel comfortable taking him home because of the amount of care he would need. She requested that he be transferred to the hospice because she wanted Roger to die in an atmosphere as much like home as possible and she wanted to be with him.

The first thing that Peggy decided to do following his arrival at the hospice center was to arrange a special reunion. She talked with the hospice nurse and got "permission" to bring in a "special" friend. Katy, Roger's buddy, was a two year old black Labrador puppy.

Katy arrived that afternoon and padded up to the bed, to sniff and scout out all the new smells. She immediately recognized the familiar scent of her master and friend and began wagging her tail briskly as she licked his hand in greeting. Roger responded by patting the side of his bed. Katy respectfully lay her head on the bed and rejoiced in the feel of Roger's hand rubbing her head. Katy was allowed to stay for about an hour, until Roger tired and fell asleep. As she left the room, she turned slowly, looked mournfully one last time at her master and then followed Peggy to the car. Katy knew.

When Peggy returned, she found Roger very restless. He seemed to be struggling to get comfortable. Once again, she walked to the nurse's desk and made a special request which also was granted. Upon returning to Roger's bedside, Peggy removed her shoes, climbed on the bed, and slid her body over next to Roger's.

# GIFTS

For the remainder of the night, Peggy lay beside her husband, cradling his head, holding his hand, rubbing his back and talking to him. She spoke of their first meeting many years before, their wedding, and their life together. She talked to him about her feelings, fear and sadness. She told him that she would miss him very much and finally, that he "could go." As she held him and talked, his struggle eased. He became more relaxed and peaceful. As morning dawned, Roger's breathing slowed and finally ceased.

Submitted by Anne Wallace Sharp

## CHESTER AND VALERIE

Chester and Valerie loved each other for fifty six years and eight months. Their love was filled with such compassion and devotion that they remained together through ten years of a cancer diagnosis.

When I first met them, I felt that they weren't very realistic about Valerie's diagnosis and prognosis. Chester would tell jokes or change the subject any time Valerie and I got into a "deep" conversation. Valerie, on the other hand, just refused to give in to her disease. The doctors had told Valerie to stop walking because her pelvis was so diseased by cancer that it was detaching from her spine

When I reviewed these instructions with her, she politely, but firmly said, "Let me get this straight. I can stop walking now and spend the rest of my life in bed—or I can walk until my pelvis detaches and then spend the rest of my life in bed." Needless to say, Valerie didn't go to bed then, or for the next three years.

Throughout the three years I cared for Valerie, she and Chester continued to focus on others, but also caring about friends, family and neighbors. Gradually her condition began to deteriorate, but it was hard for anyone to believe that Valerie was dying. She had fought so hard and so long. She had pulled through each previous crisis that it was hard to imagine that she would not pull through this one. Finally, though she said, "I'm tired." It was her way of telling Chester, myself, and all of her friends that the time was drawing near to say "good-bye."

This lady, who at times, denied the seriousness of her illness and fought it head on, was now prepared to "let go." The biggest problem, then, was to convince Chester it was time for Valerie to go. It was heartbreaking to tell an eighty-five year old man that his sweetheart of fifty-six years was dying.

It took four weeks more for Valerie's body to fail ... long enough for Chester to move from denial and hope for a cure, to peace and prayer for her comfortable death. I've found the acceptance almost always comes with little input from me.

When a patient or family member is in "denial," often it's because that is the only way they can deal with death at the time. Chester moved from denial to giving Valerie the most loving gift someone can give—permission to let go, to die.

When Valerie took her last breath, Chester consoled us, "She's in a better place, now —free from pain. She's home."

Submitted by Kim Vesey

# GIFTS

## HAPPILY MARRIED

Through my volunteering and work at a hospice, I meet
many people. Whenever I question whether there is such a thing
as a happily married couple, I remember the two extraordinary
people I met at the hospice center. I'm not talking about a couple who do nothing but smile at each other or put up a front of
happily-married bliss. What I'm talking about is a couple so in
tune with each other, so aware of each other's needs, that words
sometimes are not necessary to convey what they mean.

Leo and Edna were such a couple. Leo was a very intelligent, open minded gentleman of sixty-two. His wife, Edna, was
a pleasant intuitive woman of the same age. This was the second
marriage for both of them.

One of the chaplains had told me that Leo wanted to have
Communion every day. Leo seemed delighted that I was going to
be bringing him the Eucharist. As I left the room and turned to
tell him that I would see him the next day, both Leo and Edna
thanked me and told me they were looking forward to my next
visit. I knew instinctively that I would enjoy coming to see them.

One day when I came to visit, Leo asked me what I
thought of the sweatshirt Edna was wearing. I remarked how
beautiful her red sweatshirt with snow flakes on it was. She then
opened the closet and showed me three more sweatshirts—one
was bright blue, another a deep forest green and the last a pale
pink. Touching the pink one Edna said, "This is my favorite.
This is really my color, but Leo insists that I wear something
bright and cheerful." She gave him a wink and told him again
that the softer colors were more her style, but he insisted that she
was truly beautiful in the brighter shades. She looked at me and
shrugged her shoulders as if to say "How can you fight such a
statement?" A few days later I came in and she was wearing the
pink sweatshirt and I have to admit she did look very pretty in it.
I nudged Leo and asked how she got away with having the pink

one on.

He smiled and said, "I let her get away with a few things just to keep her around."

No matter when I came, I always felt welcomed. The weather was cold and dismal during those weeks, but the warmth between the two people in that room made me forget the weather. Sometimes it was catching sight of a look, or a pat on the hand, or seeing Edna getting Leo a glass of water without him indicating he was thirsty. Sometimes it would be a story told, a whimsical wink, or a tear running down a cheek. I felt drawn to the room because I needed and wanted to believe that two people could truly love each other on all levels and seeing Leo and Edna was confirmation that such feeling could occur.

One day while I was there, Leo was on the phone talking to his former wife. At the end of the conversation he told her that he loved her very much. After he hung up, Edna leaned down, kissed him and told him she understood his love for his first wife, but that she knew how deeply he loved her as well. There was no jealousy, anger, bitterness, just unconditional love and honest truth. How fortunate I felt to witness that. I told them how I looked forward to being there with them.

At one point Leo asked me about volunteering for the hospice. He said he would like to give back to people what he had received. That night I wrote him a letter and said he didn't need to look into volunteering because he was already giving a great deal to others. Anyone who walked into that room, always walked away feeling a little better.

Leo gave those around him three basic gifts: faith from his deep belief in God, hope that no matter what life gives one has the strength to meet it, and love.

Leo had been ready to retire when his cancer struck. He and Edna were building their retirement home. Life, instead of ending, should have just been moving into a period of reward for them. Leo's only response was, "How could I possibly be angry when I have been so blessed?"

# GIFTS

I remember Leo and Edna fondly. I miss their warmth, but to paraphrase Leo, "How can I be sad, when I've been so richly blessed in meeting them?"

Submitted by Sue Handle Terbay

## ANN

Ann Brubaker is a dynamic and attractive woman who volunteers her time to sit with and care for the terminally ill at a hospice.

"I think I just naturally gravitated to volunteer work here at a hospice," she responded, when I asked her why she chose a hospice setting. "I took care of my mother-in-law when she was dying, and I just ended up here. It seemed the right thing to do. And I love doing it," she continued.

Ann currently runs a visiting service for senior citizens, providing support, transportation and assistance to the elderly in the community. Her time with the hospice now is spent helping with meals once a week, but her involvement for many years was much deeper. I asked her to share some of her special memories.

"I remember one patient in particular. She had a lasting impact on me and I'm not sure I'll ever forget her. Marian was a fairly young woman who had ALS—a progressively debilitating neurological disease. When I first met Marian, I understood enough about the disease to know that eventually Marian wouldn't be able to speak or talk at all. I wanted to quickly get to know this woman and learn about what her future needs might be. Our relationship blossomed quickly. We would share our lunches together and I would tell her all the funny things that had happened to me during the previous few days or weeks. I can remember trying to put together all the funny stories and jokes I could think of, especially as they related to me. Marian and I would sit there eating our lunch, laughing ourselves silly and watching the people in the hall give us rather peculiar looks. I think they thought it was strange that there could be so much laughter in a place where people often came to die," Ann recalled.

'It sounds like maybe you have a gift for humor and that this is a gift you share freely with your patients. What a wonderful blessing for them,' I said.

"I do enjoy laughing and I think the people I visited cherished the opportunity to think about something other than their disease. I believe it helped for them to be able to laugh at me, with me and about me."

Ann paused for a few minutes and continued, "As I got to know Marian better, her physical condition deteriorated. She could still use her left hand, but her speech became very hard to decipher. In fact, I was one of the few people who could really understand her. I could often anticipate what she was trying to say before she even attempted to say it. Maybe one of the funniest stories about Marion and I involving something I did—or didn't do, occurred one beautiful sunny day. We had wheeled Marian's bed outside to the rose gardens. I could tell she wanted something and it dawned on me rather quickly that she wanted her head up so she could breathe better. I started cranking the bed up, but the harder I cranked and worked the controls the less progress I made. That bed wasn't budging. I was getting more frustrated by the minute when I heard Marian hysterically laughing and saw tears running down her face. I stood up and began laughing myself. Finally composing myself, I asked 'What—why are you laughing?' Marian raised her left hand and pointed. And I knew immediately what she was trying to communicate. We were outside so the bed wasn't plugged in. I could have cranked from then until eternity and that bed wouldn't have budged."

# GIFTS

Ann laughed as she told this story, then became more mellow and wistful. "I loved Marian and miss her very much. Her family did not know how to tell her they loved her. They were not a very affectionate family—not into hugs and stuff. So Marian and I really did some big time hugging. I think it helped me as much as it did Marian. I can still remember a few days before she died. She was so weak that she could barely move but her eyes were alert and her mind I think—no I know—was perfectly clear. I needed to say good-bye and I knew it and she knew it. I just looked at her and said, 'I wish I'd known you before.' She was an extraordinary woman!"

I was sitting there looking at Ann and thinking the same thing. What an extraordinary woman this volunteer had been and still was. I said this to Ann. She seemed uncomfortable with the praise.

"Thank you, but I think I got far more from any of the patients than I ever gave to them," she said.

Then she told me about another incident that she recalled with fondness. "A request had been made to the volunteer office for a visitor to go to a patient's home. I usually spent a little time with Rose, the patient and when Rose would fall asleep I would talk at length with her daughter. Her daughter, Ida, didn't drive, so I believe she enjoyed my company—just enjoyed having someone visit and talk with her. Well as you probably can tell, I do love to talk, but I also enjoy listening. I used to stop by there frequently and listen to stories of their days in Kentucky—fishing, hunting, and other funny stories about growing up. Ida shared a lot about their past life. One day I telephoned before stopping by just to touch base on how things were going. Ida was crying and obviously very upset. She told me that her family was there because her mother was doing so badly. I asked Ida if she wanted me to come out, Ida urged me to come. When I arrived the entire family was sitting around the bed. They didn't seem to know what to do or what to talk about. Even without much medical background, looking at Rose I knew that she was dying. I began to talk to Ida about all the funny things Rose had shared with me, and before I knew it, everyone there started to share their own stories. The family started to laugh and cry. As we were talking I looked over at Rose. She had quietly died in the comfort of her home, with loved ones all around trading special stories about her. What a special moment for me."

Submitted by Anne Wallace Sharp

## WALT AND PENNY

Walt and Penny met as teenagers, fell in love and got married a few years before the Second World War. They both came from broken homes and were determined that their love and marriage would endure. Their commitment to each other strengthened over the years; they worked as a team, remained aware of each other's feelings, and always kept in mind the values they shared—honesty, friendship and devotion to family.

Life, at times, was very difficult. World War II intervened and Walt had responded to his country's call. He and Penny were separated while he served as an infantryman in Europe. This was a difficult time for both of them, but they remained true to one another. Once reunited there were job losses, deaths, disappointments, major and minor tragedies and many changes, but their commitment carried them through the hard times.

In their seventies, illness and failing health affected them both. They struggled to cope with their own aging processes, while trying to remain sensitive to the needs of one another. Their bodies weakened, but not their spirits.

Penny became a hospice patient when her cancer failed to respond to treatment. Physical pain was preventing her from enjoying even the simple things in life. Fortunately, with aggressive pain management, Penny's pain was controlled and she was able to spend a few quality months with Walt, her family and friends. Quietly, she began to prepare herself and her loved ones for her inevitable death—a separation which she could not prevent.

As Penny's condition deteriorated and the "active" dying process began, Penny's loved ones rallied to meet her needs. Her daughter, son-in-law and Walt took turns with her care. They slept close by and one of them was always present with Penny.

Penny died peacefully and quietly, surrounded by her loving family. However, an important person, Walt and Penny's son, had not arrived home in time to be with his mother prior to her death. Because Penny's wish was to be cremated without any kind of public viewing, Walt was determined that his son have an opportunity to say good-bye to his mother.

Normally, following a death, the funeral home is contacted and within an hour or two, removes the deceased and begins the preparation for burial or cremation. The telephone call to the funeral home was postponed until the son arrived.

The bedroom was prepared with special care. All the medications, supplies and other hospital equipment were removed and replaced with flowers, pictures, and mementoes that Penny had cherished. Even greater care was taken preparing Penny. Walt and his daughter dressed Penny in a favorite silky mint green gown, with matching hair ribbon. Her white hair was brushed and a light amount of make-up was applied. The family spent several hours sitting around her bed patiently waiting and reminiscing about their life together. They celebrated her life and mourned her death as they waited for the son's arrival. A few hours later he came. He lingered by Penny's side, talking to her, crying, and saying his own good-byes until the funeral home personnel arrived.

I was a privileged witness to the love and commitment of these extraordinary people. They taught me about loyalty, faithfulness, and unconditional acceptance and love. These are gifts that I carry with me on my own journey.
Submitted by Elaine Wheaton

# SHARP AND TERBAY

## WILLIAM EDISON

When I read the patient census that morning I saw the name, William Edison. Years ago in my old neighborhood, there was a small, quiet man with black hair and a black moustache who lived across the street from us. He and his wife were a very nice couple who had no children of their own. As a kid growing up, you get to know which people truly like children, which people tolerate them, and those who find children a necessary evil. Mr. and Mrs. Edison genuinely liked children.

I went down to see if the William Edison on the patient list was the person I remembered. As I walked over to the bed, I recognized the face of my old neighbor. His hair was now grey and the face a little gaunt, but the patient was definitely the man who had lived across the street. A nurse was taking his blood pressure.

I reached down and touched his arm and he looked up at me. I smiled and asked if he remembered Charlie Handle (my father).

His face lit up as he said, "Yes." Of course anyone who lived in the neighborhood, knew my father.

"Well, I'm Susie," I said. I don't think he could believe that I had actually grown up! The nurse asked him what kind of a kid I'd been. He said I was a nice little girl. I stuck my tongue out at the nurse.

I told him I would visit if that was okay with him and he replied that he would certainly like that. As I left I kidded him that we would talk again over a couple of beers and he laughed. The nurse and I left together. She told me that she believed his time would be very short because his disease was rapidly progressing.

Bill was usually asleep when I stopped by. But I stayed anyway to hold his hand and talk quietly to him. He seemed so alone. His wife had died. He had a nephew somewhere, but for the most part Bill had no visitors. I told Bill I would be there for him anytime he wanted me. He gave no response, but I think he heard me. I just wanted him to know he wasn't alone.

Several days later, the nurse called me down to his bedside because Bill was dying. I ran down to be at his side, but death had already taken him. I felt that I had let him down because I wasn't there when he needed me. I stayed for a while, just standing quietly with him and thinking how sad it must be to die alone. As I was leaving the room, his nephew arrived. I felt saddened that his only family member had arrived too late also.

I like to believe that Bill felt my presence during those last few days even though he never responded to me verbally. Maybe he wasn't alone after all.

Submitted by Sue Handle Terbay

## CARRIE

Carrie was an effervescent thirty-eight-year old woman. She talked about when she first learned she had breast cancer and how she believed she could "beat it." Now, after being referred to the hospice, that belief was diminishing.

Several years before, complaining of aches and pains, she went to see her physician. She was devastated to learn that her breast cancer had metastasized to her bones.

Carrie had been divorced for six years. Her son, now age eighteen, had only been twelve at the time. Carrie had worked hard to "give him a decent life." Now she had to work hard to prepare him for her eventual death. Carrie was used to setting goals and "going for it." Her goal one September morning was to take her son Justin to Las Vegas before she died. She wanted it to be a Christmas surprise he would never forget. As she put it, "If he never forgets it, he'll never forget me."

She focused a lot of hope on making this happen, but sadly it was not to be. The week before Thanksgiving, she developed a horrible cough and acute shortness of breath. A chest X-Ray revealed a probable malignant lesion. Her condition rapidly deteriorated. It soon became evident that she would not live to see Christmas or Las Vegas.

One day before Thanksgiving, she was still set on leaving her son a memorable gift. We were considering several options when she started to cry. All of a sudden, I think she realized that this would be her last Thanksgiving with Justin.

Abruptly the tears stopped and her face lit up—she had come upon the perfect gift. She would teach Justin how to carry on the family Thanksgiving traditions. She made a grocery list and I volunteered to go to the store. We shared a hug and I wished her a beautiful celebration on Thanksgiving.

I returned to visit Carrie the Friday after Thanksgiving. She was gravely ill. I ordered oxygen and encouraged her to calm down and slow her breathing. She couldn't because she was so jubilant. As she was struggling to get her breath, she talked and cried about the beautiful day she and Justin had spent together —sharing recipes, laughs, memories. Truly a day for giving thanks.

We admitted Carrie to the hospice that Friday and she died three days later. When I visited Justin three weeks after his mother's death, I asked him what his best memory of his mother was. He tearfully replied, "Thanksgiving."

"Me, too," I added.

Submitted by Kim Vesey

# *GIFTS*

## JIM'S GIFT

I am often amazed at the control people have over the time and circumstances of their death. Some patients wait for an out-of-town relative to arrive; others want to be alone; while some choose unusual places. Jim made a unique and special selection.

His seventeen-year-old son was having an extremely difficult time coping with his father's imminent death. He had confided to his mother that he didn't want his father to die at home because he didn't think he could bear the memory of his father dying there. Jim knew this.

Jim's wife, on the other hand, wanted to keep Jim home as long as possible. She called me one morning, "I think I've waited too long. Jim's dying."

I rushed over to their home. His wife was right. He was dying. He had no blood pressure, a very thready pulse and his breathing was very erratic. I, too, was afraid she'd waited too long. I quickly arranged a transfer to the hospice center, called the ambulance and prayed that he'd live long enough to get to the center.

I'm not sure why I worried. Jim had things under control. As the ambulance crew wheeled him into the hospice, Jim gasped loudly. His wife rushed to his side, embraced him, and kissed him five times — once for herself and one for each of the four children. He died as the last kiss was given.

He had waited so he could give his son a loving, last gift.

Submitted by Anne Wallace Sharp

## CAREGIVERS

Caregivers come in all sizes, shapes and forms. They are remarkable, each in their own ways. Some are quiet, capable and energetic. Others are emotional, anxious and overwhelmed.

Occasionally, they have problems of their own which might hinder or prevent the average person from providing adequate care. But these individuals somehow rise above their own troubles and give themselves, heart and soul, to their loved ones. Most caregivers struggle to come to terms with their loved one's terminal disease. Often they deny signs that death is approaching, while trying to cope with a torrent of feelings, the most common being fear, which is often crippling. Despite the obstacles, these caregivers push on and persevere, giving of themselves and protecting their loved ones in the only ways they know how. The following are a few of their stories.

Joan was confined to a wheelchair. Degenerative arthritis had destroyed her hips and left her crippled. Crippled, but not helpless. She kept house, cooked, paid bills, cared for her husband Earl, and refused to allow her physical disability to stop her. She was seldom without a smile on her face and refused to be bitter about what was happening to her husband and to herself.

As Earl's health deteriorated, she adapted, finding ways to help him in and out of bed. She assisted him with bathing, shaving and other personal hygiene, monitored his medications and fed him. However when he become completely bedridden, she felt angry at herself.

"I wanted so badly to keep him home, but I just can't do it. I can't provide the kind of care I know he needs," she said.

Earl was transferred to the hospice. Joan stayed by his side night and day, continuing to provide for most of his needs. Recognizing her own limitations, she allowed the nurses to move him up and down in bed and to help him walk. Grateful that she could devote her energy to providing for his emotional needs, she willingly gave him love and support. When Earl died several days later, Joan was by his bedside, holding his hand.

Rosie and Jim had been married for fifty years. Their health began to deteriorate as they both aged. Jim was diagnosed with emphysema; Rosie with a progressively debilitating neurological problem. Rosie's hands shook uncontrollably and she was unable to grasp things or move her hands without severe tremors. Her hands may have been shaky, but her faith and courage were unshakable.

They had weathered a lot together. A former alcoholic, Jim had been sober for over twenty years. He was active in Alcoholics Anonymous; Rosie in Al-Anon. She spoke frequently of the support she had received from this group. Jim was vocal about the support he got from her.

"I was pretty nasty when I drank, but she wouldn't let me get by with anything. I never hit her because I knew she would not have tolerated that. I remember getting so angry once that I raised my arm at her. She grabbed a baseball bat and told me to go ahead and try it. I reconsidered. She's pretty incredible," Jim recalled.

She was incredible. Here was a woman who couldn't pour a glass of water without spilling it, yet she was providing excellent care to her husband, who was now confined to bed. She also knew how to find help—friends, neighbors and family all pitched in to prepare meals, dispense medications, etc. But it was Rosie who provided Jim's day-to-day care—physical and emotional.

One day though her incredible energy waned. "I'm exhausted," she told me. "And he's much worse. I think he needs to go to the hospice." I agreed and we arranged an admission to the center. Jim died there two days later.

I attended the funeral home visitation. Rosie was in the lobby greeting everyone. She had on a simple black pants outfit and a black derby hat. She grinned at me, took my hand and whispered in my ear, "My family are absolutely scandalized that I would wear pants and a hat, but I bet Jim's laughing his head off."

I stopped by to see Rosie a month after Jim's death.

"I'm doing okay," she said. "I've started back to my Al-Anon meetings and I'm getting on with my life." I knew that Rosie's zest and vitality would keep her going. I only hope I have that kind of spirit when I'm seventy years old.

# SHARP AND TERBAY

Helen refused to admit that Harry, her husband of forty years, was dying. Efforts on my part to bring up the subject of death were met with anger and dire warnings.

"That word will not be mentioned in this house!" Helen said.

I found this incredibly frustrating to say the least, but I respected her feelings. I knew how terrified she was of losing her spouse and decided to tread very carefully and slowly.

There were times I wanted to choke Helen or scream at her, but I bit my tongue and wisely refrained from violent acts. I'd look at Harry, see the pain reflected on his face, hear him tell me how tired he was, watch him struggle to breathe and feel frustrated as well as angry that Helen wouldn't let me do anything. Suggestions about increasing Harry's pain medication were ignored.

"The morphine makes him sleep too much," Helen told me and then looked at Harry. "And you don't really have that much pain, do you, honey?"

He'd sit there and agree with her. I did what I could, which often wasn't very much. I mentioned having one of our bereavement counselors come out and talk to them.

Helen glared at me and said, "I told you—that D-word is a dirty one. We will not talk about death or dying. He's going to get better."

I believe Helen knew the truth. No. I know she did. She just couldn't talk about her husband's death. I was very patient with Helen and Harry. I still don't know how I did it, but I managed to keep my feelings and beliefs separate from theirs. I allowed them to cope in their own way. I feel thankful I was able to do that, because when it came time to really confront Helen with the truth, she had come to trust me. She knew she could deny it no longer.

"I can't stand to see him suffering so much. Please do something," she finally said.

# GIFTS

Helen agreed that Harry should be admitted to a hospice center for pain control and more importantly, said she would talk to a counselor about him. Harry was at the hospice for three days. His pain was controlled and his breathing eased. Helen was able to tell him that if he needed to, he could "go." He died in her arms.

Audrey Gibson was a delightful seventy-year-old lady, born and bred in the South, still speaking with a pronounced Southern drawl. She and her husband, Paul, had been married over fifty years when he was diagnosed with colon cancer. Prior to his diagnosis, Paul, who was twenty years older than Audrey, had been amazingly healthy. They had traveled, played golf and been socially active, thoroughly enjoying their "twilight" years.

Paul was now confined to his home, but Audrey continued her outside interests. She and a group of female friends had lunch together at least once a month. Audrey also maintained her membership in several service and social clubs. In addition, she provided excellent care to her husband. She lovingly tolerated Paul's "grumpiness" and "nastiness."

"He gets so nasty, sometimes. Ornery, I guess, is a better word. Refusing to eat and things like that. Or I'll put him to bed and three minutes later he wants to get back up. And you wouldn't believe some of the looks he gives me or the things he says. Why they're almost hateful," she said.

"That must be hard to take," I consoled.

"Oh, no. I just let it go in one ear and out the other. That's just his way of coping, I think."

Indeed, she was right. As long as Paul could be ornery and feisty, he seemed to find life worth living. It became his "reason for being."

As his disease progressed, he withdrew into himself, becoming very quiet and no longer complaining. Audrey found this more difficult to deal with as she knew his behavior change meant that Paul had given up. Despite her frustration and grief,

Audrey's optimism and upbeat attitude continued.

After Paul's death, I talked with Audrey. She expressed her sadness, spoke of the loneliness, but added, "I'm keeping busy. I miss Paul and his orneriness, but I'm doing okay. I think the girls and I are going to travel this summer—maybe to Vegas."

George Benton was a retired aircraft engineer. He had built the house where he and his wife, Irene lived. He liked fixing things and enjoyed tinkering with the family car. He amused himself by putting together model airplanes and spent his leisure time repairing broken appliances. It extremely frustrated him that he could not "fix" his wife's cancer.

He was a devoted caregiver; always encouraging his wife to eat, walk, think positively and pursue all the treatment options available. She had undergone surgeries, chemotherapy, and radiation which kept the cancer in remission or at least "stalled", for several months. When no further treatment was possible, her physician referred Irene to a hospice.

George was appreciative of the help from the hospice, but skeptical about its philosophy. He was very honest and open with me on the day I first met them.

"I'm not ready to give up yet. Irene *is* going to get better. We have too many plans for her not to live," he said.

I made some inane comment like, "It's always good to hope" or "I wouldn't give up, either." This seemed acceptable to George, but he watched me closely—afraid, I think, that I would say something less than optimistic to his wife.

It was obvious to me that Irene didn't have much longer to live. She was extremely gaunt, pale, and looked exhausted. She had difficulty communicating verbally because of swelling in the brain, but her eyes spoke loudly. Here was a woman who knew she was dying—who was ready to die but she couldn't get that fact across to her husband. Maybe she didn't want to. I wasn't sure.

I made some suggestions about pain medication, diet and other comfort measures. I asked Irene if there was anything she needed to say and she shook her head. Further visits followed this same scenario—except her condition was rapidly deteriorating. I tried to broach the subject, but George remained adamant. "*No.* She's getting better—stronger every day," he said.

However, one fall morning he called me, in a panic. "I think she needs to go to the hospital. Her breathing is real funny," he said. I told George I would come out immediately and see what needed to be done.

As soon as I walked in the bedroom and saw Irene, I knew that she was "actively dying." Her breathing was very labored and irregular, she had a rattle in her chest, her legs were cyanotic and she was moaning and restless

"Should we take her to the emergency room?", George asked me.

I suggested that we sit down and talk. George led me to the family room where his daughter joined us.

"George," I said as gently as I could. "Irene is dying."

"No..." he began, but his daughter interrupted.

"Dad, let's hear what she has to say."

I continued. "If we take Irene to the emergency room, they may take X-rays, start IV's, do lab work, and if she stops breathing, they may put her on a respirator. Is that what she wants?"

"No, but..."

"Dad," his daughter pleaded and then motioned for me to continue.

I explained about the signs I had observed and told them both that my best guess was that Irene had only a few hours to a few days left to live.

"Do you think Irene would want to go to the hospital or be here at home with you?" I asked.

He was very thoughtful for a few minutes. "I want her here with me," he said as the tears started. His daughter comforted him and reassured him that he had made the right decision. "Does she know?", he asked.

"I think she's known for some time."

"She's been protecting me, hasn't she?"

I nodded. He excused himself and headed back towards the bedroom. Returning several minutes later, he was smiling through his tears.

"I told her it was okay—that she was going to stay right here in the house I built for her. You should have seen the smile I got," he said.

After arranging for oxygen and stronger pain medication, I left. Irene died eight hours later. George couldn't make the cancer go away, but, in a sense, he did "fix it."

Submitted by Anne Wallace Sharp


## MY BABY, MY BABY

Eleanor was one of the sweetest people I ever took care of. She was a humble woman who had raised her children with Christian principles. She quietly lived her faith and inspired those around her to do the same.

Her husband, a rough and ready truck driver, was deeply affected by Eleanor's disease and illness. He became her main caregiver and wanted to do everything for her. As he gently bathed and turned her, that big burly man with massive hands became a gentle giant.

# GIFTS

As Eleanor's death became imminent, her family contacted me. I walked into her room to see her lying unresponsive with the pallor of death on her face. Around the bed, the family and her minister had gathered to pray. All the children were present except the youngest son, who lived in Dallas, Texas. He had been contacted and was trying to fly home, but had been delayed by bad weather. Eleanor knew he was coming.

Following the ministers prayer that the youngest son arrive in time, I actually witnessed a change in Eleanor's coloring. Her skin became less gray and turned more pink. She lay in suspended animation—barely breathing, with no palpable blood pressure. I stayed through the night, monitoring her condition and thinking that any moment she could die. The family kept her constantly informed as to where her youngest son was and how much time would elapse before he arrived.

Late the next morning, he rushed into the bedroom to see his mother. He called her name and she awoke. Eleanor reached out her arms, said, "My baby, my baby!" and hugged him. She lived another twenty-four hours, alert enough to talk and take a few sips of fluid. Then she quietly and peacefully slipped away.

I attended Eleanor's funeral and was invited to share a meal with the family afterwards. One of the dishes served was corn pudding. I liked it so well I obtained Eleanor's recipe from the family. It has become a standard at my house and a real favorite of my children and friends.

Submitted by Clarissa Crooks

# SHARP AND TERBAY

## FISHING

There were two middle-aged men, one in a wheelchair, the other sitting on the ground close by, fishing. The sun reflected off their backs as the two men sat quietly watching their bobbers dip in the pond. As the water moved, their lines swayed. It was a quiet, late summer afternoon. They continued sitting there, a light summer breeze billowing their jackets. They had no time frame; no deadlines, agendas and seemingly cares. There were no lunch whistles set to blow; no mother calling them in to clean up for supper; no wife asking them to stop and fix a leaking faucet. Just two men, relaxing under an oak tree, doing what they loved the best.

Why is this scene so unusual? No reason really, except these men were not long time buddies, were not members of the same bowling team and didn't share any family experiences. They shared only one common interest—fishing. As the sun crossed the sky into early evening, the man on the ground slowly got up, and reeled in his empty line. The man in the wheelchair, with a little help, also reeled in his empty line. Somehow it really didn't make much difference that they hadn't even had a nibble. They were fishermen and loved the outdoors—the sun, the splashing of the water against the shoreline, the quiet and just sitting there, letting thoughts wander.

As the one man slowly trudged up the hill, pushing the wheelchair in front of him, a peaceful smile came over his face. The man in the chair chatted softly about the "one that got away." Finally they made their way back to the hospice center. Down the hallway, staff members queried the two about their afternoon and what they'd caught. Of course, by the time they reached their destination, the fish that got away was the size of a large tuna.

The man in the wheelchair was helped into his bed by his fishing partner and new friend. There were a few moments of light conversation and then they said good-bye.

This scenario would be repeated a few more times until the man in the chair could no longer get out of the bed to sit by the water and fish.

The man in the wheelchair is now dead. He died after fulfilling his last wish—to fish again  The man who was his partner continues to be there for others to fulfill new wishes and hopes. He's a hospice volunteer who offers the gift of himself so that others can achieve a possible dream.

Submitted by Sue Handle Terbay

## SUNSHINE

I called her "Sunshine." Her given name was Sarah, yet it was her radiant smile that lit up the room and led to the nickname. Sarah was the mother of one of our staff members. I don't really recall how our relationship developed, I only remember meeting a very sweet lady with a wonderful smile.

Sarah was a tiny person when we met, and as her cancer began consuming her body, she became even more frail. However, her spirit did not match her body, for the weaker her body became, the stronger her spirit grew.

Sarah for the most part remained in home care during the length of her illness. It was only towards the end of her life that she came to the center. I felt honored to bring her Communion daily. If ever there was a woman at peace with her Creator, it was Sarah. As I looked into her eyes proclaiming the words "The Body of Christ," her eyes penetrated my very being. I felt joy when I looked into those hazel eyes.

# SHARP AND TERBAY

It was obvious to everyone who visited her that she was a loving mother—not just to her birth children, but to everyone who came to call her "mom."

During the final days of her life, there would be times when she would be "unresponsive." And yet she always stirred when I came and said, "Hi, Sunshine." However one day I said it and she didn't move, I knew her time was close. So I leaned down to her and kissed her good-bye with a huge lump in my throat. I told her to say 'hi' to God for me.

When Sarah died, her daughter called me to her room. As I walked in, a strange feeling pierced me. I had never been in a room just after a person had died—I had never seen a dead person so soon after death. I looked at the bed and Sarah's body was lying there, her mouth slightly opened, her eyes closed. I wanted to run, but something drew me to her bedside. I watched as her daughter began to prepare her body. She lovingly straightened her hair, and washed her face. Her daughter and I talked and even made a few jokes. I started to relax. I looked up at the sky and asked Sarah if she was listening to all of this "joking" at such a sacred time? I'm not sure, but I think she was giggling with us.

In my mind I still see the radiance of Sarah as well as her silent body on the bed—such a contrast. I loved the woman who occupied that body. Often at a beautiful sunset, I remember my "Sunshine" and the love and joy she radiated.

Submitted by Sue Handle Terbay

## THE HARRISONS

Jessica Harrison was an elegant, dignified and proud woman, ravaged by a cancer that failed to strip her of those qualities that made her such a special person. She was the glue that held her family together. She was the consummate hostess who, even at the most devastating part of her disease, went out of her way to make others feel welcome. She was gentle, genteel, wise, patient, humble and an inspiration to all who knew her. She had a faith that would not be shaken by the disease that threatened her very being; and she had an indefatigable spirit that could not be broken.

She and her husband Carlton were an amazing couple whose love and devotion to one another was tested but never broken. Their interaction and behavior with one another made me laugh, cry, and at times, frustrated me to the point of wanting to scream. But their relationship worked and had worked well for them for years. Ultimately, it was that relationship that enabled them to cope with Jessica's illness and subsequent death.

When I first met Jessica at her home, she was physically debilitated. Chemotherapy and radiation had ravaged her body and depleted her energy. She was gaunt, pale and visibly uncomfortable. Despite her weakness, she rose from her bed to greet me, offering me a cup of coffee and a sandwich. I politely declined and encouraged her to lay back down. She insisted that she was fine, and sat on the edge of the bed, barely able to maintain her balance. While we talked, Carlton hovered nearby, never taking his eyes off his wife. If she started to sway, he was right there placing his hand behind her back to support her. If she reached for something, he was there to get it.

He had a list of questions about medications, vitamins, hospice services, symptoms, etc. I patiently answered as best I could. He was particularly concerned that Jessica wasn't eating.

She looked at him and grimaced, "I'm not hungry, Carl."

He replied, "But you've got to eat, Jessie, if you're going to get better."

She rolled her eyes back and repeated, "I can't eat, Carl. Food makes me sick. It doesn't taste good."

I tried to explain to both of them about the side effects of chemotherapy and radiation—that often the appetite is adversely affected and the taste of food changes. Carl was attentive, but discounted the theory.

"She just won't eat. The food tastes fine. I eat it," he said.

I explained again about the taste buds being affected, but I was speaking to a non-attentive audience. Carl was determined to make her eat. Carl walked me to the door when my visit was over. I was honest with him.

"Jessica is very sick," I said.

"She'll be fine if she just eats. She's not trying. She needs to get up and walk more or she'll never get better—never get her energy back."

"She may be too weak to do that. The cancer and treatment have really sapped her strength. Her body just can't bounce back like it used to."

"She's not trying," he said, ending the discussion.

Two days later, Jessica developed an embolism (clot) in one of the arteries going to her leg which required aggressive treatment, including surgery to save the leg. She was hospitalized in a local hospital, where she hovered near death for several days. Due to her already debilitated condition, survival was not expected. I talked to Carl in the hospital and gently approached the subject of Jessica's possible death.

He began crying and softly said, "I'm not ready to accept that. I refuse to give up hope."

Incredibly, Jessica did survive. She was transferred to the hospice center to recuperate. When she arrived at the center, she was unable to get out of bed, felt confused, and was unable to perform even the simplest self care. Carl was at her bedside night and day, feeding her, talking to her, encouraging her and praying.

He talked with the doctor and persuaded the doctor to allow him to give his wife a number of vitamins and "shark cartilage." An extensive reader, Carl had discovered from several

# GIFTS

articles about the effectiveness of using shark cartilage to arrest the spread of cancer. The doctor and nurses were skeptical, but Carl insisted.

Slowly, Jessica began to recover. Her confusion resolved, her appetite improved and she began to regain her strength. After two months in the center, she was discharged to go home. Carl insisted her recovery was due to the shark cartilage and he was optimistic that the cancer was now in remission.

I resumed home visits. Jessica looked remarkably fit for having gone through the recent surgery and recuperative period. She was weak, but able to walk with help. Carl was gloating because he had believed that she would get better when everyone else had given up hope. He never said "I told you so." He didn't have to because the evidence was plainly visible.

My visits during the next few months were, in many ways, repeats of the first one. Jessica always welcomed me to their home, offering me a beverage and lunch. She placed great importance on her appearance, dressing in slacks and a matching blouse, and taking great care with both her hair and make-up. She refused to see me in her bedroom, insisting on talking in the living room or den.

For weeks, our conversations centered around her lack of appetite and persistent weakness. Carl requested physical therapy, but Jessica refused, telling him that she'd try to do better.

"If you'd just walk more and do some exercise, you'd get your strength back," Carl repeatedly told her. "And you've got to eat."

"Harrison! Leave me alone. I'm tired and I'm not hungry."

Carl kept pushing. He asked for nutritional supplements. When Jessica complained about hating the taste, Carl would drink them, telling her how wonderful they were. He put them in her coffee and on her cereal, confiding in me that she didn't know he was doing this. She knew.

One afternoon, I brought up the subject of her disease and the deterioration in her condition that was becoming very apparent to me. Jessica started to speak, but was abruptly interrupted by Carl.

"It's not getting worse. She just won't try," he said. Once again, I explained that cancer adversely affects both the appetite and energy level. Carl didn't want any part of this. Any attempt to discuss the disease realistically was met by resistance.

"I will not give up hope," he said. "I will not let her give up. She's got a bad attitude. If she won't fight, I will."

But Jessica's condition had worsened. She was getting progressively more short of breath, and was coughing constantly. I knew, as did Jessica, that the cancer in her lungs was growing. Carl, however, insisted she had a cold. We tried antibiotics, sinus capsules, home remedies—all to no avail. And, in what I consider one of the most loving and bizarre gestures I have ever witnessed, Carl came down with the same symptoms.

"See, Jessie, I told you it was a cold. I've got it too," he said.

Carl's symptoms resolved themselves. Jessica's did not. Reluctantly, she agreed to oxygen as her breathing worsened. She was now so weak that she could not get out of bed. I could see the struggle and the fear on her face. I was worried about her and felt an overwhelming need to talk about her feelings. I wanted to talk to do this when Jessica and I were alone. This wasn't possible, because Carl hovered around us. I'm convinced he was making sure that I didn't take a "negative" attitude and bring up subjects that were "taboo"—like death and dying.

Carl's daughter intervened, convincing him to allow Jessica some privacy—to let her talk to me openly. Jessica took immediate advantage of this opportunity. "I'm getting much worse, aren't I?"

"Yes, you are. And I need to know how you're feeling and what you want me to do. Should I confront Carl—make him listen to me?"

"No. He can't handle it. He's coping the only way he knows how."

"But aren't you getting tired?"

"Yes — but I'll keep going as long as I can. And when I can't go any longer, I'll tell you."

Carl called me five days later and asked me to come out to see Jessica. She was lying in bed very peacefully with a smile on her face. "Anne," she said, "it's time. I want to go back to the hospice center."

Upon arriving at the center, she looked at me and said very quietly, "Okay. Let's get this show on the road." Two days later, she died very peacefully with Carl at her bedside.

At the funeral, her daughter took me aside. "Thank you for everything. But most of all for not pushing. Dad needed to think he was controlling everything. But Mom was in charge. They've been that way for as long as I can remember. He pushed. She resisted. But she always got her way. I'm not sure he ever realized that. It was a game with them—it's how they coped. But once Mom got to the center, she really took charge. She even told Dad when she was going to die and she was right. And by then, I think he was ready—as ready as he was going to be."

Jessica and Carl were an amazing couple. They taught me about acceptance, about allowing people to cope in ways that work for them. They taught me lessons in patience, love and devotion, about teamwork and relationship. They were unique individuals, but as a couple they were extraordinary. They truly complimented each other—in a relationship that worked very well for them. They were inseparable, until death.

Submitted by Anne Wallace Sharp

# SHARP AND TERBAY

## MARGIE

The In-Patient Unit staff had told me that Margie wanted daily communion. As I made my way to her room that first day, I wondered what to expect. I tapped on the door and heard a quiet little voice telling me to come in. Lying there in the hospital bed was a frail, silver haired woman in her late sixty's. The first thing I noticed about her was her beautiful and flawless complexion. The second was her steel blue eyes.

My visits with Margie were short in the beginning because of her pain. I was distressed by the expression on her face as she grimaced with every movement and I kept my visits brief and to the point.

One day on entering her room, I found the bed empty. For a moment my heart stopped, but then I saw her. Margie was sitting on the couch by the window in a royal blue robe. The color of her robe accentuated her silver hair and deep blue eyes. I almost didn't recognize her ... she looked so beautiful.

With a huge smile on her face, Margie told me she was going home the next day. She asked me for communion and then said, "If you have a minute ..."

For the next thirty minutes I sat and listened to her concerns, worries, loves and hopes.

She told me that for the last three years she had been a widow. Shortly after the death of her husband, she had moved to be near her son. Within weeks of moving, she had been diagnosed with cancer. Margie told me that she feared she would be a burden to her son and daughter-in-law. She wanted to return to her own home, but weakness prevented her from living alone. She was to go home to her son's house and this worried her. I reminded her that it was her son who was insisting she live with them, but this did little to ease Margie's anxiety.

As Margie talked that day, she seemed to find it a relief to "unburden" herself. At the same time, she kept apologizing for keeping me from my work. I tried again to reassure her, but this did little to relieve her worry.

Margie and I made a special connection that day. It wouldn't be until a few weeks later that I would begin to understand why.

The next day Margie was discharged and went to live with her son. Two weeks later, she was back at the hospice center. She was once again in horrible pain. The nurses and chaplain quietly told me it was doubtful that Margie would be able to go back home.

I went downstairs to the center to see her the next day. The same frail woman with the beautiful complexion and blue eyes awaited me. But this time, she reached out her hand to me and a small tear rolled down her cheek.

Her pain once again under control, she insisted on getting up everyday and sitting in the chair. "I hate this bed, Sue!" she proclaimed to me one day. "And I don't want to be here. I want to go home!"

She was very depressed. As we were talking one day she told me, "I keep asking God why this is happening to me ... He won't answer me." The tears flowed. "I keep praying everyday ... and still no response. Why won't God answer me?"

She asked me this same question each day when I saw her ... almost pleading with me to find an answer for her. Finally, I said, "Maybe God is answering you, but you're not listening."

She looked at me quizzically. So I told her a little about my own experience with prayer. "Sometimes I look for answers in one area ... while God is actually revealing Himself somewhere else."

I asked her if she believed that God loved her. "Most definitely," she replied.

"I think so, too. But since God is a spirit, he can't show us directly. So what I think God does is send us His love in the beauty of flowers ... in music .. but most of all in the loving presence of friends and family. I think that's how God is showing his love for you, Margie ... through the love I see from your son and all your friends and also I think from the staff here who loves you, too." I paused, winked at her, and said, "So maybe there's one of your answers."

The days that followed were hard for Margie. She told me how much she looked forward to my visits and my bringing her the Eucharist. She would start getting anxious if I was late. So I assured her that I would not forget her, but that I just couldn't always be right on time.

As her cancer progressed, the tumor began to cause pressure on her nervous system. She began dropping things. Being a proud and meticulous woman, this caused her great anguish and concern. One day when I walked into her room, she was crying.

"What's the matter?" I asked.

"I spilled my coffee all over the floor this morning ... and last night, I dropped some of my dinner," she said through her tears.

I knew these mishaps were devastating to Margie. I sat beside her, held her hand and told her how sorry I was that such things were happening. I told her that I wished it could somehow be different.

Each day after that whenever I walked in Margie asked me the same question. "Why are these things happening to me?" And each day, my eyes would fill with tears and I would respond, "I don't know."

Finally, Margie stopped asking why. I'm not sure if she had reached a peace about what was happening, or if she just didn't want to see the tears in my eyes and hear the frustration in my voice. Now bed bound, Margie reached out her hands very shakily and I held them as we talked

By this time the two of us had developed a special bond. When our visits were done, I'd kiss her on the forehead saying, "I love you, Margie." She would respond in kind.

# GIFTS

It was a Thursday, I remember. I walked in for our daily visit to find Margie's son and her sister at the bedside. They looked at me and shook their heads.

"Mom is dying, Sue. She's not responding anymore," her son said, sadly.

Quietly, I went over to the bed, bent down and said, "Margie, I'm here. And I've got Communion here for you if you want it, but you don't have to take it."

I was surprised when Margie opened her eyes, and in a very weak voice, said, "Please, Sue, I need it."

I broke off a tiny piece of the communion host and placed it on her tongue, with a little sip of water to help her swallow it. I kissed her forehead, and said, "I love you, Margie." She slowly reached her hands out to me and I placed mine in hers. She held them gently. Then with one hand, I began to gently brush her forehead. "You're doing just fine, Margie," I whispered and kept repeating the same words over and over. I was reminded of the time when I was in labor with my first child. I was a very frightened young woman and I remember the nurse saying those same words to me. As I sat there holding Margie's hand, I knew that she believed firmly in her heart that she was giving birth to a new life and I knew that she was also frightened. I kept repeating my answer to her unspoken question ... "Yes, Margie, you're doing just fine."

As I slowly pulled my hands away, her last words to me were, "I love you, Sue." My tears flowed as I walked away.

Margie was finally within reach of God's open arms ... and she had turned her face away from Him just long enough to say those final words to me. Those are the most profound and meaningful words I've ever heard. They still bring tears to my eyes.

Margie, like me, questioned God. We both asked why this was happening; we both realized sometimes there are no answers. That was hard for Margie and for me to accept.

# SHARP AND TERBAY

Margie was forced to succumb to a disease that showed no respect for her. But the cancer couldn't destroy her spirit nor the gift of love she offered. It was the ability to love and to be loved that in the end won out.

Margie came into and left my life in a very short period of time, but her words, "I love you, Sue" will live with me for an eternity.

Submitted by Susan Handle Terbay

## SPECIAL GIFTS

One of the most frequently asked questions of hospice public relations and marketing staff is: "How can a hospice afford to stay in existence?" Good question. Our hospice is a non-profit organization and it is our philosophy not to turn anyone away for any reason, financial or otherwise. Insurance companies re-imburse us for a lot of our services, but we also rely heavily on fund raising activities, United Way contributions, corporate support, and individual donations.

The large contributions received from area corporations are certainly welcome and enable the hospice to continue to provide high quality care and service to the community. But these large endowments are only part of the story. It is often the small donations, the gifts from the heart, that leave the greatest impact.

For example, one morning, an elderly gentleman arrived at the reception desk. In his hand was a check that he wished to contribute in memory of his dead wife. He explained that his wife of fifty years had died recently and he praised the care she had received while in the hospice. Somewhat embarrassed, he confessed that he didn't have very much money, but stressed how strongly he felt about giving "something." He had taken his wife's clothing to one of the consignment stores in the area and sold them all for a few dollars. He proudly handed over his check.

"My wife would have wanted me to do this," he said, and with tears in his eyes he departed.

Many donors prefer to remain anonymous. For almost a year, a young man in his early twenties would stop by the office once a month and leave a contribution anywhere from ten to twenty-five dollars. We never knew his name or the reason for his donation.

Special people—that's how we stay in existence!

Submitted by Sue Handle Terbay

# 5

# Glimpses of Humor

*The authors and other hospice workers contribute stories which reveal the surprising role laughter plays in our darkest hours.*

## THE KEYS

I went to Jennifer's, a patient of mine, funeral and spent a few minutes with the family before I walked up to the casket. I lingered there several moments, before I walked away and I realized that I could not find my car keys. I had had them in my hand earlier, and with a sinking sensation in the pit of my stomach, I immediately knew I had dropped them in the casket. I was in a panic. How could I explain this to the family? I didn't think it would be proper etiquette to "root" around in somebody's coffin? Embarrassed, I didn't know quite what to do. Out of the corner of my eye, I spotted the hospice chaplain and rather sheepishly told him what had happened. I have to give him credit because he didn't laugh, but merely smiled.

He said, "I'll take care of it." A few minutes later he returned with my keys. I asked him how he had accomplished this feat? He responded, "I merely told the family I was saying a special prayer which involved the 'laying on of hands.' Now I keep my keys in my pockets—where they belong!
Submitted by Anne Kuntz

## THE GOSSIP

They were an extremely improbable pair. She was a small, frail, elderly woman with thinning white hair, dressed in a blue flowered, floor length robe. He was a tall, slender, long blond haired man of thirty, clad in faded jeans and a black leather jacket.

They were sitting side by side on a worn sofa in the lounge area of the nursing home where she was living. She was talking very animatedly and he was listening attentively, occasionally asking a question, nodding his head, or making a brief comment.

She was a hospice patient with terminal cancer. He was a volunteer, making his weekly visit to "Granny." They had been meeting together for several weeks. She looked forward to his visits almost as much as he enjoyed making them.

She moved a little closer to him, whispering conspiratorially in his ear. "See that woman over there in the red dress by the television?" He nodded. "She's the biggest gossip here and it's driving her absolutely nuts."

"What's driving her nuts?"

"Not knowing who you are." She laughed and continued, "I can just imagine what she must think!"

"You haven't told her who I am?"

"Oh, no! That wouldn't be any fun. It's much better to keep her guessing."

"You wicked woman!" he nudged her affectionately and joined in the laughter.

Their visit over, she walked him to the front door, gave him a kiss and hugged him good-bye. She watched him cross the parking lot, climb on his motorcycle and speed away. She turned to re-enter the nursing home and nearly ran into the woman about whom she had just been talking.

"Who was that, Irma? Is he a relative?" the woman asked.

# GIFTS

*Wouldn't you like to know*, Irma thought. Instead, she said, "Just a friend, Clara. Just a friend." Walking to her room, she could barely contain her laughter.

She told me later, "It was much better to let her guess."

Submitted by Anne Wallace Sharp

## RESPONSES

"My husband's not responding!" a panicky voice cried at the other end of the telephone.

"I'll page your nurse right away, Mrs. Jones," I assured her and hung up the phone. As receptionist, I often receive distress calls about a patient dying, a family not coping or someone not breathing right. My responsibility then is to "double beep" the nurse to let her know it's an emergency and that she should call me immediately. As soon as I hung up with Mrs. Jones, I double beeped the nurse. Kathy was very prompt and phoned in within minutes. I relayed the urgent message and Kathy told me she would go see the patient immediately.

The woman's panic had been contagious and I had found myself, wondering anxiously about the Joneses many times during the day.

Several hours later, I saw Kathy in the office and asked her how the patient was doing? Kathy's response startled me. She began giggling and said, "You told me that Mrs. Jones's husband wasn't responding ..."

"Right," I interrupted and then thought, *Oh-oh. Did I make a mistake? Maybe he was already dead. Maybe I misinterpreted what she said.*

"Well, he sure wasn't responding. I'm not sure I blame him. That woman talks a blue streak. She never stops. Drives me crazy sometimes. And it must drive him nuts. Anyway, I guess poor old Mr. Jones just tuned her out today. He wouldn't talk to her. In fact, he wasn't even listening or paying the smallest bit of attention to her. That must have made her madder than a wet hen. So, she started asking him questions, wanting to know what was wrong. No response."

I began to get the picture.

"No response?" I asked with a laugh. "He wasn't unconscious at all, was he?"

"Nowhere near unconscious," Kathy laughed. "Although at times I bet he wishes he were comatose. But Mrs. Jones was right. He wasn't responding—not one little bit. So she thought maybe I could make him talk or make him respond to her questions."

The word "unresponsive" has taken on a totally new meaning for me. It brings to mind a talkative woman and a husband tuning her out. It no longer has connotations of the death process at all, but a survival process.

Submitted by Sue Handle Terbay

## IN A HURRY

I was a few minutes late arriving at the cemetery. The mourners had already gathered around the graveside. The funeral home representatives were standing quietly by the hearse waiting for the completion of the prayer service. As I was getting out of my car, I noticed a man running down the hill toward the hearse. He was waving his hands in the air and yelling something that I couldn't make out. The funeral directors must have understood, however, because they all started running up the hill toward the grave.

My first thought was that somebody must have fainted. As I neared the congregation of mourners, I could hear a babble of voices, coming from the casket area, but I couldn't see the casket.

Two of the funeral directors were deep in conversation beside the grave and were trying desperately to "retrieve" the casket. One of the mourners told me what had happened.

"The preacher was just finishing his prayer when all of a sudden the casket just dropped into that grave with a thud," he explained.

Fortunately the family adapted well to this mishap. A son laughingly commented, "Dad always was in *such* a hurry to get to new places!"

Submitted by Oda Holliday


## SPEEDING

Hattie was a feisty lady of seventy-two, who refused to let her disease and terminal diagnosis deter her from going to church. One Sunday she was returning home, when she was pulled over by a policeman.

This is the story she told me:

"I heard the siren, saw the flashing lights and immediately wondered what I had done wrong. I pulled over and a young policeman walked over to my car. He asked me if I knew how fast I'd been going.

"I responded that I had no idea. I told him, 'I've just been to church and it was such a wonderful celebration. I'm so filled with the spirit that I had no idea I was speeding.'

"That policeman just smiled and said, 'Well, ma'am, you were going nearly seventy-five. If you could just pull over for a few minutes until that spirit passes, I won't give you a ticket. Have a nice day.'"

Submitted by Sonia Kreider

## TRAPPED

"Help me," the male voice pleaded on the telephone.

"What's wrong?" the nurse asked.

"I'm trapped here in my trailer in this harness and I can't get out," he said, barely able to get the words out.

"Is anybody there with you?"

"No. I don't know where my wife is."

"Okay, sir. Try to calm down a little bit. What's your name?"

"Bill Smith," he stammered.

The nurse leafed through the pages of patient information sheets and found the appropriate one. She quickly noted that Mr. Smith did live in a trailer and could very well have fallen and pulled something down on top of him. Concern and compassion filled her voice as she asked, "Are you hurt, Mr. Smith?"

"No. I just can't get out."

"Okay. Just stay calm and I'll get somebody out there to you, right away."

"Please hurry," he said and hung up.

# GIFTS

The nurse gathered up her purse and nurse's bag and was headed out the door when something inside her made her pause. She picked up the phone and dialed Mr. Smith's number, wanting to verify for herself that no one else was home. She thought his wife might be outside or in another room and just couldn't hear him."

A woman's voice answered.

"Mrs. Smith?"

"Yes."

"This is Martha at the hospice. Is your husband all right? He just called and said he was trapped there in your trailer. Have you checked on him lately?"

"Why, honey, he's out there."

"I beg your pardon, he's out where?"

"Why, he's been at your hospital for a couple of days."

The nurse could feel the flush of embarrassment creeping up her throat and face. She apologized for the phone call and silently gave thanks that she had called before going out to the trailer. She hung up the phone and decided to investigate.

Downstairs in the hospice center, she found Mr. Smith harnessed in with a safety belt to a special chair. He was yelling into the phone. He had propelled himself around the bed, found the telephone and dialed his home number — the first three digits of which were coincidentally the nurse's extension. She spoke briefly with the patient, hung up his phone, notified the nurse of his restlessness and confusion, and returned to her office, chuckling about her close call. "What if I'd gone out there? His wife would have thought I was *nuts*!"

Submitted by Anne Wallace Sharp

# SHARP AND TERBAY

## ONE OF THOSE DAYS

My first job when I came to the hospice at which I still work, was as a receptionist. I was responsible for answering the phone, taking messages and paging the nurses and other staff on their beepers as needed. Once paged, the staff member would call in and I would relay whatever message might have been left.

Not long after I started this job, one of the home care nurses stopped by my desk on her way out the front door. She sighed heavily and looked tired. "What's the matter?" I asked.

"Oh, it's been one of those days!" Sue exclaimed. "I can't get anything done. This darned beeper keeps going off." She paused momentarily, "I'm just here to get supplies—then I'm off again." And she was gone, with diapers and bedpads under both arms.

A few minutes later, I looked up to see a somewhat frazzled looking Sue standing in front of my desk. In a tired, impatient and whining voice, she asked, "What?"

I was confused and it must have shown on my face for Sue continued, "You beeped me. What did you want?"

"I didn't beep you," I protested. She shrugged her shoulders and headed towards the parking lot. Within two minutes, she was back. Now she was mad.

"I was just here. And already you're beeping me. What is the message?"

Again, I looked at her dumfounded and proclaimed my innocence. She stood there for a minute or so staring me down with a bewildered blank look on her face. Finally, muttering to herself, she left.

Two minutes later, she was back again. The anger was gone. In its place was laughter. She was laughing so hard, she was almost crying. As she flopped down in a chair near my desk, she tossed her head back and laughed even harder.

"You'll never believe this!"

Between giggles and laughs, she was finally able to blurt the story out. "I feel so stupid," she said. "I kept hearing that darned beeper going off and it was making me so angry. Then I realized what was going on. It wasn't my beeper making that noise. It was my seat belt buzzing to remind me to buckle up? Can you believe that? Do I feel stupid or what?"

As we laughed together, Sue seemed to relax. Someone once said that laughter is the best medicine. That day for Sue, it certainly proved to be an effective stress reliever.

Submitted by Sue Handle Terbay

## ELMER

My experiences as a volunteer at the hospice have proven to be the most rewarding activities of my life. As a golfer I have had three holes-in-one. As a sales manager, I once successfully negotiated a contract worth ten million dollars. But none of these experiences compares to the smiles of appreciation and pleasure I have received from patients during my visits with them.

Even though we are engaged in a serious business, I always try, whenever possible, to bring some humor into my conversations with patients, and I have found that many of the patients themselves have a wonderful sense of humor.

Here are some of my experiences:

One of my "assignments" has been to transport patients to hospitals for various treatments. Once such transport involved a patient named "Daisy." When I arrived at her home and introduced myself, she said, very clearly and with just a hint of a smile on her face, "So you are 'Driving Miss Daisy' today."

# SHARP AND TERBAY

On many occasions I have been the "goat" of the story. Once, I was visiting a patient who decided to go upstairs for a nap. I remained in the living room watching television and soon dropped off to sleep myself. It wasn't too long before I was awakened by a hand on my shoulder. "Ah-ha!," the patient said, "I caught you sleeping on the job this time." Getting caught wasn't too bad (I had done it before), but I'll never know how he knew I was sleeping. The patient was blind!

Another time that I was the "victim" occurred just after I started doing the food shopping for the Inpatient Unit. Before working for the hospice I had never done any grocery shopping so I found myself being "educated." One day, I made a trip to a local grocer and began loading the groceries into paper bags for the trip back to the hospice. I had a large order this particular day: eight one gallon glass jugs of apple juice. I was using my wife Eleanor's car. Since the tank was nearly empty I had promised to fill the car with gasoline before grocery shopping, because it was a task my wife disliked. After loading everything into the trunk, I returned to the hospice.

When I opened the trunk, I discovered one of the jugs had broken. What a mess! There were two lessons learned that day: surround all glass containers with soft materials such as bread or paper towels and no longer volunteer to fill my wife's gas tank. Eleanor, my wife, learned to pump her own gas.

One of the warmest feelings from my work at the hospice came after a particularly long visit with a male patient. As I was leaving, his wife stopped me by the door. "That's the first time I've seen Bill smile in three months. Thank you." That's what working at a hospice is all about.

Submitted by Elmer Sensel

# GIFTS

## THE GOOSE

In early spring two years ago, we, at the hospice, surrounded by death and sadness, became witnesses to the miracle of birth. While the trees and gardens were springing forth new buds, a young mother goose began her nesting vigil. For approximately six weeks, we watched as she sat on her nest, periodically getting up to stretch her wings, turn her eggs, squawk a little and, attack anyone who came too close.

Of course, most of us humans knew that momma goose was doing it all wrong. We certainly would not have selected her nesting spot. After all, having babies should be in a private out-of-the-way corner—certainly not in front of a walkway and in broad view of the entire staff, patients and families.

Furthermore, where were the father and other family members? Shouldn't she have a coach urging her on? And what about family and friends stopping in, fixing some food or straightening the garden area? What about the sterile conditions, breathing techniques, pain relievers, an obstetrician, anesthesiologist, nurses and pediatricians? Was this any way to give birth?

Fortunately, momma goose knew what she was doing and a week after Easter gave birth to four goslings. For the next two weeks, we watched as her babies grew stronger and more independent. Employees, patients, families and guests stood at the windows watching the growth of the little goslings. At first, they could hardly stand up, but soon we were fascinated as we watched them follow momma goose around the courtyard. Periodically, the goslings would strike out on their own adventures, only to fall in line at momma's beck and call. Sometimes, it was more fascinating just to watch the watchers.

It was truly the greatest show on earth that spring because of the joy on people's faces, the laughter, the oohing and aahing and the looks of fascination. Some brought cameras and videos. Strangers even stopped to ask each other how the babies were doing. No one walked by the windows without stopping to check on the little goslings.

Momma and her babies are gone now. They have been transported to a farm in the country where there is a pond. There, in the country, the geese can have the freedom to grow strong—away from the traffic that would, otherwise, threaten their existence. Their departure was greeted with as much sadness as the joy experienced at the goslings birth.

For those few weeks, a simple creature of nature brought happiness to a place where, the miracle of life is cherished on a day-to-day basis.

Submitted by Susan Handle Terbay

## RACHEL

It was a dark and stormy night when Rachel and Gertrude waddled from the banks of the pond up towards the brightly lit hospice. Voices were calling them, something deep from within themselves over which they had no control. Like a magnet, the hospice drew them.

The two geese crept from flower garden to flower garden, being careful not to draw attention from patients and families in the building. They were wearing outfits taken from two cement geese they had found on nearby neighborhood porches. Rachel was dressed as a cowgirl and Gertrude had on a yellow raincoat and rubber boots. They were hoping to "just blend in."

Where was the perfect spot? It was not easy looking for a nesting spot at night, but they had no choice. If they were on the grounds during the day, surely Mike, the building manager whose keen eyes missed nothing, would spot them and they would face certain deportation.

The trek to the building was important, especially for Rachel. She had flown in from South Carolina where she had spent most of her five years. She was hatched here, but relatives took her to the Carolinas when she was knee-high to a duck. Since she was growing old she had few eggs left. She had returned home to lay what the last one.

The building offered nice little protective corners for the geese. And the flower beds gave up little nuggets of worms for tasty snacks. The geese could also forage in the lawns which surrounded the center.

After many nights of preparation, the nest was ready for Rachel. With an almost inaudible "swoosh" the little egg was deposited in the nest. Rachel fluffed her feathers, settled herself over the egg and began her vigil of many days and nights to protect and hatch this special egg. She slept off and on through the night as a spring rain pelted her snowy white feathers. She slept and she dreamed of what her small duckling would grow to be

Submitted anonymously

## BUGGED

It was my third home visit to see Jack Austin and his wife, Irene. Jack was quickly losing his battle with lung cancer. Extremely short of breath, in pain, and becoming weaker by the day, Jack was struggling to reach an acceptance of his inevitable death. He was still in the late stages of "denial," fluctuating between despair to hope. He was angry at the disease, the doctors who had told him there was nothing else that could be done, and at his increasing weakness and lack of energy.

# SHARP AND TERBAY

The three of us were sitting outside on their covered patio. Jack, with his ever-present oxygen, was talking about his frustration with the persistent pain. He seemed more open about discussing the course of his disease. We were beginning to get very intense and close to some really significant issues and feelings.

I was listening intently, offering re-assurance when I could and encouraging him to vent and express his feelings. As I opened my mouth to ask a particularly poignant question, a large gnat flew in and set up residence in my throat. I started to choke and gasp. I couldn't swallow the gnat because it felt like the bug had actually attached itself to the lining of my throat. I couldn't cough the invader up either, for the same reason. I was choking helplessly—trying to cough, trying to dislodge the gnat. My face turned red and I thought, *Oh, this is just great. I'm going to choke right here in front of these people and all because of a stupid bug. And we were making such progress!*

Meanwhile, Irene had rushed inside and returned with a glass of water. Jack had managed, with great difficulty, to get up from his chair and was hovering over me with the oxygen tubing dangling around his neck. I'm sure he thought he was going to have to perform the Heimlich maneuver or cardio pulmonary resuscitation. Fortunately the water forced the gnat to slide smoothly down my throat and into my stomach.

Once I recovered my composure I attempted to "pick up" where we had left off. Unfortunately the mood had passed, as did the gnat.

Submitted by Dee Baughman

# GIFTS

## ETHEL

Ethel Carson, terminally ill, was a determined woman. She was also extremely fastidious about her cleanliness. Despite her weakened condition, she insisted on taking a bath every day. I suggested one day to Ethel that perhaps a daily bath wasn't necessary.

"Oh, no, Debbie. You never know when the Lord is going to call you," she said.

Ethel wasn't about to get to the pearly gates and be turned away by St. Peter because she wasn't clean.

Submitted by Debbie McMillan

## BEEPERS

People who don't carry beepers don't know the fun or the problems they're missing. For instance, you're driving down a country road and the beeper goes off. Trying to find a phone booth is almost an impossible task and a great annoyance. Many of our home care nurses could tell you exactly where every pay phone in their "territory" is located. This problem has been somewhat resolved with the advent of car phones, but the beeper continues to bring with it other problems.

One of the nurses, upon receiving a new beeper, was trying to figure out how to make it stop beeping. She pressed the appropriate button, but the beeping noise persisted. She became so intent on working with her beeper that she inadvertently took her foot off the brake pedal and hit the car in front of her.

# SHARP AND TERBAY

Another nurse stopped for lunch at a local shopping center and, on her way out to the car, decided to look at a dress she saw in the window of an exclusive dress shop. It was one of those stores where all the merchandise is electronically tagged so it can't be removed from the premises. Her beeper went off and, within seconds, she was surrounded by several burly security guards. She had to talk very fast, and convincingly, to persuade them not to arrest her for shoplifting.

Submitted by Anne Sharp and Sue Terbay

## HOME ALONE

The "old timers" at the hospice where I work still talk about my first patient visit when I joined the organization ten years ago.

It was a warm summer day and I had spent the previous day getting used to the paper work and the routine of the office. I had met the various nurses, social workers, home health aides and office personnel. I had filled out the mandatory insurance forms, had an interview with the executive director and had filled my trunk with various items which I had been told would be essential for home care nursing. With my mandatory catheters, enema bags, bedpans and diapers, I felt prepared for any emergency (any "normal" emergency, that is).

I set out with the nurse who was orienting me to the job. Margery had been with the hospice for four years and was moving to another state. I would be taking over her case load so she was taking me around to meet her patients. Margery was also filling me in on what to expect. When we arrived at a modest little home I had expectations of a "normal" visit. Margery told me that the lady I was about to meet was a "character." She had colon cancer

226

and was doing fairly well. The patient lived with her daughter but managed to retain a lot of independence.

"She can be pretty crusty. I think her daughter went back to work to give herself a little break," Margery commented as we got out of the car.

I knocked on the door expecting the patient to greet us with a smile and invite us in. A few minutes passed with no answer. We became somewhat alarmed and rang the bell again. From within the house came a muffled voice, "I've fallen and I don't think I can get up. I think I may have broken my hip." We tried the front door but it was locked. We called out to the patient, asking if she could crawl somehow to the door and unlock it. She said she couldn't and suggested we go around back and come in that way.

Sounded easy enough. But we both noticed rather quickly that there was a five foot fence all around the house. To further complicate the situation there was a large padlock on the fence gate.

Margery and I looked at each other and she said very quietly and very seriously, "Welcome to home care." And then, she added, "You'll have to climb the fence."

I looked at her and realized this was probably the best thing. First of all, I was twenty years younger, but more importantly I was probably one hundred pounds lighter. So over the fence I went—not very gracefully perhaps, but I did manage to scale the fence without injury to myself or to my pride. Once over, I made my way to the back door. Sure enough, there was a screen door which was locked tight as a drum. So out came my trusty nurse's scissors. In the best tradition of all home care nurses—and professional burglars—I cut a small hole in the screen, reached in and unlatched the door and prepared to make my entry. It was at this point that the patient's ten pound guard dog decided her house was being invaded. She began barking and attacked me with a vicious snarl. Thank goodness her idea of attacking was to leap into my arms and lick me to death.

Finally I was able to get to the patient. She had fallen but by some miracle had not broken anything. Somewhat bruised and shaken, she was very embarrassed but appreciative. The broken screen door was replaced before my next visit. Thank goodness not all home care visits involve breaking and entering. But I suppose if I ever get tired of nursing, I can always fall back on my initiation into the world of suburban crime. Who knows—I might have a great future as a cat burglar.

Submitted by Anne Wallace Sharp

## CONDOLENCES

I try to attend most of the funerals and viewings for my patients. This enables me to put some closure on our relationship, and also allows me to process my own grief. At the same time, I am able to provide support to the family and let them know that their loved one was important and will be missed.

I debated about going to Mrs. Barker's funeral, however. I had talked to Mrs. Barker several times while she was in the hospice, but had not met her husband or family. Ultimately, I decided to attend the funeral out of respect for the patient and so I could offer the family my condolences.

I checked the newspaper obituary column, noted the time and place for the service and headed out. The listing indicated a brief prayer service at the First Baptist Church. I hadn't been there before, but knew it was located on Main Street.

As I drove down Main Street, I saw the church, the funeral home hearse and a parking lot full of cars. I parked, entered the church and walked slowly towards the front to view the casket and see the family. The casket was closed, so I offered a silent prayer and turned to the family. I introduced myself to an older man who I assumed was Mr. Barker. I expressed my sympathy about his loss and invited him to contact me if he needed anything. He seemed appreciative of my words and thanked me for coming.

I found a seat towards the back of the church and waited for the minister to begin the service. A short, bald-headed man approached the pulpit. He offered a prayer and then read several passages from the Bible. "Any death is difficult, but when one is so young..." began his eulogy. I didn't hear what he said next as my mind was busy thinking about his first words. I was confused.

*Funny—Mrs. Barker was in her seventies—not exactly young. Well, I suppose it could be perceived by some as young.* I focused again on the minister.

"...killed tragically in an automobile accident, the victim of another..."

I looked around as he continued.

"Sheila Jones, a young woman, a daughter, a friend..." The truth hit me. I was at the wrong funeral. My face must have turned a million shades of red and I wanted to sink beneath the pews and vanish. But I stuck it out, listening to the rest of the eulogy, and the closing prayer. When the mourners were invited to pass once more before the casket, I quietly slipped out the door, hoping I was unnoticed.

By the time I reached the right church, farther down Main Street, the funeral was over and the procession had left for the cemetery. I sent Mr. Barker a nice note and called him several days later to offer my sympathy and condolences for his loss.

When it came time to attend my next funeral, I checked the church address three times. I wanted to make sure I went to the right place.

I comforted myself that I'm not the only one who gets confused. I once attended a funeral where the minister called the patient by the wrong name throughout the entire service. Not one person ever corrected him.

Submitted by Oda Holliday

## JELLO

Iva was a woman with pancreatic cancer. As her condition deteriorated, she lost her appetite. This was a big concern for her family and, in an effort to help, I suggested that Iva try different foods. One of the suggestions I made was jello.

"Oh, no. I never eat jello." Iva said adamantly with a grimace.

"Why is that?" I asked.

"I've never eaten jello. When I was a kid, my father always used to say that he just would not eat anything that was more nervous than he was. And I won't either."

Submitted by Debbie McMillan

## DEPARTING "GIFTS"

The snow was blowing outside, but the small humble house was filled with warmth and love for a father and a husband who was making his final earthly journey. He lay on the couch in the small living room, always surrounded by at least one family member. Words of love and comfort were spoken continuously. As this was happening, one of the children kept going into the bathroom with bottles of Drano. Finally, his wife bent over him, saying, "You know, George, you're leaving me with a stopped up drain..."

Submitted by Roberta Erwin

## NEW KID AT SCHOOL

One day while at lunch, one of the nurses came in with a story he wanted to share with me about his little girl.

His daughter, who was six and in the first grade, had come home from school the previous day and excitedly announced that there was a new boy at school who had "aids". Somewhat taken back, Carl was surprised at his daughter's openness about this new student. He inquired how she knew this. She told her father that the teacher had told the class.

Carl was quite impressed with this open policy at the school, thinking that finally public acknowledgment and education might break down the barriers of ignorance surrounding this disease. He asked his daughter, "So what did you learn about this boy?"

"He had 'aids' in both ears," she announced. A little stunned by her response, he asked how she had come to this conclusion.

"He showed us." Carl chuckled quietly to himself as he realized the "aids" his daughter had mentioned were of the hearing variety. His vision of an open school policy was a bit premature.

Submitted by Sue Handle Terbay

## SOAP OPERA

It was late in the afternoon and I was glad to be getting around to my last new patient assessment of the day. I drove to the west side of town, found the street I was looking for and slowly picked out the house that I was to visit. It was a neat little white house with a front porch that was enclosed, I knocked on the outside door and a friendly voice called, "Come on in."

I opened the outside door and struggled in with my medical bag and then entered a second door into the living room of the home.

An elderly lady was sitting in a chair to my left. I stood by the door waiting for her to invite me to sit down. She had a wonderful smile, but really did not give me much attention as she could hardly take her eyes off the television, which had a popular soap opera on.

Now, I am used to many different people and their "ways." I tried to ignore the fact that she didn't seem the least bit interested whether I sat down or not. In fact, she was doing a good job of totally ignoring me. So I resolved to draw her attention back to me by showing interest in her soap opera.

"Victor certainly is in another mess again, isn't he?"

"Yep," she replied without looking at me.

"His daughter is really going to be mad, isn't she?"

"Yep."

My strategy simply wasn't working. While she continued to keep an eye on that soap opera, I looked around the neat little house for "the patient." After working at the hospice for a few months, I knew what to look for—a significantly thin person, someone who has no hair (and doesn't appear to be one who would have his/her head shaved just to be fashionable), or just someone with that certain look in their eyes that says *I've been through a lot.* No one was in sight, no one called out from any other rooms and I was starting to get more uncomfortable by the minute. During the painful and prolonged silence, the lady seemed to be getting a little more interested in me and maybe just a bit uncomfortable too. She gave me a strange sideways glance that said, "What you sellin'?" And I returned that glance with one that said, *Lady, won't you help me just a little here?*

I looked at my watch and knew it was time to get down to business. So I asked, "Is your husband in bed?"

With this question I got full eye contact and her full attention. The soap opera suddenly ceased to be important. Her eyebrows went up and she turned in her chair. "I don't have a husband!"

My bag became very heavy, the room suddenly felt one hundred degrees Fahrenheit and I could feel the redness starting to creep up my body from my feet.

"Are you Mrs. Morgan?"

"No, I don't know any Mrs. Morgan. I thought you were my daughter when I told you to come in."

Things just weren't making any sense. I quickly looked at my referral sheet. I was in the right city and on the right street.

"Is this 321?"

"No, this is 231."

I explained that I was a hospice nurse looking for a patient and apologized for intruding. I was somewhat relieved, although greatly embarrassed. The lady smiled again and turned back to the soap opera. As I was leaving I said quietly, "Hope everything works out okay on that soap opera."

"Yep," she replied.

Submitted by Kathy Yowler

# 6

# Glimpses of Wisdom

*The authors distill the most important of the coping advice
from the accounts of the hospice workers.*

## SAYING GOODBYE

Tom taught me a valuable lesson about the importance of saying good-bye. I had been visiting Tom for several months and had developed an admiration and respect for him and his family. I learned a lot from them, especially since Tom was only my second hospice patient.

My most important lesson, one that has affected the care I've given hundreds of patients since then, came on the night before his death. Our visits had always ended with a ritualistic kiss on the forehead. On this particular day, I felt I was coming down with a cold, so I skipped "our" kiss.

I guess I knew he was dying, but I didn't want to risk giving him my cold. When I got the call the next morning from the on duty nurse telling me he had died, I was stunned. Later, as I discussed how awful I felt with the hospice chaplain, I began to sob. As I spoke about Tom, I stumbled over the words, "And I never even got to say good-bye!"

# SHARP AND TERBAY

I don't let that happen anymore. In both my personal and professional life, I always try to say "Good-bye" in such a way that I can live with it for the rest of my life—no matter what happens.

Submitted by Kim Vesey

## YOUNG TEACHERS

Our hospice offers bereavement services for people of all ages, not only patients, but those who must cope with grief. I have been fortunate in that I have been able to work with several different youth groups. During these sessions, the children often become teachers. Eddie was such a teacher.

It was my first group of "kids"—ages ten to twelve—and I had five patients. Three of the children had lost a parent to death, one a grandmother, and another an uncle. At the first meeting, we sat in a small circle and introduced ourselves. We took a "quiz" and answered such questions as our favorite color, favorite song, food likes and dislikes, and other facts that allowed us to get to know each other.

After a few "ice breakers," we reflected on why we had come to this support group and who in our family had died. I led off, sharing that I had lost my mother as a young girl. After my introduction, each child shared their own losses. When it came to Eddie, he sat very quietly and stated that his uncle had come to live with his family and had died of AIDS.

Immediately, the rest of children focused their attention on Eddie. It was obvious to me that Eddie had dealt with similar reactions before. He went on in a very nonchalant manner about his uncle, how much he had loved him, and described the fun they had had. He said that he missed him very much.

# GIFTS

Throughout the remaining sessions, Eddie and the children discussed their loved ones, what they missed the most and how they felt about their family member. Periodically, the children would ask Eddie about living with a person who has AIDS. They did not appear insensitive—merely curious. Eddie answered all their questions very matter-of-factly.

He admitted to being disturbed about what a lot of people thought concerning AIDS. He seemed very honest and forthright in his answers.

"You can't get AIDS by hugging," he stated. "We all used the same dishes and silverware. My uncle didn't have to use special towels only for him: he was my uncle and he was dying from an illness."

Eddie educated all of us during those sessions together. It was obvious that he dearly loved his uncle and missed him deeply. The idea of never hugging his uncle would have been absurd to him.

It was also obvious that he had more insight into human kindness than many of the adults he had encountered. Eddie's uncle died of a terrible disease, the others had suffered losses from different causes. In the end, it mattered little to the children the cause of death because they were all hurting and shared that pain.

Submitted by Sue Handle Terbay

# SHARP AND TERBAY

## A LITTLE CHILD SHALL TEACH US*

Often when a loved one has a terminal illness, we "wiser" adults usher children out of the "sick room," remind them to be quiet and tell them to keep out of the way. Frequently, this "rational" approach does a real disservice to all involved. The child's need to grieve is ignored and, in the process, we often fail to take advantage of what children can teach us about coping with death and the dying process. In our efforts to shield children from the reality of death, we miss out on their gifts, insights and creativity.

As a hospice home care nurse, I have witnessed many miracles and seen many wondrous acts and gestures by patients and caregivers. I have seen people act and react both rationally and irrationally, appropriately and not so appropriately. I have often wondered. Perhaps the most remarkable story belongs to Gary, a three-year-old, whose joy, spontaneity and creativity were allowed expression by his family. His innate wisdom helped relieve an extremely frightening situation and taught me a valuable lesson about the "nursing process."

Gary's great-grandmother was dying of pancreatic cancer. She was being cared for at home by Gary's grandmother, Joan. In addition to caring for her mother, Joan was also caring for Gary during the daytime while his own mother worked.

Gary had been an active participant in his great-grandmother's care almost from the beginning of her illness. He would bring her water and food, sit by her bedside playing, talk to her and entertain her with his stories.

Gary's great-grandmother complained to me about how long it was taking her to die, how miserable she was, about the hardships of her life, and about the dysfunction within her family. But her face would always light up when Gary arrived. He would bound into the bedroom—a ball of energy and enthusiasm. We would talk a few minutes while Gary waited

 *Appeared originally in *Nursing 95* magazine. Reprinted with permission of the Springhouse Corporation.

for the physical assessment.

"I'm ready to help you Nurse Anne. Is it time yet to listen?"

I would get out my stethoscope and take Gran's vital signs, while Gary "assisted" me. He was an eager helper, using my flashlight to look in Gran's ears, mouth and nose.

"Yep, she's okay," he would solemnly pronounce and then run out to play.

As her illness advanced, Gary's great-grandmother became weaker. She was spending more time in bed and approaching the final stages of her disease. She also began to have vivid and sometimes terrifying dreams and hallucinations. During one afternoon visit while I was talking to Joan in the living room, Gran began screaming for her daughter. Joan, Gary and I ran to the bedroom to discover Gran flailing wildly about in the hospital bed, trying to get up, and reaching for something that only she could see. Joan and I tried to calm her down by speaking soothingly and rationally. This didn't work.

"What do you see, Mom?" asked Joan.

"I can't get this boat down the stream," Gran screamed, "And all those babies in the water will drown." She was nearly hysterical, still flailing, reaching wildly and frantically.

Joan tried again to reassure her mother that everything was okay. This only made the older woman scream louder.

Suddenly Gary jumped in the bed with his great-grandmother. He began to paddle imaginary oars.

"It's okay, Gran," he said, "We'll get there." He began "casting" with the dog's leash he had in his hand.

"Oh, Gran, look, I got one," he said as he pulled one of the babies onto the bed and gently placed it in his great-grandmother's arms.

He continued paddling and casting and rescuing babies until his great-grandmother breathed quietly and drifted off to sleep. I stood there in utter amazement, profoundly moved by Gary's wisdom and intuition. Sadly, I was never taught this technique in nursing school and I doubt that it will become part of the curriculum. However, I have filed this approach away in my memory bank. Who knows when it might be needed again.

We as adults can learn much from children if we only observed and allowed them to gift us with their incredible innocence, wisdom and spontaneity. Perhaps, children are the *real* teachers and healers.

Submitted by Anne Wallace Sharp


## ADVICE

An insightful patient once told me, a few days before he died: "When something is troubling you ... ask yourself, will this really matter to me on the day I die?"

I've repeated that question many times and it certainly keeps things in perspective.

Submitted by Kim Vesey


## MOM

Those of us working at a the hospice, especially those of us who have direct patient care, use much of our energy dealing with the emotional issues that face our patients and families. It becomes extremely important for us to have time away from the hospice to rejuvenate ourselves. But what happens to us when

240

our own families have need of hospice care? Can we still work effectively with the terminally ill? And more importantly, how do we take care of ourselves and our own family members?

While I was working at the hospice, my mother-in-law was diagnosed with terminal cancer and became a hospice patient in another state. I was extremely close to my mother-in-law, who had, in fact, become a second mother to me. I was amazed at how much energy I needed just to cope with the grief of losing a loved one even though I was not providing any of the actual physical care. I was unable to be with my mother-in-law until the last week of her life, but I focused an incredible amount of my energy upon her even though I was miles away. This energy was spent worrying about whether she was receiving the proper care and trying to support my husband, father-in-law and the rest of the family, since they considered me, the "all knowing hospice professional." It was an expertise the family seemed to want and need from me.

Because I was no longer involved with direct patient care, I was able to view my "real" job, as a home care co-ordinator, as a "break" from the pressures at home. I am convinced that if I had to deal with my mother-in-law dying while I was caring for and losing patients, I would have had to leave the hospice. I don't believe I could have dealt with the combined stress and fear would I have needed to take a leave of absence, or perhaps even find other work, at least temporarily.

I learned a lot from my experience of being on the receiving end of hospice care. I have come to appreciate even more the grief that families experience when a family member is sick and then dies. While this particular out-of-state hospice provided adequate home care, I was appalled that no one came out when my mother-in-law died. The nurses at the hospice where I worked always respond personally to a patient's death. I expected this same support for myself and my family.

I had the impression that because I was a health care professional, I was somehow expected "to do it all." I didn't think I needed any support because I could deal with everyone else's grief, as well as my own. This was simply not the case. In the case of my loved one dying, I was not a registered nurse, but merely a grieving family member. This experience has caused me to appreciate the hospice and its policies. I also realized that all too frequently nurses take for granted that health care professionals are strong and in control of their emotions, because they know what to expect. However, even health care professionals need support.

Losing a family member has also made me more sensitive to the needs of hospice families. A nurse's support is crucial during the illness, at the time of death, and in the days and weeks afterwards.

Submitted by Kathy Skarzynski

## THE "KNOW IT ALL" NURSE

Big Momma was nearly ninety years old (and weighed about ninety pounds). She had lived in a tiny metropolitan housing apartment for over thirty years, despite the area's reputation for having the highest murder rate in the city. She had lived there alone since her husband's death many years before.

From the time of my first visit, I was impressed with the loving attention her family lavished upon her. There were always several children or grandchildren sitting in her living room waiting for the chance to "wait on her." However, they were in the living room because her bedroom was so tiny there was barely enough room for her bed and a small dresser. The children had to stand in the doorway to talk to her or else she would have to exert herself to talk loud enough for them to hear her a room away.

From my position of "middle-aged-middle-class-know-what's-best-for-everyone-nurse," the solution was easy. I ordered a hospital bed, chose the perfect location for it in the living room and supervised grandsons in moving her old fashioned furniture to set up a new place for Big Momma to survey and supervise her kingdom. Then she became truculent. She didn't want the hospital bed. She was very polite, gentle and soft-spoken about it, but she just didn't want to get into that bed.

Instead of removing the hospital bed, I cajoled and encouraged her. After a week or two, I enlisted the help of her family to convince her. They told her that if she would only give it a try, she would love being in that nice electric bed. Finally, she agreed and promised to move to the hospital bed. I left feeling especially smug about my ability to improve the quality of my patients' lives in ways they hadn't dreamed of.

First thing the following morning, I was called to Big Momma's home because she had died. I was stunned. I had been sure she still had weeks left to live. I felt as shocked and bewildered as her family. They talked about the last day of her life. She had been alert and kept putting them off about moving to the hospital bed. Finally, late in the evening, she had reluctantly moved.

We sat huddled around her bed reviewing her life as we waited for the funeral home people to arrive. The talk eventually got around to Big Daddy's death so many years before. The oldest daughter said the talk about him brought back vivid memories of his death. She asked the others if they remembered the nurse who started to come to the house when Big Daddy got sick and how this nurse said she thought Big Daddy ought to be in a hospital bed in the living room. Apparently, the nurse arranged the furniture (this same furniture!) exactly the way it was now. Big Daddy also died soon after he moved to that bed.

Submitted by Maggie Bauer

## EXTRA EFFORT

Caring for patients sometimes requires the extra effort of finding some special way to meet their needs or perhaps, to meet an unusual request in an unique manner.

Donna was a mental health student doing a three month internship at a hospice in the Bereavement Department. One of her patients was a woman named Delores. Delores had alienated many of the staff with her critical comments and often unreasonable demands. She had also struggled with both her disease and her relationship with her children. In addition, she had difficulty communicating her needs and feelings.

Donna had tried many different approaches to "reach" Delores, but all had failed. Delores remained isolated, fearful and non-communicative and yet, very needy.

One Wednesday afternoon, Donna walked into Delores's room at the hospice to find Delores propped up in bed, watching her soaps.

"Hi, Delores, how are you today?"

"Miserable."

"Well, let's see ... what can I do to make you feel better?"

Delores turned off the television set and was quiet for a few moments. Finally she said in a very soft, yet challenging voice, "Entertain me."

Another employee might have floundered but Donna was definitely up to the challenge.

"All right," she said, "Wait right there. I'll be right back."

Donna exited the room, closing the door behind her. Within minutes, she was ready. She swung the door open with a swooping motion, and tap danced her way into Delores' room, singing a lively version of "New York, New York."

# GIFTS

Delores' mouth dropped open and she started laughing until tears began rolling down her face. She applauded loudly as Donna tap danced around the room, finishing with a flourish, and plopped down in the chair by the window.

Donna's unique method of "reaching" her patient worked. Delores opened up and began talking about her past, her relationships, her disease and her feelings. A truly novel approach and a most effective one.

Submitted by Anne Wallace Sharp (as related by Donna Smith)

## KIDS

One of my volunteer duties involves helping children deal with the loss of a loved one. Our hospice has support groups for children, ages five to young adult. These groups bring in kids from around the community and provide a setting where individuals can share their experiences and feelings with those.

I work with the eleven and twelve-year-olds the same age I was when my own mother died. Of course in those years there was no such thing as children support groups. Children's grief for the most part were just not considered. Fortunately, times have changed and it is now recognized that children have their own grief issues with which to contend.

At the first meeting of our group there is always a sense of uneasiness from the children, because they don't know what to expect, and also from the counselors, wondering how the children will respond. The first week is spent just getting to know one another. By the third week it is obvious what profound support these kids are offering each other. Often they will remark about seeing their loved ones or feeling their presence. Instead of being made to feel that these must be "weird" experiences, these kids relate to each other and what they are feeling.

Children bring in music tapes and recordings their loved ones liked and share it with the group. They bring in pictures, mementoes, art work, and drawings as well. They share their stories and their emotions, understanding each other's sadness, loss and anger. They discover it is okay to cry. They know they have to go on and that at times it isn't going to be easy. The counselors suggest the use of memory books in which the children write down everything they can remember. I reveal to all the children in my group how sorry I am that I did not join them. After so many years, my memories of my mother are very few.

It never ceases to amaze me how these perfect strangers from all areas of town can meet for a few hours, for a few weeks and bond so quickly and strongly. They leave the group feeling that someone their own age understands them.

I ask each child if they could have one wish, for what would they wish? One young man wished that no kid would ever have to experience the pain of losing their dad. Some wished for cures. Some wanted their loved one to come back. Nearly all asked for "normalcy."

Sometimes they asked questions. Often feeling burdened by adult expectations, their questions reflect guilt. For example, a common question is: "I didn't cry at the funeral—is there something wrong with me?" Just to hear someone say "No." and to hear that everyone grieves differently seems to remove some of the burden from their shoulders. Others ask, "Will I die young?", "Will I get leukemia?", "What will happen if Dad dies too?" These are very real questions and concerns. We may not be able to squelch their fears, but at least we listen and address the issues.

Some of these children deal not only with death issues but social issues. Sometimes the sessions involve talking about the pressures of pre-teenage years. I walk away from some of the sessions totally drained, yet incredibly inspired.

246

# GIFTS

The bereavement program for children addresses the very real need for kids to have someone who cares listen to them. And yet, it is more than that, it is kids reaching out to other kids. It's knowing death is part of life and that death hurts and that they are not alone.

The wonderful result of these brief few weeks together is that the children always state they want to come back and help others. I think of these young people often—hoping they are well, hoping they remember, hoping that when their grief starts to hurt again, they can cope with it in healthy ways.

The past two and a half years have been a learning experience for me. By being there for these youngsters, I have been able to help the little twelve-year-old girl inside of me, who was never allowed to grieve or talk about my feelings concerning my mother's death.

Submitted by Sue Terbay

# 7

# Glimpses of Courage

*The dying process is, finally, about courage. This is revealed in a final set of stories from the authors and other professionals.*

## HEROES

We honor heroes by placing them on pedestals. We quote presidents, senators, and other great statesmen. We honor our inventors, artists, scientists, writers, poets and actors by filling museums with remembrances of these great men and women. Great people are etched in history and will not be forgotten because we have recorded their existence, either in stone or in books as a visible reminder of their lives and contributions to society.

But what about the person who does not achieve fame? The father who works forty hours a week, coaches his childrens' soccer team, volunteers at his church and obeys the law. The mother who alone must raise her children, work outside the home to provide food and be both mother and father, while teaching her children the importance of self-worth. The young person who strives to attain his or her goals. The grandmother or grandfather who leaves a legacy of love and dignity for his/her children and grandchildren. Because these people are not great statesmen or artists, are they any less heroic? When their lives have ended where will their memories be etched? Will they be forgotten?

At the hospice where I work, such ordinary heroes are remembered. Winding its way through the beautiful gardens outside the hospice is a brick walkway of memories—a walkway of heroes.

Families are invited to purchase a brick in memory of their loved ones. The bricks vary in size and price and the engravings are left up to the family. This idea has been wonderfully received.

I often walk the pathways reading the bricks. "Oh, I remember John," I murmur glancing at a particular stone. I will smile as I think of him and his family and the extraordinary story that is theirs alone. I see nurses and other staff doing the same thing.

The impact of this walkway hit me the other morning as I read an article in the Sunday newspaper about a soldier weeping at the Vietnam Memorial Wall in Washington, D. C. His friend's name was engraved in stone for everyone to read and it resurrected the young dead soldier for his friend to remember. The young soldier listed on the wall will never be read about in our history books, yet he is and was a hero. The names of people written on the bricks at the hospice will never have a biography written about them, yet their lives have an enduring story and they are remembered.

Years from now the names on the wall and the names on the bricks may not be recognized by many people, but as we at the hospice touch and read the wall—as we walk and read the names—they are remembered. They lived, died and are remembered. The memory of these humble heroes remains with us forever as tributes to their ordinary—but extraordinary—lives.

Submitted by Susan Handle Terbay

# GIFTS

## CINDY

The first time I met Cindy I was mesmerized by her bright blue eyes and yet it really wasn't the color that caught my attention. It was the depth of pain and sorrow that I saw there that haunted me. Yet side by side with the sorrow was something else —a twinkle, a glimmering of her indefatigable spirit. Those eyes had a story to tell, but I wondered if I would ever know it because Cindy could not speak. Her only communication was through writing. She had advanced throat cancer that had taken her voice and would ultimately take her life.

My heart went out to this woman who was trapped inside her body with so much to say and so little opportunity to say it. Several years ago, Cindy had begun a long series of surgeries, radiation treatments and chemotherapy. Despite treatment, the cancer had continued to spread. A tracheotomy had been performed to help her breathe and a feeding tube had been surgically implanted into her stomach for purposes of nutrition. She was unable to swallow even her own secretions and she had been taught to suction herself, do her own tube feedings and clean the tracheotomy. Several weeks before I met Cindy, she was still able, with her husband's help, to care for herself. However, increasing weakness and pain led to a decision that she needed hospice home care.

Death alone tugs at one's heart but as the story of Cindy's struggle unfolded, the tragedy deepened into terror and disbelief that such evil could exist. She was dying, but she was also being emotionally and physically abused by her husband.

As the truth began to emerge in small bits and pieces, I was appalled and indignant. Cindy was able to reveal very little because of her inability to talk. During home visits, her husband hovered by her bedside and she was unable to communicate anything privately even by writing. For a long time she was unable to confirm or deny the suspicions. However, there were signs present that ultimately could not be ignored. Bruises that could not be explained appeared with increasing frequency. Pain medication was being withheld. Tube feedings were given with such frequency that Cindy was vomiting daily. But perhaps the cruelest thing of all was that her husband had forbidden her to see her son from her previous marriage. On one occasion when the young man had attempted to visit, the police had been called to expel him. Her phone calls were monitored, her letters were opened: little communication was possible. Cindy was isolated but her spirit refused to die.

Cindy began to write notes when her husband wasn't around and then passed these surreptitiously to me and her friend, Audrey. The notes never addressed the abuse directly. She wrote of wanting her son there with her, her pain to be eased, that she was tired of fighting and struggling. In one extraordinary note, she wrote "I can't wait to get to heaven and see Jesus. In heaven I'll be safe and then I can talk again and say all the things I want to say. I'll even be able to sing." Other notes also expressed her strong faith.

"*Ben keeps telling me my faith is weak. If I'd only pray more I'd get better. He tells me I don't really want to get well,*" she wrote.

I talked to her of these things and told her what a remarkable woman she was, what a beautiful spirit she possessed and what an unshakable faith she had. Her eyes teared up and glistened.

On one of the few occasions when I was allowed to see Cindy alone, I asked her if she was safe or if Ben was hurting her. I also asked if she wanted me to do something. She was adamant that she was fine and that Ben was not harming her. She wanted to stay home. I asked her if she would let me know when it was no longer safe or comfortable to be at home. She nodded affirmatively.

# GIFTS

In the meantime Cindy's friend Audrey was denied access to the house for initiating a contact with Cindy's son. Cindy was distraught. Audrey had been her life-line. Cindy became even more isolated when my visits were reduced. Any interaction I had was closely scrutinized.

A conference was held at the hospice and we contacted the appropriate protective service organizations, looking for a way to help. We were told that unless Cindy admitted the abuse and asked for help, their hands, as well as our hands, were tied. I was extremely frustrated and angry that I had to sit back and do nothing. But, we at the hospice made plans, for I was sure at some point that Cindy would ask for help and I wanted to be ready. We decided on an Inpatient Unit admission. Once Cindy was in this safe place, further intervention could be made.

We waited. I continued to visit and questioned Cindy when I could. She and I developed ways to communicate that didn't involve Ben and I knew she would let me know when she was ready. The signal came one Saturday morning. I was on-call when a call came in from Ben that Cindy's pain was escalating and she was having trouble breathing.

I set the wheels in motion. When I arrived at Cindy's home, I found her lying in bed gasping for air. Ben was downstairs and I took advantage of the moment. I asked her one question only—"Do you want to get out of here?" Cindy nodded vigorously. I told Ben that her pain and breathing could not be handled at home and that perhaps a couple of days in the hospital would help. He agreed somewhat reluctantly that I could arrange a hospital admission.

Once in my car, I followed the ambulance to the hospital and helped Cindy get settled in to the hospice unit. While Ben was downstairs taking care of the paperwork, I sat by Cindy's bedside. I told her she was safe now. She nodded and indicated she wanted to write something down. She took the pencil in her shaking hands and wrote seven words. "Call Audrey, and my son. Thank you!" Then she grabbed my hand and held. I watched the pain slip from her eyes and body.

When Ben returned he told Cindy that she could stay one night and that he would be back the next day to take her home and he left. I called Audrey and Cindy's son.

"No one can hurt you here." I promised her. I told her that her son and Audrey were on their way.

Late that night, after seeing Audrey and her son, Cindy died. She had said her good-byes, found the safety she needed and made the decision not to go home to Ben. She died in peace, surrounded by those she loved.

Her courage and determination in the face of unbelievable odds were nothing short of inspiring. Her spirit could not be broken and her faith could not be diminished. She fought until she was ready to let go. Then she chose the time, place and circumstances of her death. She was a remarkable woman whose death provided "a happy ending" to a tragic story. Her last words to me as I left that day, the last of her life were, "I'll be talking again soon and singing."

Submitted by Anne Wallace Sharp

## ANDREA

Andrea was twenty-three-years-old when she developed a persistent cough and shortness of breath. She went to a local clinic and was given antibiotics. However, her condition worsened. She went to the emergency room where she was admitted for intravenous medication and oxygen and told she had pneumonia. The sad faced doctor walked in two days later and told Andrea and her mother the bad news. "You have AIDS," he said without looking her in the eyes.

# GIFTS

Andrea tried hard to come to grips with her diagnosis. *How did I get it? Why did I get it? Could I have passed it on to my children? Did I have the virus while I was pregnant?* After much consideration, she had her children tested. They were not HIV positive.

Andrea's recovery was slow and the doctor felt her prognosis was grim. He made a referral to a nearby hospice. Andrea told the nurse that only her mother and sisters knew the real diagnosis. She felt she and her family would be harassed if people knew the truth. She feared that her children would face hatred. So they told friends and neighbors that Andrea had been diagnosed with terminal cancer because it was a much more "acceptable" disease.

Over the six months that followed, Andrea's health improved and her condition stabilized. It was agreed that she was no longer appropriate for hospice services—at least for the time being.

There was no contact with Andrea for twenty one months. Then she was referred back to the hospice program because of her deteriorated health. Her home care nurse, upon seeing Andrea again, said she was *not* prepared for the deterioration that Andrea had experienced.

I had trouble concealing my reaction and I have seen a lot of sad and shocking situations. This once beautiful young woman was now fifty-six pounds of gray colored flesh, tautly stretched over a five foot seven inch frame. She was confused, weak and constantly coughing," the nurse explained.

Andrea's desire to keep her diagnosis from others failed. One afternoon, her children walked in the house in tears. They had been approached and teased on the playground with "Your Mommy has AIDS! Your Mommy has AIDS!" Even at the young ages of six and eight, they knew that AIDS was something terrible.

The home care nurse, social worker and bereavement counselors worked hard to finalize care arrangements for Andrea's children and to prepare them for their mother's leaving them. They struggled to answer the questions asked by the children, including, "Is our Mommy going to die?"

In the gentlest way possible, they were told "Yes."

Two weeks later, Andrea died.

Walking into the funeral home, the nurse was met by Andrea's eight-year-old, Patrick. He took her hand, saying, "Come on. You have to see Mommy. She died, but God made her pretty again."

He was right. God had made Andrea beautiful again, because she no longer suffered from pain and hatred due to AIDS prejudice.

Submitted by Kim Vesey

## SHERRY

As I sat and listened to Sherry's story, I was amazed at the strength and courage of the woman who sat before me. At fifty-two, she was dying of cancer, but she had struggled with it for the last eighteen years. Diagnosed with breast cancer at the age of thirty-four, she had successfully endured surgery, radiation and chemotherapy, only to have the cancer recur time and time again. This time she was facing metastatic lesions in her eyes, brain, bones and lungs. She knew in her heart, that the illness was a terminal one, but her attitude was one of hope and determination. She had 'licked' it before and she would continue to fight.

# GIFTS

I looked forward to our weekly visits. Sherry would talk of growing up, her marriage at age fourteen to husband, Cliff; her pregnancies; her jobs; her friendships and the death of her son due to AIDS. She had certainly had her share of life's tragedies, but she kept smiling and moving forward, voicing a firm belief in God. She could still laugh and repeatedly told me, "Life is good."

Her husband was still working, so for the most part Sherry was home alone. She was fiercely independent, wanting to care for herself and her husband as long as she was physically able. She'd prepare dinner, and then take an hour nap before sharing the meal with Cliff. Repeated offers to send in volunteers or home health aides to help with these chores were declined. Sherry wanted to do it her way or not at all.

As her disease progressed, Sherry was forced to become dependent on others. She hated this. Her husband began to administer her medications—and he never did this quite properly—at least not to Sherry's satisfaction. We arranged for volunteers and home health aides to visit. Sherry enjoyed their company, but was very reluctant to allow them to help with her personal care.

Her tumors began to encroach on her airway. She became very short of breath, her voice quivered and was hoarse, and her appetite vanished. She could barely swallow and was gagging constantly. She was admitted to the Hospice In-Patient Unit. Various options were discussed and a decision was made to insert a G-Tube (a feeding tube inserted directly into the stomach, bypassing the esophagus). She began a series of radiation treatments on her skull in the hopes of diminishing the rapidly spreading cancer and keeping her airway open. The radiation was partially successful.

Sherry was extremely sick while in the hospice unit. She required continuous medication for nausea and vomiting and her pain had escalated and was growing increasingly difficult to control. Despite these symptoms, Sherry maintained a positive attitude and demanding that she be allowed to get up and do as much for herself as she was able.

She loved to go down to the "break room" and have a cup of coffee and a cigarette. At all hours of the night, the nurses would find her there with a cup of coffee in one hand and a cigarette in the other. While there, she met a young man named Rick. He had AIDS.

She shared her feelings about her own son with Rick. She had been the primary caregiver for a while, until he had chosen to go live with his significant other. From that time on, Sherry had been denied access to her son. She had not been allowed to talk to him, see him or be with him when he died. His death had devastated Sherry. There had been some extremely bitter confrontations with her son's partner, including threatening phone calls and requests for money, etc.

As Sherry spoke of these things to her new friend Rick, she allowed herself to cry and grieve. She also offered Rick her friendship, total acceptance and love. He told her that his own mother had more or less disowned him and that her story of love for her own son touched him deeply. They met daily. Prior to his discharge, he told her that he wished she were his mom. He hugged her and cried with her. They stayed in touch—Sherry called him every few days and continued to do this when she was finally able to return home.

She was only able to be home for a short while. Her disease was spreading rapidly and she weakened dramatically. She spoke to me of her fears and her readiness to die. Her biggest fear was that she would linger on and on, becoming totally dependent on others. Her other fear was of becoming confused. She spoke openly of how much this terrified her.

"I can't stand the thought of not knowing what I'm doing. I pray that my mind doesn't go," she told me.

Sadly, she did become confused. Her family could no longer care for her at home and she was returned to the hospice center for "terminal care." She was admitted on a Saturday and was virtually non-responsive for several days. When I saw her on that Tuesday, she opened her eyes, called me by name, and told me she had somehow lost three days in her life. I reassured her and we talked of her physical deterioration. She said she was ready to go.

Later that day, she became very agitated and restless. She began having dreadful hallucinations and paranoid delusions. She hadn't wanted to live like that. Within twenty four hours, Sherry was dead by her own choice, I believe.

I mourned and grieved Sherry's death. She was an extraordinary woman, a fighter, a fiercely independent woman, a loving mother and a wonderful friend.

Submitted by Anne Wallace Sharp

## ALICE

When I first met Alice, I was taken aback—she was twenty-eight years old and facing more tragedy than many people face in a lifetime. Her youngest son, aged six, was dying of a rare genetic disease, while his brother, age nine, was dying a slow death from Muscular Dystrophy.

I never heard a "poor me" from Alice. She just went about her day-to-day living, providing excellent and loving care to both sons on her own. There was little I could teach her that she didn't already know. She was an expert with the children's tube feedings, suctioning and physical care. She knew the signs and symptoms of infections, respiratory distress and the indications of approaching death.

# SHARP AND TERBAY

My role was to walk with her through her sons' deaths and cheer her on. I applauded and celebrated with her as she learned to drive. I praised her when she announced proudly that she had lost sixty pounds. And I encouraged her as she sought part time work, ultimately finding a job she loved. I mourned with her when her children died.

When I saw Alice a few weeks after the death of her second son, she hugged me and thanked me.

"You helped me find myself and my identity. I wondered if I would have anything left after the boys died. So much of me had gone into their care, but you helped me learn to take care of me. And now, I can go on. Thank you."

Submitted by Roberta Erwin

## SOUP

"I've been a nurse for over thirty years, you'd think I'd know what to do." These words came from a woman in her late fifties, dying of lung cancer. "I don't understand what's happening or what to do next. And I don't know what to expect I don't like that."

We talked about what was happening: her disease was progressing and she was beginning the "dying process." I answered all her questions as best I could. As I finished, she began to tell me about a dream she'd had the night before.

"My family thinks I'm nuts or maybe just confused, but this dream felt real important. I need to understand it. Maybe you can help," she said.

"I'll try," I told her.

# GIFTS

"I'm in the kitchen and I want to make vegetable soup. I go to the cabinet and start pulling out cans of this and cans of that. I'm nearly frantic, trying to find just the right ingredients. And I'm so afraid I won't be able to find them all. Sounds silly, doesn't it? What do you think it means?" she asked.

"It sounds like you're trying to get things together—making sure you have everything you need. Maybe putting your affairs in order, saying good-bye." I suggested "Does that sound right?"

She sighed loudly. "Exactly! My God, that's it exactly! I need to put everything in order so I can die." She seemed relieved, and after talking for a few more minutes, fell into a deep, relaxed sleep.

The next day, she began "gathering the ingredients" by making phone calls and inviting people over to her house. One by one, she said good-bye to colleagues, friends, and family. Saying good-bye to her parents was difficult, but finally her mother was able to tell her it was okay to "let go." Children, grandchildren and husband were all gathered by her bedside for last words and tears.

When her "ingredients" were gathered and her job was done, she died peacefully. She had known exactly what to do—she just needed a little help with the recipe.

Submitted by Anne Wallace Sharp

# SHARP AND TERBAY

## AN ORDINARY DAY

Please tell my family, my friends, my doctors,

"I really am doing okay,
I just need to have an
ordinary day, from now
until my journey's through.

Let me tire myself doing things
I'll all too soon, not be
able to do.

Say what you need to me, any way
you can.
Leaving isn't easy ...
but if I can have an ordinary
day
You'll see how strong I really am.
Being tired isn't bad
I'll rest when I must

And when it's not such
an ordinary day
And the time has come
to move on, to move away
Sit by my side, hold my
hand
And remember with me
how glorious is an ordinary day."

Submitted by Jan Jessen

# GIFTS

## A LONG WALK

Sakoung is a young native born Cambodian woman. She was referred to our hospice program in January 1995. At that time she was only expected to live a few days—as her kidneys were failing as a result of abdominal cancer. Because her death was so imminent, no further testing was done to determine the primary site of her disease or its extent.

However, Sakoung didn't die. She gradually regained her strength and began to resume her normal life-style—being the matriarch to a family of "refugees."

It is now March, 1996 and Sakoung's health has deteriorated, but she continues to defy that original prognosis. Several times in the last year, I have thought her to be close to death. Yet each time she has "bounced back." The extraordinary thing is that she has done this without any help from me or the medical profession.

I have been both inspired by and frustrated with Sakoung and her family. There is a language problem between us. They communicate in Cambodian—I, in English. Luckily, Sakoung's daughter is fairly fluent in English. Sakoung, herself, speaks and understands some English, but I'm never sure how much they comprehend. I've repeatedly tried to discuss Sakoung's terminal status, but am continually met with smiles, nods of the head and blank stare. Do they understand that Sakoung has cancer and will die? I don't know and maybe it doesn't really matter.

Recently, Sakoung developed a high fever. Her blood work showed she had a massive infection of the bloodstream. I once again "prepared" Sakoung and her family for the worst.

"Your Mom may die if this infection isn't treated," I told Sakoung's daughter. She nodded her head and told me she understood, but her Mom didn't want to go to the hospital and didn't need any medicine. I expected any day to receive a call telling me that Sakoung had died.

The call didn't come. When I saw Sakoung a week later, she seemed stronger and free of fever and infection.

I asked the family what they had done—if there were any special "healings" they had utilized from their own culture. They shook their heads. It was during this visit that I found out a little bit about their family history. Sakoung told me she had been to see her sister and that they had talked about how much they both missed their home country, Cambodia.

I asked Sakoung why she had left. She answered my question, and with the help and translation of her daughter, I began to understand a little of Sakoung's extraordinary will to live.

"We left because there was nothing to eat and because of the killing and the war," she said.

I had already learned that Sakoung's husband had been killed by soldiers. I also knew that several of Sakoung's children had died. Now I learned they had died of starvation, victims of the Khmer Rouge's genocide campaign.

"How did you get out of Cambodia and to the United States?" I asked.

"We walked from Cambodia to Thailand. We ate berries and hid in the woods."

Apparently Sakoung and her children, the oldest of whom was eleven, had walked the whole way. Sakoung carried the youngest who had polio and was still unable to walk. Sakoung had led them to freedom.

I looked at this woman with a new respect and understanding.

Sakoung is still alive. She continues to refuse my suggestions about stronger pain medication. She's going to do "this" her way. And who am I to argue with a woman who defied the odds once before and made it to freedom and life. It's her journey. I feel fortunate to be walking with her and for now, I'm content to follow, letting her "call the shots." Maybe she knows something I don't.

Submitted by Anne Wallace Sharp

# GIFTS

## MILDRED

I only saw Mildred twice before her death, but the manner of her dying left a lasting impression.

I arrived at her home for my second visit to find Mildred in the final stages of dying. Her breathing was very shallow and her extremities were cold and discolored. Yet, she was wide awake and totally alert. Her husband, Robert, was standing by her bedside. When I approached the bed, he asked if I minded staying with her a few moments while he ran quickly to the grocery store. I looked at Mildred and asked her if that was all right with her. She nodded her head and he quickly departed. Mildred pointed to a chair by the bedside and I sat down. She grabbed my hand and looked me straight in the eyes.

"I'm dying," she said clearly and calmly.

"I know. Does Robert know?" I asked.

"No," she said softly, "I can't tell him. Will you?"

I assured her that I would and asked if there was anyone else I needed to call or notify. She told me to call her daughters, but only after I told her husband.

"Anyone else?" I asked.

"I'd really like to talk to a minister, if that's possible, but I don't know one." I informed her that I could call the hospice chaplain and see if he was available.

"That's fine," she said, and closed her eyes. She was signaling me that we were done talking for the moment.

I called the hospice chaplain while I waited for her husband to return home, and the chaplain told me he would come out right away. When Robert returned, I talked to him quietly and honestly in the kitchen.

"Mildred wants me to tell you something," I said. I went on to explain that she was dying, but seemed at peace and that she wanted her daughters and the chaplain to come out. He teared up, then regained his composure and went to telephone his daughters. He then joined his wife in the bedroom. I left them alone and waited.

Mildred's daughters arrived and joined their father in the bedroom. I continued waiting. The chaplain soon arrived and we both proceeded into the bedroom. The chaplain spent a few minutes alone with Mildred while I talked to Robert and the daughters. It wasn't long before the chaplain beckoned all of us into Mildred's bedroom and explained that Mildred had requested a prayer. He said a beautiful prayer and then we all joined hands and recited The Lord's Prayer together. As we ended with our "amens," Mildred looked around the room and said in a voice that was still remarkably clear, "If you don't mind, I'd like to be alone for a few moments."

Robert, the girls, the chaplain and I retired to the kitchen where we talked quietly. Robert talked of what a private person his wife had always been. After ten minutes had passed I excused myself to go check on Mildred. She had died as she lived—very privately.

Submitted by Anne Wallace Sharp

## MELTING POT

It has been my privilege to care for many patients and families who have been of different ethnic backgrounds: a Greek woman, who was able to tape a record, in Greek, of personal messages for her children to savor and remember her by; a Vietnamese gentleman, who shared parts of his life as a soldier in France and spoke of the fall of Communism; a German caregiver, who lived on the wrong side of the Berlin Wall, and her joy as she learned of the fall.

These and others help me realize how fortunate I am to live in America.

Submitted by Roberta Erwin

## THE ACCIDENT

Hospice work is not without its dangers because home care nurses are constantly on the road in all kinds of weather and places. I had worked at the hospice for several years and had never been involved in a car accident, not even a fender bender. As it turned out my first accident was not to be a minor one.

It was a warm and sunny day. I had just attended one patient's funeral and was on my way to see another patient, before finishing the day with a third patient's viewing at the funeral home. I was on the interstate in the center lane when a semi-truck came from behind me in the right lane. As he passed me his vehicle came over into my lane.

I saw the center of his truck hit my right front side. My car spun around one or two times, then slid backwards across all three lanes and hit the cement divider. As my car was going across, another semi-truck was coming from behind me in the center lane. I was sure he would hit my vehicle too. By some miracle he was able to maintain control of his truck and stop.

As my car was sliding out of control across the interstate, I felt sure I was going to die and I can remember calmly and somewhat detached, thinking *So this is how it feels to die in an auto accident.* As my car hit the wall the back window shattered and my first thought was, *Thank God my children aren't with me.*

# SHARP AND TERBAY

Immediately after that thought, I became extremely concerned about my patients and what I would do if my beeper went off. I was so concerned about answering the beeper that one of my first requests to the ambulance crew was for them to call my supervisor at work. It is funny how we set our priorities in emergencies. When I arrived at the hospital, I repeated this request. I was so focused on and obsessed about the beeper that I did not allow the doctors and nurses to examine me until I was sure my patients were okay.

Later as I related the story of my accident to family and friends they were amazed and had difficulty understanding why I would be so worried about my patients. It seemed strange to them that I would worry about others before worrying about myself. This is something though that many hospice people understand. Patients many times become a priority in our lives —after our families, but before ourselves.

As it turned out, I was able to focus on myself as soon as I was assured that my patients' needs were in another hospice nurse's hands. I was very shaken from the accident, and somewhat battered and bruised. Fortunately there were no serious injuries. A few days rest and some physical therapy led to a complete, rapid physical recovery. The emotional damage required a little more time. I had to overcome my fear of driving and riding on highways, especially near trucks. I was so determined to overcome this fear that I refused to even consider any change in my home care status for a year. I insisted I would get back on the road again—and so I did—but the memory remains a part of me and probably always will.

Submitted by Kathy Skarzynski

# GIFTS

## "HI, MY NAME'S PHIL"

My first impression of Phil was that he had everything.

He had been a successful salesman and he lived in an expensive, professionally decorated home, with a beautiful wife who obviously treasured him. They had lovely children and grandchildren. He appeared to have lived the American Dream.

One day when I was visiting, I was shocked when two "scroungy-looking" Hell's Angels-type guys dropped in for a visit and were welcomed as bosom buddies. Although I tried to mask my surprise, Phil realized I was curious. He and his friends told me their story.

Phil had had a terrible battle with alcoholism which had nearly cost him his career and his family. Through Alcoholics Anonymous, he had found peace and the desire to help others. After the recovery period, he went looking for other drunks, not among his business associates, but in the roughest bars in town. He built up his own "gang" of recovering alcoholics who, several nights a week, donned their colors, climbed onto their Harleys and went offering hope to others. By the time I knew Phil, his gang consisted of several tattooed former ruffians, as well as a banker and a high school principal. The gang was very large.

His funeral was the most moving one I've ever seen. It was a private ceremony attended by members of the family, the gang, and somehow, me.

After a short service led by a minister, the service was turned over to Phil's buddies. They stood in unison, each dressed in leather, patched denim, bandannas, earrings and sun glasses, and filed past the open coffin of their leader, each one in turn giving him a crisp military salute. They carried his coffin to the hearse and then mounted their Harleys to form the loudest, most respectful honor guard I have seen for a man's final earthly journey. When we arrived at the cemetery, I realized what I hadn't noticed at the funeral home. The lead rider was Phil's son, dressed in Phil's colors.

As I watched I concluded that I was right in the beginning. Phil probably did have everything a person could want!

Submitted by Maggie Bauer


## THE MANY FACES OF AIDS

A young father whose life was destroyed by a tainted blood transfusion for treatment of hemophilia ... whose loving wife could not face her friends because of the social stigma and fear of losing her job ... whose teenage son was kept in the dark about the disease that was killing his father in order to spare the boy the pain of rejection by his friends ...

A son who had been adopted into a loving family, but had gone astray, trying the world of crime and drugs ... only to be welcomed back with open arms by a loving mother who cared for him physically and emotionally until the end of his life.

A lover who was brilliant—a classical pianist, fluent in seven languages, artistic and able to decorate a room with hand-sewn bedspreads and drapes and wonderful artwork ... whose favorite color was lavender which he kept in the form of herbs strewn with amethyst stones in a bowl at his bedside ... who taught all those who met him to look at the beautiful things in the world ... the sky, the beauty of nature, and the beauty inside all people.

A son who was HIV positive ... but who served lovingly as a caregiver to a dying father ... knowing that the future held a similar end for him.

Submitted by Roberta Erwin

# GIFTS

## MICHAEL

Michael, age nine, was one of five young boys I met while helping to facilitate the formalation of a young peoples' grief group. All of the children had experienced the loss of a parent and were attending these sessions to help them cope with their parent's death.

Michael's Mom had recently died—although he never spoke of it. In fact, he sat in our group silently and somewhat isolated. His sadness seemed profound and unreachable.

Michael confided privately to one of the bereavement counselors that he felt invisible. The counselor encouraged him to share his feelings with the group, but Michael remained silent.

On our last night together, the boys exchanged phone numbers and "warm fuzzies." I had decided it would be nice if we all wrote down something positive about each other—that way, when we felt kind of down, we could read something "nice" from someone who understood our feelings.

As we were getting ready to leave, one of the boys (whose father had died) was telling me how his mom had grounded him just the night before. Michael looked at him, then at me and said, quietly, "I guess my mom can't do that to me anymore." I hugged him and said, "No, I guess not." Michael finally broke his silence, acknowledging his mom had died—all in one simple stated fact. I wanted to laugh and cry at the same time. It was a small step, but a giant leap for Michael.

Michael, I think, is slowly coming around. When his path becomes too difficult, I hope he pulls out a note from one of his special friends and knows he's not invisible. I hope he realizes grief is okay and that there are four other little boys who feel the same way he does at times.

I wrote this poem for Michael.

# SHARP AND TERBAY

## MICHAEL

Tousled hair
Passive eyes
Somber face
Silent lips
A child in pain.
He stands.
He sits.
He walks.
And sometimes he talks.
But
He does not remember
He does not reflect
He does not cry
He does not express.
He is a child in pain.
He's alone in a crowd.
A body seen by everyone.
A child hiding within.
Where no one can observe him.
He functions
But he does not feel.
He participates
But he does not care.
He follows
But it does not matter.
For if he feels
or cares
or loves,
He won't allow it.
For
He is a child in pain.

What will happen to this

tousled hair, silent, little boy?
Who will notice him?
How will he continue?
Where will he retreat?
Why is the pain so extensive?

Will he ever reflect and remember?
Will he ever cry?
Will he ever care or love?
Will he ever touch the pain?
Only time and Michael know
For he is the child
And he is in pain.

Submitted by Susan Handle Terbay

## BILL AND TIM

Bill and Tim had been partners for twenty-five years. Twenty-five years is a long time for any couple in this day and age, but even more difficult for a homosexual couple. At my first visit, which I felt was going well, Bill stopped me in the middle of a sentence.

"I have to ask you something, and please be honest. Are you just paying me lip service or do you really care about us?" he asked.

I was shocked. What did he mean? Here I was voluntarily coming into their home to care for an end-stage patient with AIDS, anxious to help them and was being verbally drilled by the patient's partner, Bill. What followed was eye opening and heart breaking. I began to understand why Bill wanted to be sure I wasn't just giving "lip-service."

In the next months, I heard about and observed the hatred and prejudice they encountered, not only because of the AIDS diagnosis, but also because of their homosexuality. Once I saw through Bill's anger and pain, I saw a person who just wanted to be accepted and treated as a human being. I saw someone who was losing his life-long partner. I also saw how he was hurting.

We focused our plan of care not only on Tim's physical needs, but also on dealing with both partners' emotional needs. I encouraged them to spend time together and to be honest with each other. Bill was devoted in the care he provided to Tim. Around the clock feedings through a tube, decubitus ulcer care, bathing, control of bleeding problems, and on and on.

Maybe it's the courage and strength they found in facing society together for twenty-five years that gave them the foundation to get through Tim's battle with AIDS. No matter what the circumstances, I found that dealing with a loved one who has been diagnosed with AIDS is one of the greatest challenges a person can face. It is a disease that destroys a person physically and emotionally. We may not be able to cure the disease, but we can at least focus our energies on healing the emotional scars.

Submitted by Kim Vesey

## GARY

Gary lives in a clean, newly painted, two-story white frame house in a quiet neighborhood. I am surprised to find the rooms cluttered and dirty. Laundry is strewn on the floor, sofa, chairs and in every corner. Dirty dishes are piled in the sink, crumbs and dog food litter the floor, and boxes by the hundreds are stacked everywhere. Gary's wife apologizes for the mess, "I just can't keep up with everything."

She directs me up the stairs to Gary's room. The stairs and upper hallway are also packed from floor to ceiling with clutter. Boxes, old newspapers, magazines, clothing and paper bags litter the way. Coming to a door, I knock and receive a hearty "Come in."

Gary greets me with a warm and firm handshake. He is a large man, dressed neatly in plaid pajamas, slippers, and a baseball cap. He laughs when he notices me looking at the hat. Removing it to reveal his bald head, he says, "I can't stand looking at it. I think the proper word for me is vain."

I sit down on a folding chair as he takes a seat in a large tan recliner. I look at the long, narrow room. A hospital bed and oxygen condenser occupy one end, while the recliner and a dresser fill the other. Running along the outer wall is a long wooden work table with shelves. Despite the cramped spaces, everything is in its place—it's not immaculate, but it's orderly. Tapes, books, magazines, clothing and personal items fill the shelves. The walls are covered with framed photos and souvenirs of other times.

As his wife has done before him, Gary apologizes for the messy appearance.

"My wife is not a very good housekeeper. This house is just too small for all of us," he says. He goes on to explain that his daughter and her children live in the house, as well. "And my son arrived yesterday. He's going to be here awhile, too."

On subsequent visits, I learn more about Gary and his family. He talks openly about his past—a high paying, prestigious government job, a drinking problem, and a disastrous financial deal that had left him facing bankruptcy. His life has changed dramatically and he is still struggling to reconcile the many feelings he has.

His relationships with his daughters has mellowed, but his son remains a source of frustration and concern. Gary freely admits not being there for his children when they were growing up and now he voices bitterness that his family isn't there for him.

Gary seems so isolated and alone. He spends his days in this long, narrow room with the door always closed. If he needs his wife, he bangs on the floor with his cane. And occasionally, he drives to the store or to the doctor's office. But with the disease progressing, these trips become less frequent. He seems reconciled to being alone. He repeatedly tells me, "It's okay. I accept this." But I also sense a real sense of loneliness. His wife and family are meeting his physical needs, but his emotional needs seem to be forgotten.

He seems genuinely glad to see me each week. Gary never fails to rise from his chair, shake my hand and smile. He invariably launches into one story after another and the time slips by very quickly. I enjoy his stories. But I also read a lot between the lines. Gary is trying very hard to reconcile his past, forgive himself, and be honest about his feelings. This is something, I suspect, with which he does not have much experience. He is struggling, but making a genuine effort.

The baseball cap is eventually forgotten as his comfort level with me—and with himself—increases. At some point, he realizes I don't care whether his head is bald or not and stops being so concerned about his appearance.

Following a course of chemotherapy, his blood count drops dangerously and he requires a blood transfusion. He is admitted to a hospice for twenty-four hours. I see him several days later and ask him how things are going. A huge smile appears on his face as he begins to describe his experience at the hospice. He boasts about the food and the accommodations, "But the best part was the people. Everyone was so nice. I sat out on the terrace and three or four different people came up and talked to me. Of course, I started in with my stories. But they seemed to enjoy them," he says.

He goes on to describe the several volunteers who stopped to chat with him and how the dietician had visited to help him fill out his menu. His smile fades as he adds, "I didn't want to leave ..."

# GIFTS

My heart breaks for him as I reflect again on how isolated this man is. He is like a prisoner in his own home. Whether self-imposed or not, now he is in solitary confinement. His cell is a small upstairs room. His jailer is either the cancer, his family, or his own sense of guilt. I'm still not sure.

Gary will die soon. I wonder how and where? Will it be in this small upstairs room? Or will it be at the hospice center? Will he reconcile with his family? Will he forgive himself? Will his family forgive him? I don't have the answers to these questions. In the meantime, I continue to visit Gary each week. I listen to his stories for an hour or so, allowing him to leave his solitary confinement and enter a realm where someone is concerned about his feelings and emotional needs. I leave, feeling frustrated that I can't do more ....

Submitted by Anne Wallace Sharp

Postscript: Gary died in the hospice at his own request. Three days before his death, he called me. He told me he could barely breathe or eat and that it was time to return to the hospice. Within an hour of his arrival, he slipped into a coma and ultimately died. I rejoice that he wasn't alone.

## NOEL

"I have a new referral for you," the discharge planner from one of the local hospitals told me. As I took out the appropriate form, she continued. "He has AIDS. His name is Noel Green."

I gasped. Noel was a friend of mine. I hadn't seen him since high school. Somewhere along the way, we had lost touch with one another. Trancelike, I wrote down the rest of the information provided by the discharge planner, but my thoughts were elsewhere. I could see Noel and his crazy antics, which had always reminded me of Jerry Lewis. I could see his whimsical smile and twinkling blue eyes. There had always been laughter when Noel was around. Surely, there must be some mistake!

I wanted very badly to see and talk to Noel, but I was also reluctant to intrude. I wasn't sure whether he'd want to see me. I approached his home care nurse, explained my feelings and asked her to tell Noel that I was thinking of him. "I'm not sure he'll even remember me," I added.

Several days later the nurse stopped by my desk and said, "Noel not only remembers you but wants to know if you'll join the two of us for lunch next week."

I was delighted, but apprehensive. I knew a little about AIDS and a lot about the stigma attached to it. I had lots of questions and concerns. Noel's nurse was very patient with me, listening to my fears, answering my questions and alleviating my doubt. She was honest and straightforward. By the date of our luncheon, I felt reassured and much less anxious.

The remainder of my fear evaporated as soon as I saw Noel. He was standing on his front porch waiting for us. The nurse immediately walked up to him and gave him a hug. Noel turned to me, smiling, "Sue, it's good to see you," he held out his arms and I embraced him warmly. It felt good to hug an old friend.

As we sat around the table eating our lunch, I learned about Noel's tragic story. A few years earlier he had his whole life before him—a promising career and a beautiful fiance. The expectation of marriage, children and a long life together awaited them. Shortly before their marriage, Noel's fiance had been killed in an automobile accident. Despondent, Noel decided that his life was not worth living and attempted suicide. He took a gun and fired a single bullet into his head. Incredibly, he survived, but suffered irreversible brain damage. While hospitalized in a rehabilitation facility, he was diagnosed with AIDS.

As Noel recounted this story, I was watching his eyes. I yearned for the old twinkle and gleam, but it was gone. All I could see was the emptiness and sadness. Every now and then a small smile would cross his face and the old Noel would shine through the clouded mask. As I listened to Noel, I knew, without a doubt, that the young clown I had known in high school was gone forever.

Noel talked openly about his disease and his chances for recovery. He mentioned suicide, but then added, "I would never try that again—I'm too afraid I'd fail." Then a smile appeared. "And besides—it won't be long before I'm with her again, anyway."

He proudly showed me the gold chain that hung around his neck. Which told the history of his past. The chain carried a small locket with a picture of his girl friend, a ring and a medal.

As we hugged each other good-bye, we both sensed this would probably be the last time we saw one another. When I heard the news that he was gone, I felt an enormous emptiness inside me and grieved for the loss of the boy I grew up with. His empty eyes still haunt me, but I rejoice in my memories of the young man who had such a wonderful gift for making others laugh. Whenever I see a clown, I think of Noel and how the sound of laughter must be resounding through heaven.

Submitted by Sue Handle Terbay

## DYING WITH DIGNITY

When I was forty-seven years old, my doctor told me I had incurable cancer of the colon with metastasis to the surrounding lymph nodes and to both ovaries. The prognosis was six months. If I lived longer than six months, the doctors told me my quality of life would be very poor.

Here I am, at fifty-seven, without my colon, ovaries, spleen, and many lymph nodes. I have had three series of chemotherapy, four surgeries and countless experimental treatments. Still I go on.

As I begin my third year of liver cancer with additional tumors on my stomach, the lining of my abdominal wall, aorta and lymph nodes, I find myself waiting again. I have forgotten how many times I have been told six months, one year, etc., etc. ...

I sometimes feel embarrassed or worse yet, freakish, that I am still alive. I have been asked often how I deal with this everyday. The answer for me is God. I believe God still has plans for me, that I have not yet finished my work here on earth. The other reason I have survived is my attitude and approach.

As a child, I was afraid of the dark and of death. As an adult, I have added the IRS to my list. I have always considered myself to be a spiritual person, but not particularly big on organized religion. That day ten years ago, when the doctors were discussing my prognosis with me, I was praying for God to give me the strength to deal with my fear of death. I also wanted to be strong in front of the doctors. God touched me on the shoulder. To date, I have been okay with the "death" part. I feel the way you might feel when you are going to do something for the first time. I'm a little nervous, but looking forward to this next new experience. For me, that next step in my life is dying.

I have been warned to minimize stress because it would only make my cancer worse. Unfortunately, stress hasn't been real co-operative. I've had more than my share and more than I could adequately deal with at time. There was a marriage, the suicide of my cancer stricken husband, my father-in-law's suicide, and many more episodes of emotional turmoil.

Perhaps my most difficult task has been to prepare myself for death so many times through the years, only to get better again. I feel sometimes like I'm on a roller coaster and I can't get off!

Ten years ago the doctors told me to go on a cruise assuring I wouldn't be able to go back to work. I asked which of them were willing to support me in the style to which I want to get accustomed. No one volunteered to support me, but they did assure me I was going to die but I didn't die. So I went back to work.

# GIFTS

After much thinking, crying, and re-evaluation, I have tried my best to live by the following guidelines:

1. Life isn't always fair, so I don't waste time saying "why me?" And, no, I'm not being punished for anything. My God doesn't punish.

2. I am determined to live my life as fully as possible. I don't let "cancer" control my life. I have never gotten up in the morning thinking, "Oh, I have cancer." I get up and go on with my day as if I didn't have cancer.

3. I've planned my life. I travel. I go out shopping. I go to dinner. I entertain. And when my body made me change this lifestyle, I created another lifestyle. I'm not going to quit living.

4. I refuse to be a "Pitiful Pearl." If I acted that way, I believe people would turn away from me. People do not want to listen to every detail of my disease. I let people tell me about their aches, pains and problems. I'm interested in other people. I smile a lot. I say, "I'm doing as well as I can."

5. I believe it is harder for my loved ones watching me die, than what I'm going through. I hate to see the pain, helplessness and fear in their eyes. I try to make it as easy for them as I can.

6. I've never lost my sense of humor. And I would recommend to people "If you don't have a sense of humor, get one." Laughter is the best possible medicine. There are lots of funny things out there if you look.

7. I've forgiven people—those who say the wrong things and those who don't know what to say. I know that sometimes being with me frightens them. I think it makes them think of their own mortality.

8. I took charge of my illness. I demanded to be part of my treatment. I asked questions. I know what medications I'm taking and why. I refuse to be intimidated by the medical community. By the same token, I don't blame my doctors. They are trying their best to help me. I try to help them help me by doing as I'm supposed to do and by being a nice person instead of a

pesky patient.

9. Every pain isn't cancer. When I get a new ache or pain, I wait a week or two and if it doesn't go away, then I go to the doctor. I don't spend my life worrying.

10. I've taken care of business. I have my affairs in order. I've left instructions for my family. I have a will, a living will. I refuse to leave a mess for my family to clean up.

11. I try to have a project going on to keep myself busy when I'm not feeling well.

12. I've written notes to my loved ones. It was difficult to do, but I know they will be happy when they read my notes.

13. I read. I keep myself informed about what is going on in the world because there is more to conversation and life than cancer.

14. I try to put other people first. I don't waste my energy feeling sorry for myself. Everyday, I count my blessings— and I have so many!

15. Lastly, if I've had a rotten day and I've failed at everything on this list—I forgive myself. I apologize and go on— determined to do better tomorrow. I try not to beat myself up because I know I'm entitled to a bad day every now and then.

I realize I am nearing my last days. I hope that I will be able to be brave. I want to die with dignity and I never want to forget the blessings I have had along the way. I have been blessed with excellent care and for that I am eternally grateful. I am counting on God to help me in this final journey.

My favorite line is "Men make plans and God smiles." I wonder if He was smiling the day I rented the beach house for next August?

Submitted by a hospice patient

# A Few
# Last Words

## From Susan:

As I reflected recently on the past few years I have worked
at a hospice, I thought of all the wonderful people who have journeyed with me—patients, family members, caregivers and staff.
In particular, I thought about a dedication and memorial service
we had just this week.

The service was a celebration of life. It took place outside
on the walkway of the hospice, surrounded by all of Nature's
beauty—ponds, gardens, flowers and birds.

On this particular day, the sun had shown brightly until
late afternoon when clouds drifted in bringing with them the
threat of rain. As the service neared, the rain started and staff
and visitors scurried for the nearest shelter. The violinist continued playing for those gathered under the big tent, while
others waited inside the building for the rain to cease.

Just as quickly as the rain came, it began to ebb. Slowly
families came out of the building and joined those already outside. Everyone visited with one another and wandered down the
walkway. A gentleman who had lost his wife earlier this year

began a short tribute to his wife. Just as he started his remarks, the sun came out. The sunlight caused the raindrops to shimmer in the trees and the walkway glistened in the early evening light. The breathtaking beauty of the moment did not go unnoticed. The spirits of all those present and those remembered filled the air. The rain relinquished its grip and gave way to the glow of the sun as the celebration continued.

That evening was very symbolic for me. I realized that the spirits of the patients are undaunted by the "rains" of their disease. It is the glow from within that reflects the beauty of the people.

Sometimes I'm overwhelmed by the presence of death. As I walk down the walkway or through the hallways of the hospice center, the rain seems to dampen my spirit. But ... when I encounter the people in those rooms and their loved ones, the rain seems to stop and the sun begins to glow.

How blessed I feel to have known so many beautiful spirits. They have become a part of me. While I am forced to say good-bye to their physical form, their spirit remains with me for a lifetime.

## From Anne:

It is difficult to know exactly how to conclude this book. Writing and compiling the stories has been a labor of love. As I have read and re-read each story, I have experienced the person, his or her family, with its pain and joy. Each person impacted my life in some way. The lessons I learned were many—unconditional love, acceptance, courage, humor, honesty ... and so much more.

As a result, I carry each person's story with me on my own journey through life. Some of the stories have had a more profound impact than others, but each one changed me in some small way.

The initial preparation for this book began over several years ago. Since that time I have cared for many patients whose stories do not appear in these pages. Yet their courage and love are not lesser gifts than those about which I've written. Each one is a hero or heroine in his or her own way. Each one struggled to deal with his or her disease and impending death in the best way he or she knew how. I feel privileged to have been part of their lives, if only for a brief time.

Currently I am taking care of a fifty-two-year-old woman with advanced colon cancer. Her life's battle is nearly over. As I write these words, Carol lies in a coma in her home with her husband by her side. I still remember fondly the first day I met her. I felt like I'd known Carol all my life. Her first words came through tears, "Can I have a hug? I'm scared."

Over the last six months, Carol and I have walked together hand in hand. We have become good friends. Carol has slowly reached an acceptance of her impending death. She has dealt with her fears while, at the same time, celebrating and enjoying everyday she has been given. She has *lived* these last six months—sometimes in pain, but always in joy and with an attitude of thankfulness and appreciation. She has been totally open and honest with her feelings, sharing her fears, hopes, joys and disappointments with equal candor. In the process, she has helped me to be more open and honest with my own feelings.

Three days ago, I knew that Carol was entering the last phase of her disease and that I might not see her again. I hugged Carol, kissed her good-bye, and told her I loved her

"You have touched my heart," I said, with tears rolling down my cheeks. "And I will never forget you. I don't want you to die ... but I know you're tired and need to go. I will miss you ... but I will carry part of you right here," I said as I put my hand over my heart. I stroked her forehead and kissed her again.

A small smile appeared on her face through her own tears. In a small, weak voice, she said, "I love you, Anne."

That night I awoke at four in the morning. My friend had come to me in a dream and I knew that she was saying her last goodbye. A few hours later Carol slipped into a coma. She lingered on. Her breathing came slow and shallow and her body was shutting down.

I will miss her hugs, her smile and her spunk ... but a part of her spirit will live with me always.

Susan, my co-author, recently showed me a poem she'd written about masks which I thought was fitting because my friend and I had been able to meet each other without masks. There was no need to be anyone other than who we really were. There were no pretenses, hidden agendas or games—just honest, open sharing of feelings from one friend to another.

### The Mask

*On the night stand, close within reach, lay the mask. A little worn from usage over the years. The magic of the mask lay in its ability to transform like a chameleon whenever she held it in her hands and placed it on her face.*

*It first was the creation of a lonely little girl, full of imagination. Some days she was a "mommy" taking care of her dolls —other days, a teacher, a trucker, a dancer, a singer, an actress— a shadow.*

*Later the mask became a shelter, a shield from the pain, from screams, from tears. A way to hide while being seen.*

*As time passed, the mask disguised fears, uncertainties and shyness. It became a protection to buffet words, accusations and anger.*

*Life was a masquerade party of laughter through tears, smiles through sadness, composure through anger, love through aversion.*

*After a while, the mask totally concealed the real person inside; the lonely little girl, the uncertain teen, the frightened youth, the weary woman.*

286

*Each morning, she reached over to the night stand and placed the mask upon her face. She became whoever it was she had to be at that moment. No one ever saw her without the mask. It became her survival technique.*

*Now, as she lies dying, the mask is bothersome; it no longer conforms to her face, disguises her pain, covers her loneliness. For it is no longer necessary to survive.*

*For the first time in many years, the mask lays abandoned on the night stand. Death, unlike life, has freed her from disguises. She is finally allowed to be as the mask shatters, setting her free.*

Sue has expressed an important part of what a hospice is all about. Allowing our own masks to come down as we meet people who no longer have need of theirs. Real people with real feelings who are ending their life battle and setting out on a new journey—an unfolding process of personal and spiritual discovery of eternity.